# ANCHORAGES OF THE BRITISH ISLES

## OVER 100 BEAUTIFUL HAVENS, COVES AND ESCAPES

JANE CUMBERLIDGE, DICK DURHAM, NORMAN KEAN,
JONTY PEARCE AND DAG PIKE

ADLARD COLES

LONDON · OXFORD · NEW YORK · NEW DELHI · SYDNEY

ADLARD COLES
Bloomsbury Publishing Plc
50 Bedford Square, London, WC1B 3DP, UK
Bloomsbury Publishing Ireland Limited,
29 Earlsfort Terrace, Dublin 2, D02 AY28, Ireland

BLOOMSBURY, ADLARD COLES and the Adlard Coles logo are trademarks of
Bloomsbury Publishing Plc

First published in Great Britain 2026

Copyright © Jane Cumberlidge, Dick Durham, Norman Kean,
Jonty Pearce and Dag Pike, 2026
Maps © Richard Thomson, rt-imagery.com, 2026

Jane Cumberlidge, Dick Durham, Norman Kean, Jonty Pearce and Dag Pike
have asserted their right under the Copyright, Designs and Patents Act, 1988, to
be identified as Authors of this work

Sections of this book were previously published, in adapted form,
in *Yachting Monthly* magazine

All rights reserved. No part of this publication may be: i) reproduced or transmitted in any form, electronic or mechanical, including photocopying, recording or by means of any information storage or retrieval system without prior permission in writing from the publishers; or ii) used or reproduced in any way for the training, development or operation of artificial intelligence (AI) technologies, including generative AI technologies. The rights holders expressly reserve this publication from the text and data mining exception as per Article 4(3) of the Digital Single Market Directive (EU) 2019/790

A catalogue record for this book is available from the British Library

ISBN: PB: 978-1-3994-2354-0; eBook: 978-1-3994-2353-3;
ePDF: 978-1-3994-2352-6

2 4 6 8 10 9 7 5 3 1

Designed by Nick Avery
Typeset in Isidora Sans by Kirsty Hunter
Printed and bound in Thailand by Sirivatana Interprint

Bloomsbury Publishing Plc makes every effort to ensure that the papers used in the manufacture of our books are natural, recyclable products made from wood grown in well-managed forests. Our manufacturing processes conform to the environmental regulations of the country of origin.

To find out more about our authors and books visit www.bloomsbury.com
and sign up for our newsletters
For product safety related questions contact productsafety@bloomsbury.com
Title page photograph: Percuil River, Cornwall

# CONTENTS

Author profiles....................................................................1
Introduction.......................................................................4

## NORTH EAST
1 **HOLY ISLAND HARBOUR**, Lindisfarne, Northumberland...10
2 **NEWTON HAVEN**, Northumberland.........................................12
3 **NEWBIGGIN BAY**, Northumberland.........................................14

## EAST AND SOUTH EAST
1 **SPURN HEAD**, River Humber, Yorkshire........................................18
2 **NORTON HOLE**, Brancaster, Norfolk............................................20
3 **IKEN CLIFF**, River Alde, Suffolk..................................................22
4 **BUTLEY RIVER**, River Ore, Suffolk..............................................24
5 **THE ROCKS**, River Deben, Suffolk..............................................26
6 **STONE HEAPS**, River Orwell, Suffolk..........................................28
7 **ERWARTON NESS**, River Stour, Suffolk.......................................30
8 **STONE POINT**, Walton Backwaters, Essex..................................32
9 **KIRBY CREEK**, Walton Backwaters, Essex..................................34
10 **PYEFLEET CREEK**, River Colne, Essex........................................36
11 **OSEA ISLAND**, River Blackwater, Essex......................................38
12 **CLIFF REACH**, River Crouch, Essex.............................................40
13 **YOKESFLEET CREEK**, River Roach, Essex..................................42
14 **RAY GUT**, River Thames, Essex...................................................44
15 **SOUTH DEEP**, The Swale, Kent....................................................46
16 **SHARFLEET CREEK**, River Medway, Kent.................................48
17 **LYDD-ON-SEA**, Dungeness, Kent.................................................50
18 **WEST ITCHENOR**, Chichester Harbour, West Sussex..........52
19 **BEAULIEU RIVER**, Hampshire........................................................54
20 **NEWTOWN RIVER**, Isle of Wight..................................................56

## CHANNEL ISLANDS

1. **SAYE BAY**, Alderney..................60
2. **FERMAIN BAY**, Guernsey..................62
3. **PETIT PORT**, Guernsey..................64
4. **ROSAIRE**, Herm..................66
5. **EAST COAST**, Herm..................68
6. **LA GRAND GRÈVE**, Sark..................70
7. **PORT GOREY**, Sark..................72
8. **DIXCART AND DERRIBLE BAYS**, Sark..................74
9. **MARMOTIÈRE**, Les Ecrehous..................76
10. **ROZEL AND BOULEY BAY**, Jersey..................79
11. **ST CATHERINE'S BAY**, Jersey..................81
12. **BEAUPORT BAY**, Jersey..................82

## WEST COUNTRY

1. **STUDLAND BAY**, Dorset..................86
2. **CHAPMAN'S POOL**, Isle of Purbeck, Dorset..................88
3. **LULWORTH COVE**, Jurassic Coast, Dorset..................90
4. **BEER**, Jurassic Coast, Devon..................92
5. **BABBACOMBE BAY**, Torquay, Devon..................94
6. **BLACKPOOL SANDS**, Dartmouth, Devon..................96
7. **ELENDER COVE**, Prawle Point, Devon..................98
8. **HOPE COVE**, Salcombe, Devon..................100
9. **CAWSAND BAY**, Plymouth Sound, Cornwall..................102
10. **POLPERRO**, Cornwall..................104
11. **PERCUIL RIVER**, Falmouth, Cornwall..................106
12. **HELFORD RIVER**, Cornwall..................108
13. **LAMORNA COVE**, Penzance, Cornwall..................110
14. **GREEN BAY**, Bryher, Isles of Scilly..................112
15. **ST HELEN'S POOL**, Isles of Scilly..................114
16. **CARBIS BAY**, St Ives, Cornwall..................116
17. **PORT GAVERNE**, Cornwall..................118
18. **LUNDY**, Bristol Channel..................120
19. **BUCK'S MILL**, Devon..................122
20. **ILFRACOMBE**, Devon..................124

## IRELAND

1. **DRAKE'S POOL**, Crosshaven, Co. Cork..................128
2. **COURTMACSHERRY**, Co. Cork..................130
3. **CASTLE HAVEN**, Castletownshend, Co. Cork..................132
4. **BARLOGE**, Co. Cork..................134
5. **CROOKHAVEN**, Mizen Peninsula, Co. Cork..................136
6. **KITCHEN COVE**, Dunmanus Bay, Co. Cork..................138
7. **GLENGARRIFF HARBOUR**, Bantry Bay, Co. Cork..................140
8. **DUNBOY BAY**, Co. Cork..................142
9. **ARDGROOM HARBOUR**, Kenmare Bay, Co. Cork/Co. Kerry..................144
10. **DERRYNANE HARBOUR**, Co. Kerry..................146
11. **PORTMAGEE**, Co. Kerry..................148
12. **PARADISE**, River Fergus, Co. Clare..................150
13. **ROUNDSTONE**, Co. Galway..................152
14. **TOBERDENNY HARBOUR**, Co. Galway..................154
15. **INISHBOFIN**, Co. Galway..................156
16. **BURTONPORT**, Co. Donegal..................158
17. **GOLA**, Gola Sound, Co. Donegal..................160
18. **LOUGH SWILLY**, Co. Donegal..................162
19. **PORTMORE**, Inishtrahull, Co. Donegal..................164
20. **STRANGFORD LOUGH**, Co. Down..................166

## WALES

1. **PORT EYNON**, Gower Peninsula, Swansea..................170
2. **PRIORY BAY**, Caldey Island, Pembrokeshire..................172
3. **WATWICK BAY**, Milford Haven, Pembrokeshire..................174
4. **SOUTH HAVEN**, Skomer, Pembrokeshire..................176
5. **MARTIN'S HAVEN**, Haverfordwest, Pembrokeshire..................178
6. **SOLVA**, Pembrokeshire..................180
7. **BARDSEY ISLAND**, Gwynedd..................182
8. **ABERDARON**, Llŷn Peninsula, Gwynedd..................184
9. **PORTH DINLLAEN**, Gwynedd..................186
10. **CEMLYN BAY**, Anglesey..................188
11. **FORT BELAN**, Menai Strait, Gwynedd..................190
12. **RHOS ON SEA**, Conwy..................192

## NORTH WEST

1. **PIEL ISLAND**, Morecambe Bay, Lancashire....................196
2. **PORT ERIN**, Isle of Man..........................................198
3. **DERBYHAVEN**, Isle of Man.....................................201

## SCOTLAND

1. **LOCH SCADABAY**, Harris, Outer Hebrides..................206
2. **SHIANT ISLANDS**, Outer Hebrides.............................208
3. **WIZARD POOL, LOCH SKIPPORT**, South Uist, Outer Hebrides..............................................................210
4. **ACAIRSEID MHOR**, Rona, Highland.............................212
5. **POLL CREADHA**, Applecross Peninsula, Highland.......214
6. **CROWLIN ISLANDS**, Inner Sound, Highland................216
7. **LOCH NA CUILCE**, Skye, Inner Hebrides.....................218
8. **SOAY HARBOUR**, Soay, Inner Hebrides......................220
9. **CANNA**, Small Isles, Inner Hebrides............................222
10. **HYSKEIR LIGHTHOUSE**, Inner Hebrides....................224
11. **EIGG**, Small Isles, Inner Hebrides...............................226
12. **ARISAIG**, Loch nan Ceall, Highland............................228
13. **LOCH MOIDART**, Highland.......................................230
14. **SANNA BAY**, Ardnamurchan Peninsula, Highland.....233
15. **LOCH NA DROMA BUIDHE**, Highland......................235
16. **TINKER'S HOLE**, Mull, Inner Hebrides.......................237
17. **PUILLADOBHRAIN**, Seil, Argyll and Bute..................239
18. **BARMORE ISLAND**, Lower Loch Fyne, Argyll and Bute.............241
19. **MILLPORT**, Great Cumbrae, Argyll and Bute.............243
20. **ISLE OF WHITHORN**, Solway Firth, Dumfries and Galloway...245

Acknowledgements..............................................................247
Picture credits....................................................................247
Index..................................................................................248

# AUTHOR PROFILES

----

The anchorages in this book have been written by a panel of experienced cruising sailors with each signed off by the author's initials for clarity.

**JANE CUMBERLIDGE** (JC) started sailing while at university and then cruised extensively with her husband, Peter Cumberlidge. In *Stormalong*, their gaff cutter, they regularly visited Brittany and the Channel Islands, went up to the Danish islands, across to north-west Spain and the Biscay coast of France, the Basque coast of Spain, as well as the West Country, where *Stormalong* was based. They often delivered boats for friends and chartered, enabling them to sail further afield including on the New England coast and in all the Scandinavian countries, where anchoring is a way of life. For many years Jane has been a freelance writer and photographer contributing to various boating magazines, both inland and offshore.

▲ Jane Cumberlidge

**DICK DURHAM** (DD) started sailing aged 12 and, as a teenager, served as mate in the last cargo sailing ship in the UK, the Thames barge *Cambria*. He has cruised from Norway to Gibraltar; been at the end of a lifeboat tow-rope in the Bay of Biscay when a force 10 storm disabled the 55ft brigantine, *Black Pearl*; raced in the America's Cup Jubilee aboard the 12m *Victory*; and aboard *Warpath*, a 41ft Bashford Howison during the 2001 Fastnet Race. He acted as watch leader aboard *Gipsy Moth IV* on two legs of her second circumnavigation, and crewed for Sir Robin Knox-Johnston aboard *Suhaili*. He has written six sailing books including the biographies of the last sailing captain Bob Roberts, yacht designer Maurice Griffiths and yachting cartoonist Mike Peyton. A *Yachting Monthly* columnist, Dick sails his 25ft gaff cutter, *Betty II*, around the Thames Estuary.

▼ Dick Durham

▼ Norman Kean

**NORMAN KEAN** (NK) grew up on the shores of the Firth of Clyde and has been messing about in boats since childhood. He went to work in Ireland in 1980, and fitted out his first cruising boat – a Sadler 25 – beside his house. He sailed her round Ireland and to France, up the coast of Scotland and out to St Kilda and the Faroes. After three years working in the USA, he and his wife Geraldine bought a classic steel Frers ketch, which Norman and four friends sailed home to Ireland in 2001. In 2005 Norman became editor of the Irish Cruising Club Sailing Directions, and he and Geraldine have now downsized to a sensible plastic Warrior 40. He is a Yachtmaster Offshore and a Fellow of the Royal Institute of Navigation, and was co-author in 2012, with the late Mike Balmforth, of *Cruising Ireland*. He writes frequently for *Yachting Monthly*.

**JONTY PEARCE** (JP) A retired GP living far from the sea in the Malvern Hills, Jonty and his wife, Carol, own *Aurial*, a Southerly 105 ketch, based in Pembrokeshire. He is an ex-commodore of the Penguin Cruising Club (a group of sailing enthusiasts who charter to cruise in interesting locations, frequently the Scottish islands) and dabbled in yachting journalism as a contributor to *Yachting Monthly* for over 12 years. The couple contributed to the Cruising Association's MOB seminar following their practical 'Expert on Board' YM article 'How an 8st woman recovers a 20st man' and also gave lectures to sailing clubs on the subject. Their favourite cruising grounds cover the Welsh coast with occasional trips to the West Country, the Isles of Scilly and Ireland. They have chartered widely in the Lofoten Islands, Sweden, Shetland and Orkney, and north-west Scotland. Their main sailing interest is safe coastal cruising aboard their own and chartered yachts.

▽ Jonty Pearce

▽ Dag Pike

**DAG PIKE** (DP) began his career as a merchant captain. He went on to test RNLI lifeboats, and took up fast boat navigation, winning a string of trophies for powerboat races around the world, including navigating Richard Branson's *Virgin Atlantic Challenger* on the record-breaking fastest Atlantic crossing by powerboat. He later became a navigation and powerboat journalist in demand all over the world. He also built up 20 years' experience in marine surveying, covering yachts, fishing and workboats of all types. Dag was an internationally renowned sailing and motorboating expert with extensive experience of offshore racing, cruising and boat testing. He was the author of over 40 books including *The Complete RIB Manual*, *Be Your Own Boat Surveyor*, *Powerboat Design and Performance* and *Cruising Under Power*. He also wrote articles for the leading nautical magazines around the world.

# INTRODUCTION

**DISCOVERING A REMOTE** anchorage and dropping the hook there for the first time must be one of the most satisfying feelings for any cruising sailor. The sense of achievement and independence when you have spotted a potential location on a chart, navigated to it and then gently worked your way in is nothing short of magical. Many coastal anchorages have been safe havens for sailing vessels for centuries and pilot books invariably describe popular, reliable coves or creeks, though a lot of these have now begun to fill up with moorings.

Peter Cumberlidge, a well-known yachtsman, yachting journalist and cruising author, always said an anchorage hunter's best tools were a large-scale paper chart, a magnifying glass and a pair of compasses. Choosing a paper chart isn't a Luddite reaction; they furnish the greatest degree of information, something the small screens of plotters just cannot provide. When ferreting out anchorages, coastal waters present numerous possibilities.

▼ La Grande Grève on the west coast of Sark

▲ Sheltered behind Sketrick Island is Ballydorn, in Strangford Lough, with its lightship clubhouse

**Major headlands** can offer shelter on their lee side, particularly as a place to wait between tides. Dungeness is one such unlikely possibility where pilot cutters used to wait. Start Point is a classic choice in westerlies or north-westerlies when Hallsands is a good spot.

The **mouths of minor rivers** can provide shelter in offshore winds, though you need to work your way in carefully using your echo sounder as they tend to bring down silt, potentially making depths less than indicated.

Looking at a river chart with bends and mud banks, you might spot a **charted pool** that has been used by generations of boat skippers. On the Dart there's one in Mill Creek near Dittisham and another close to Stoke Gabriel. Heading further west, off the Tamar, you can edge into the St Germans River and find Dandy Hole. On Ireland's south coast, if you turn to port as you enter Cork Harbour you can wind up the River Owenboy to Drake's Pool.

In and around islands, the Channel Islands, Isles of Scilly, west coast of Ireland or the Hebrides, **rocky lagoons** can be fascinating places to anchor, depending

▼ Dried out in Green Bay, off Bryher in the Isles of Scilly

▼ Almost enclosed by rocks in Scadabay on the Isle of Harris

on the nature of the seabed. Looking at a chart and seeing all those rocks may seem intimidating, but at low water (LW), rocks and reefs make great breakwaters.

**Bars and spits** can also give shelter; think of the Cove and Port Conger between Saint Agnes and Gugh in the Isles of Scilly, or the amazing sandy curve of Spurn Head. In this type of anchorage you need to be alert for sudden wind shifts; you don't want to end up on a lee shore so you may need to use a kedge.

**Sandbanks** abound on the east coast, all around the Thames Estuary, Essex and into the Wash. Just off the north Norfolk coast you can find Daseley's Sled and Cork Hole in the Wash, both anchorages nuzzled between sandbanks.

Some anchorages are only available at **neap tides**, so if you stay too long you may ground at LW as the tides edge towards springs.

Coming into an unfamiliar natural anchorage for the first time you should take careful soundings, note the shallowest depths and the time and then, using tide tables and the rule of twelfths, work out the minimum depth at LW. This, with the tidal range, will also help you to determine swinging room, how much anchor cable to let out and if you should buoy the anchor. You should also consider how feasible it is to leave at night if a wind shift should force you to clear out. Always fix a riding light if anchoring at night and a black ball during daylight.

In this book we have brought together a great range of interesting locations for dropping the hook. It doesn't claim to be an exhaustive list and any choice of anchorage is dependent on the conditions occurring on the day, as well as individual preferences.

Between them the contributors have many years' experience of cruising and picking suitable anchorages but, as with restaurants, not everyone will agree with our selection. Many old favourites are either too popular or now overcrowded with moorings, so those have been left out, and there's always an argument for not telling everyone else about your 'secret' anchorage in case too many people believe you and spoil it.

Sailors based in these islands are spoilt for choice with such a spectacular and intricate coastline, so we hope the anchorages we have featured will whet your appetite to try some out or explore in a new cruising area. Ultimately the safety of a boat is down to the skipper so, although every effort has been taken to ensure these suggestions are safe and practical, *you* must make the final decision based on the prevailing conditions and your boat and crew.

Anchoring offers something intangible, keeping you in touch with the sea and the elements as sailors have done for hundreds of years. So once the anchor is well dug in, sit back in the cockpit and listen to the quiet chuckle of the water trickling past the hull.

▽ Anchored in Sharfleet Creek

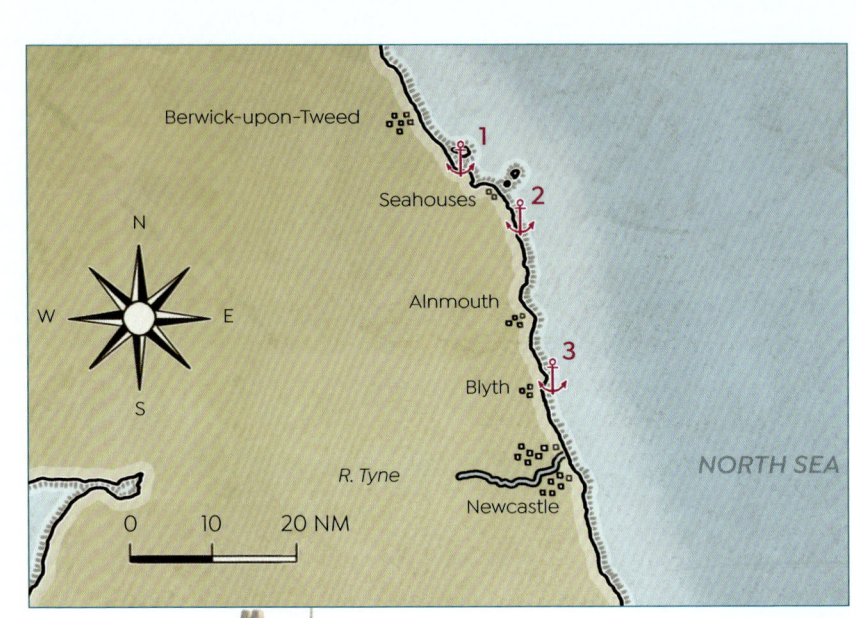

▼ The anchorage at Holy Island

# NORTH EAST

## SCOTTISH BORDER TO SPURN HEAD

----------------------------------

The Northumberland coast is designated an Area of Outstanding Natural Beauty (AONB) and attracts many walkers along its spectacular cliffs, but for anyone afloat, safe havens aren't all that prolific. The dramatic cliffs and impressive headlands can offer a variety of temporary anchorages and there are possibilities for overnight stays when the weather permits. This beautiful coastline has a wealth of history and should not be overlooked.

Grateful thanks go to Ray McGinty and Lester Sher of the Royal Northumberland Yacht Club for their advice and the Club's excellent Sailing Directions, first created in 1902 and regularly updated ever since. 'Navigation is straightforward. The tides are not strong and there are few off-lying dangers,' they advise. That said, the simple anchorages used by fishing craft, while a tranquil refuge in any westerly conditions, are to be avoided in strong easterly winds.

# HOLY ISLAND HARBOUR

LINDISFARNE, NORTHUMBERLAND

---

**THE SAILOR SECURELY** anchored between Lindisfarne Castle and St Cuthbert's Island can revel in a sense of isolation because two hours either side of high water (HW) the causeway, which leads pilgrims from all over the world to the cradle of English Christianity, is cut off by the tide. Motorists trying to outrun the flooding North Sea have been rescued from the roof of their swamped vehicles, and pedestrians trying to outpace the incoming tide along the posted path have taken refuge in a shed on legs.

The day I called, there was a smart white ketch anchored off the Heugh and she had the whole anchorage to herself. An inflatable on the beach below was evidence that this crew were enjoying a lone pilgrimage.

To enter from seaward you pick up the east cardinal Ridge End buoy on the 5m contour and then line up the west and east beacons on Old Law – in transit they will put you on 260°T (True bearing) and this will carry you in over the Triton Shoal bar, marked with a green conical buoy.

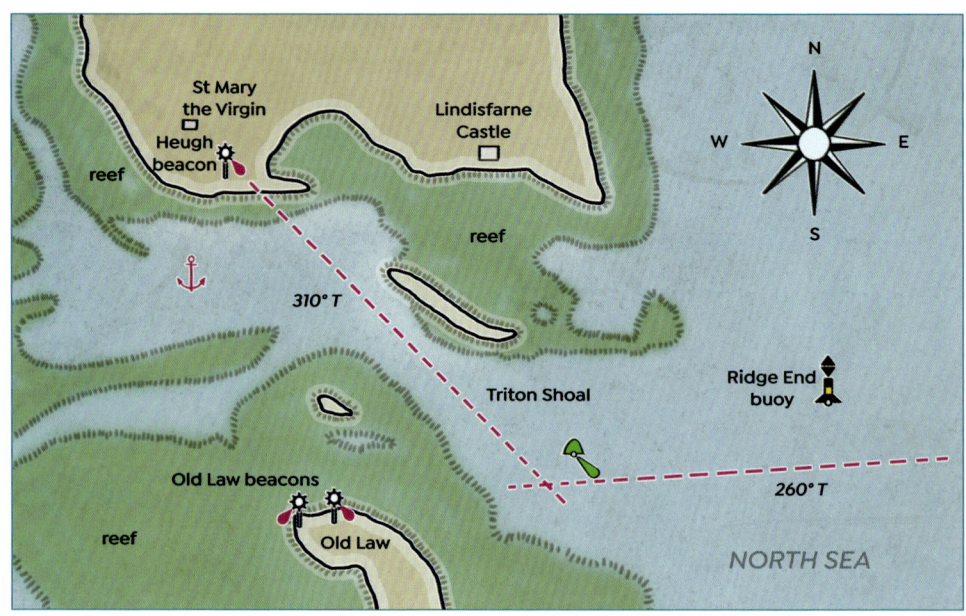

▲ Lindisfarne Castle is a distinctive mark

Once the church belfry and beacon on the Heugh cliff come into line you turn on to 310°T and after five cables (930m, 3,050ft) will be in the anchorage in 3–6m. Holding is in sand and kelp can be a problem. Tides run fast here so either set two anchors – one up and the other down tide, or be prepared to re-set your bower anchor when the tide turns.

Shelter is good in all winds from west through north to east but the anchorage is open to the south-east. When the tide covers the reefs to the south and south-west, winds from that quarter will also kick up a sea until the tide drops below the Long Batt sand once more.

Lindisfarne Castle sits on a crag and is now owned by the National Trust, but the Benedictine Abbey ruins – home to Saints Aidan and Cuthbert – nestle not far from pubs and stores.

Holy Island, with the Cheviot Hills as a backdrop, is one of the most beautiful anchorages on the east coast, and its isolation from the mainland makes it a bridgehead for wildfowl of all descriptions.

▲ The beautiful anchorage at Holy Island

At the turn of the 19th century the area supported drifters, and long-lining boats known as Holy Island keels, which chased herring. They were influenced by Scandinavian design: completely open, double-ended, beamy and with a fine sheer and setting a dipping lugsail. These craft were good at holding directional stability while running into shallow harbours, such as Holy Island, and could be stopped quickly by casting off a single halyard and dumping the sail. Some of these types of hull can be seen to this day as upturned netting sheds and storage huts used by contemporary fishermen. **– DD**

# NEWTON HAVEN

NORTHUMBERLAND

------------

**SILHOUETTED HIGH ON** a crag to the south of Newton Haven are the ruins of Dunstanburgh Castle, its towers never rebuilt after constant sieges by both armies of Lancaster and York as the fortress changed hands during the Wars of the Roses.

For any sailor seeking a romantic selfie backdrop this is the perfect anchorage, nestled between Newton Point to the north and the Emblestone Rock to the south, which dries 4m.

The hamlet of Newton Square offers a handy transit – by lining up the blue doors of the last house with the higher gable end of the neighbouring house you will find yourself on 240°T. Continue along this line until Dunstanburgh Castle bears 155°T – which will be in transit with the western edge of Emblestone Rock – then turn south on this line and anchor anywhere along it. You will find good holding in sand, but an anchor watch is recommended around HW in case of incoming swell.

There is good shelter with a combination of cliffs and rocks giving protection from winds from north-west to south-west via west and, unusually for this coast, there

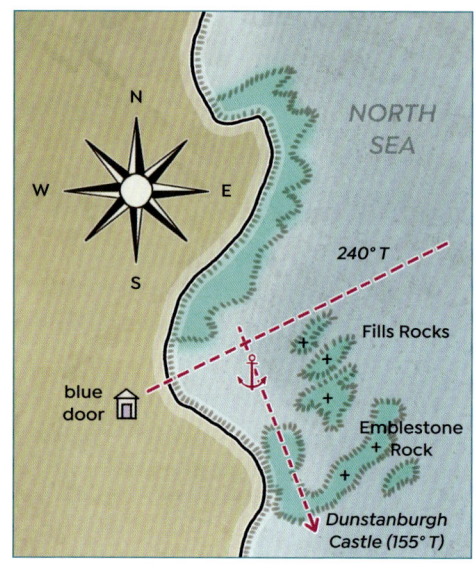

is shelter from the south-east and even east when the Fills Rocks – which cover on the top of the tide – dry. There is no shelter from the north-east.

The saucer-shaped bay has a break in the rocky shoreline that boasts a beach. You can land here by dinghy for a run into *The Ship Inn*, which brews its own beer, serves hot food and has framed copies of large-scale charts hanging from the bar wall from which you can reinforce your navigational prowess. There has been a hostelry here since the late 1700s when it

▼ Newton Haven with Dunstanburgh Castle in the background

was called the Smack. A short mile (1.5km) inland is Embleton village, which has a farm shop where you can stock up on local produce.

During the 1700s smuggling was virtually a way of life, as in many fishing communities. The Coastguard was supposed to stop the delivery of contraband ashore by fishing boat, and in 1828 a row of Coastguard cottages was built outside the village in an attempt to keep tabs on what was happening.

Dunstanburgh Castle is a 1.5-mile (2.4km) coastal walk through National Trust grounds, but worth the effort if you agree as I do with English Heritage's description of it as 'One of the most atmospheric castles in England'. The 14th-century pile, built by Thomas Earl of Lancaster, later beheaded for rebelling against King Edward II, became so battered from sieges that by the time it came into King James I's ownership he sold it off. Much later, however, it's semi-ruined outline provided inspiration for painters including JMW Turner. The castle once had its own harbour but only an overgrown quay remains. The redoubt was used as a fortress again during the Second World War – albeit without cannons – when it was the site of a minefield in case of landings by the Kriegsmarine. **– DD**

▼ *The Ship Inn* is a welcoming hostelry

NORTHUMBERLAND | **NORTH EAST** | 13

# NEWBIGGIN BAY

NORTHUMBERLAND

-------------

**THE LARGE BALTIC** ketch sat with her mizzen set just to nudge her bow towards the early sea breeze coming into Newbiggin Bay. It was prudent seamanship keeping the vessel head-to-wind to prevent her sailing round her anchor. The real wind was west, providing the anchorage with perfect shelter, which the bay enjoys from north through west to south-west.

Newbiggin Bay is easy to identify from seaward from the dun-coloured St Bartholomew's Church crowning

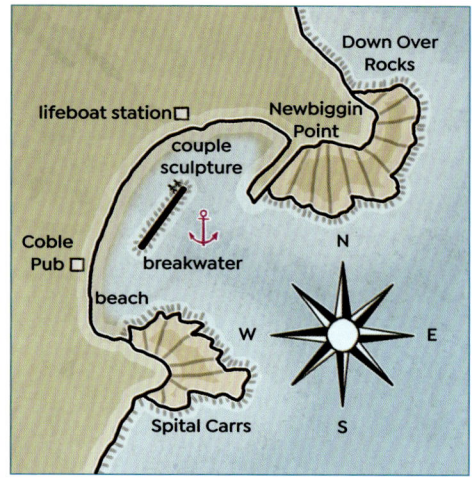

▼ The anchorage at Newbiggin Bay

14 | ANCHORAGES OF THE BRITISH ISLES

▼ The *Couple* statue on the breakwater

Newbiggin Point. That is the northern side of the bay with an outcrop of reef – Down Over Rocks – atop which a disembodied causeway sits with a 4m-high green light (Fl G 10s).

Just south of this is the anchorage in 4m outside a breakwater which runs north–south; the holding in sand is good but it is advisable to buoy the anchor. The breakwater was built in the early 2000s after the town was flooded in the 1990s. It sports a red light on each end (Fl 2 R 5s) and on top of it is a giant statue of a couple, called, appropriately enough, *Couple*, an art installation by sculptor Sean Henry and Britain's first off-shore sculpture.

At the southern end of the bay is Spital Point with an extending reef – Spital Carrs.

Landing can be made by dinghy onto soft sand where the RNLI station is and where fishing boats are hauled out on travel hoists. This is Britain's oldest operational lifeboat house, built in 1851 (the RNLI took over the station in 1867). The current lifeboat is an Atlantic 85 B class, *Richard Wake Burdon*, which has been on station since 2012. Ashore is the Newbiggin Sailing Club HQ, a maritime centre with history of the fishing industry, and a busy town with all amenities. Newbiggin was an early holiday destination with an annual street fair that attracted thousands of visitors until 2004.

The nearest pub is the aptly named *Coble Inn*. It is worth noting that the coble is a unique craft which, like an inanimate Darwinian object, came about through survival of the fittest; that survival taking years to perfect. By the mid-1800s the fishing cobles peaked at over 140 but there are now fewer than 10. Anything from 27ft to 33ft length overall (LOA), a coble was built with a flared, high, planked bow and deep forefoot, but with a ram plank instead of a keel, to cleave through the big seas that pound the Northumberland and Yorkshire coast in heavy onshore conditions when launching. Yet she had a shoal flat bottom aft and a raked transom so that, coming through the breakers stern first, she can be beached on a wave and immediately dragged up the sand. Although the coble was considered the greatest open sailing boat of her time – both on and offshore – if handled improperly she could easily broach. It was in a coble that Grace Darling and her father made their legendary 1838 rescue of survivors from the steamer *Forfarshire* in the Farne Islands. Lieutenant EE Middleton made a yacht cruise around England in 1869 in a coble described in his book *The Cruise of the Kate*. – **DD**

# EAST AND SOUTH EAST

SPURN HEAD TO THE SOLENT

---

The sailor's East Coast lies between Yorkshire's Spurn Head and Kent's South Foreland, encompassing 20 rivers, three inland seas, hundreds of creeks, any number of swatchways – Essex alone has the longest coastline in the country – and is, therefore, a lost world of anchorages. From the Wash to the Humber, the coast feels rather exposed and there is little shelter for an overnight stop. Once into the Humber, most of the rivers are now behind locks, so timing is critical. Coming down the Norfolk and Suffolk coasts the possibilities begin to open up.

Past South Foreland and the Dover Strait, finding comfortable anchorages is rather more challenging until you reach the Solent. Here the greater problem is the sheer number of yachts and the traditional anchorages that have now been filled up with moorings, but it's still possible to nudge into a quiet corner or two.

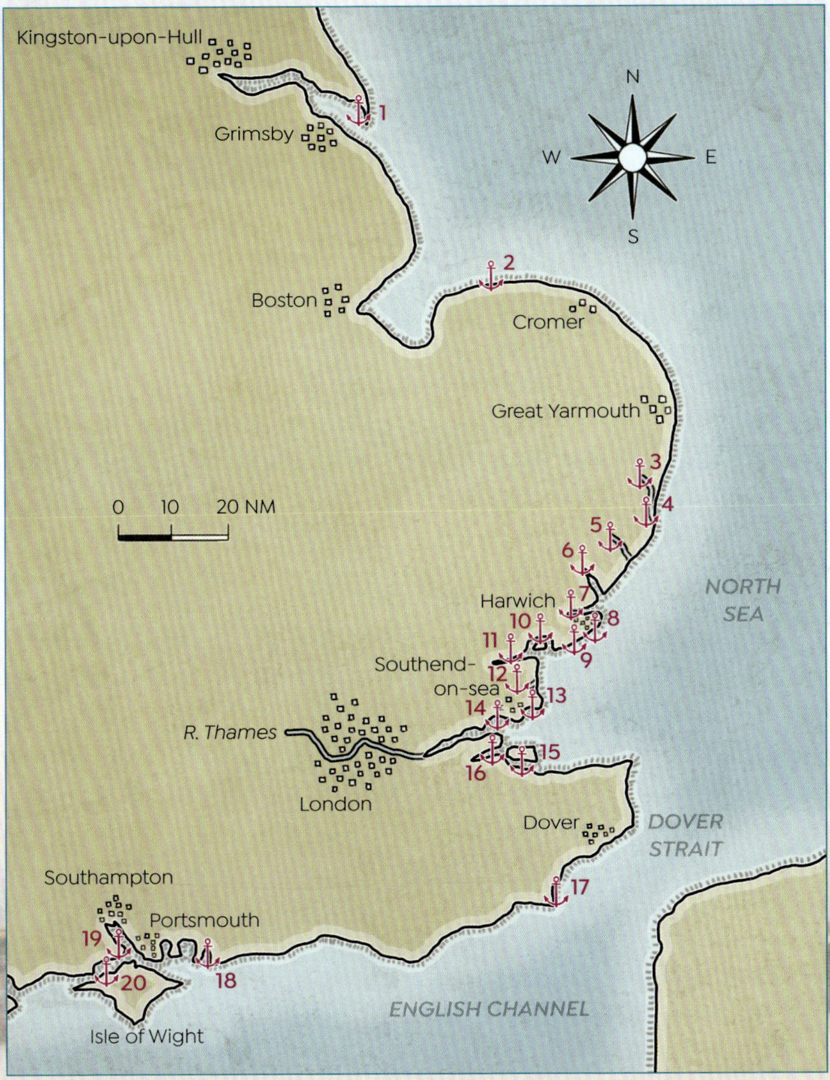

▼ *Wendy May* anchored in Sharfleet Creek with a transit beacon in the distance

# SPURN HEAD

RIVER HUMBER, YORKSHIRE

---

**THE BUOYS MARKING** the channel of the River Humber sit on boat-shaped hulls, so fiercely runs the tide here. Therefore, I had been rather pleased with myself when *Wendy May*, my Maurice Griffiths'-designed 26ft gaff cutter, arrived off the lock gates at Grimsby with half an hour to spare before HW. The timing was near perfect, I thought. However, my smug demeanour evaporated when I discovered that the lock gates would not open until *after* HW. This is because during spring tides, which it was, a flood barrier is also in operation and would not be opened until after the tide started dropping.

I explained patiently, over the VHF, that my passage plan had been drawn up to fit in with 'opening time' and that once the ebb came away my boat's small auxiliary engine would not be man enough to stem the furious Humber tide, and that the open river was no place to anchor. Did the harbourmaster have any suggestions as to where we should go?

'We know of no safe haven,' came the unhelpful reply.

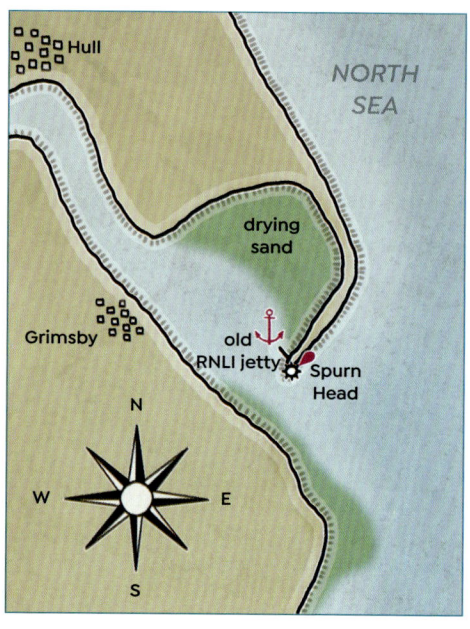

But my crew and I had already scoped out an anchorage, on the way up river, should we need it.

Inside the black and white hooped tower of Spurn Head lighthouse is a neat little bay in estuarine clay. The bight in Trinity Sand opposite the Hawke east cardinal is situated directly across the river from Bull Sand Fort and is formed by the curled finger of Spurn Head. You can anchor here in a couple of metres at LWS inside the 12m Hawke Channel, with the

▼ Spurn Head anchorage with its two disused lighthouses in the distance

two disused lighthouses in transit, but not further north. You're sheltered in all winds, from north through east, but in strong winds from west to south, although you are only facing a short scend of 10 miles (18.5km) to the protective coastline of Lincolnshire on the south side of the Humber, a serious swell can roll in.

It's obvious from the chart that on flood tides there will be a clockwise back-eddy and on the ebb the reverse, but that should not be an issue as this is a temporary anchorage used as a jump-off point for yachts heading out of the Humber, or, as we faced that day, for yachts trying to negotiate the locked ports of this commercially busy and strongly flowing river. It is, therefore, an anchorage where you would not leave your boat unattended.

Ashore there's a nature reserve run by Yorkshire Wildlife Trust. The RNLI station, which was the only one manned full-time in the UK, has closed down because the launching pier is in bad repair. The lifeboat is now based at Grimsby.

As things turned out, we managed eventually to lock into Grimsby and, that night, in the convivial company of sailors from the Humber Cruising Association, learned that most places are behind lock gates on the River Humber. As one hoary old mariner put it: 'You don't expect us to drown our town for one southern yachty, do you?' Anchoring havens are rare in these parts, so it's worth taking note of this one. **– DD**

▼ Spurn Head as it appears as you enter the Humber

# NORTON HOLE

BRANCASTER, NORFOLK

--------------

**THIS SAND-DUNE INFESTED** port sends enough fishing boats to sea to bring home the largest catch of whelks – after Wells – in Norfolk. And if you're a whelk then there's enough water in Brancaster's sandy creeks to keep you covered; if not, you need to find Norton Hole to stay afloat.

I nosed *Wendy May*, my 26ft gaff cutter, in there at dusk just as the east-going tidal stream died away. You approach just north of west, leaving Scolt Head, with its beaconed wreck to port, through a buoyed channel (not lit) and make three turns in the channel before arriving at the (comparatively) deep anchorage of Norton Hole, where there's about 1.8m (6ft) of water at LW.

When we arrived, in the month of May, Norton Hole was busy with moored fishing dories and so, convinced I had enough water beneath my 4ft 3in draught to stay at least no more than tilted gently at LW, we backed down the channel again and dropped the CQR anchor, with enough swinging room, in the entry channel.

That this was a mistake I discovered around 0100, when first the pump handle

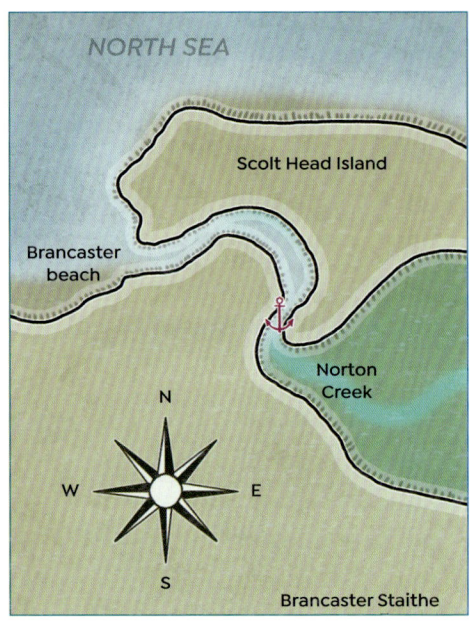

rolled across the bridge deck with a clonk, then came a splishing sound as weather-side bilge water trickled leeward, and finally a thump as my crew slid effortlessly from his berth onto the cabin sole. As I was in the leeward bunk, I suffered no more discomfort than to roll around onto the topside lining.

When next morning the tide returned, its powerful run wrung the boat on her keel and sent whirlpools and eddies around her until she lifted. I was relieved

▲ The tide whipping out at Brancaster

that I had not shipped the boat's legs, as there's a chance they would have been wrenched off. Unless you sail a bilge keeler, barge yacht or centre-boarder, you definitely need to anchor in Norton Hole when visiting Brancaster!

That said, the visit is worth the vexation: nature has been reserved by the National Trust on Scolt Head Island, and a walk ashore is an arcadian idyll. The island is a long sandbank that protects both Brancaster and its easterly neighbour, Burnham Overy Staithe. It is constantly moving westward, though pretty slowly, and has amazing dunes, salt marshes, flora and fauna, and is particularly noted for its terns. Alternatively, you can head up to Brancaster Staithe, a hamlet where the local sailing club, when open, has a bar and showers, and the Jolly Sailor keeps customers smiling with platters of local seafood.

▼ The Brancaster channel buoy

These places are ideally reached by tender, as all the approach creeks dry out. All the North Norfolk coastal ports are like this – with the exception of Wells, where you can lie afloat on the visitor's pontoon. **– DD**

# IKEN CLIFF

RIVER ALDE, SUFFOLK

-------------

**IF YOU COULD** anchor in the Garden of Eden, then Iken Cliff would be where, as you nosed into the treeline, Adam or Eve would take your dinghy painter – just a monkey fist's lob from your foredeck.

Without question, Iken Cliff is the most perfectly sheltered anchorage I've ever visited. To the south, beneath the cliff, drooping trees almost touch the water and, to the north, marsh islands lie like bristling lily pads marking the last of the snaking River Alde up to Snape. You'll not find much more than a metre here at LW, but the bottom is liquidised mud and your keel will nestle gently in the ooze.

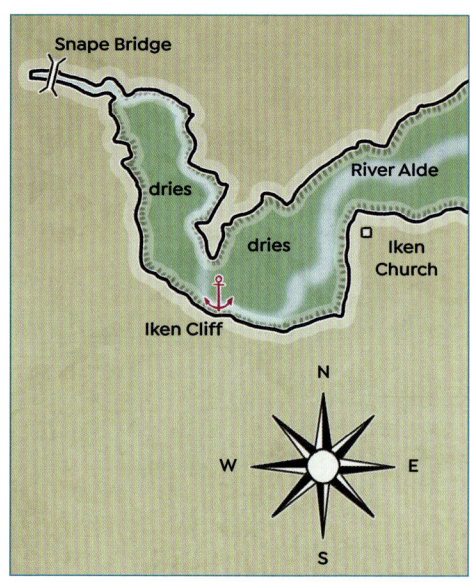

▼ The anchorage from the shore

▼ Peace and quiet at Iken Cliff

You can walk along the banks of the river to Snape and its famous Maltings, converted in 1948 into a world-renowned concert hall created by composer Benjamin Britten and his lover, the tenor Peter Pears, who lived in nearby Aldeburgh. It's also possible to sail right up to the quay at Snape and dry out alongside, as the Thames sailing barges once did to load malt, but you would ground here in soft mud and part of the quay is reserved.

A major cruising benefit of sailing up to Iken Cliff is that you get two hours extra flood tide (over the HW at the River Ore entrance) to carry you up river through the withy sticks, which mark the waterway's tortuous progress – the most labyrinthine known as Little Japan – through reed beds, saltings and sedge. The port-hand withies are marked with red plastic bottles cable-tied to saplings stripped of twigs; the starboard-hand withies are saplings left with their twigs intact and facing the way nature intended.

St Botolph's Church stands up over the river just before you get to Iken Cliff and marks the start of Troublesome Reach. It actually isn't troublesome any more thanks to the efforts of local sailors who replace the 'planted' withies on each side of the serpentine creek each year, as many get flattened by charter barges that fail to make the tight turns when visiting Snape. The church is built on a knoll sticking out into the river and is thought to be where St Botolph landed in AD 654. Much of what you see today is from a Victorian restoration. It has a thatched nave but there was a fire in 1968 gutting this part of the church which was later restored.

Above the reach on the south shore is Iken Hall. Some Victorian farm buildings have been converted for holiday accommodation with views of the river and easy access to the riverside path.
**– DD**

# BUTLEY RIVER

RIVER ORE, SUFFOLK

----

**THE SUMMER NIGHT** was so warm that I lay on top of my sleeping bag listening to a gentle swish of water somewhere away in the darkness. As I dozed there, I realised the swish had a symmetrical pattern, too regular for the surf rinsing through the shingle of Orford spit, which I had earlier assumed it was. No, this swish was the controlled spray of a giant hose wetting the bone-dry fields struggling to push up corn, north of Gedgrave Marsh.

There is nowhere on the East Coast where plough gets closer to sail than the Butley River, a mere creek given the grand title of river because it has water aplenty for any yacht at all stages of the tide.

Earlier my daughter Emily, my son Richard and I made the 2-mile (3.2km) trudge from the small fisherman's landing on the east side of the creek, along a sandy path to Orford village – dominated by the stone polygon of King Henry II's castle, so designed to prevent besiegers undermining the footings, a breach possible with square towers – where we dined at a local pub. There are three to choose from – the King's Head, the Crown and Castle, and the Jolly Sailor, which has links to smuggler's girl Margaret Catchpole whose transportation to Australia for the theft of a horse brings a tear to the eye of the most brutal observer. There is a fine restaurant here, too – the Butley Oysterage, specialising in the local bivalves.

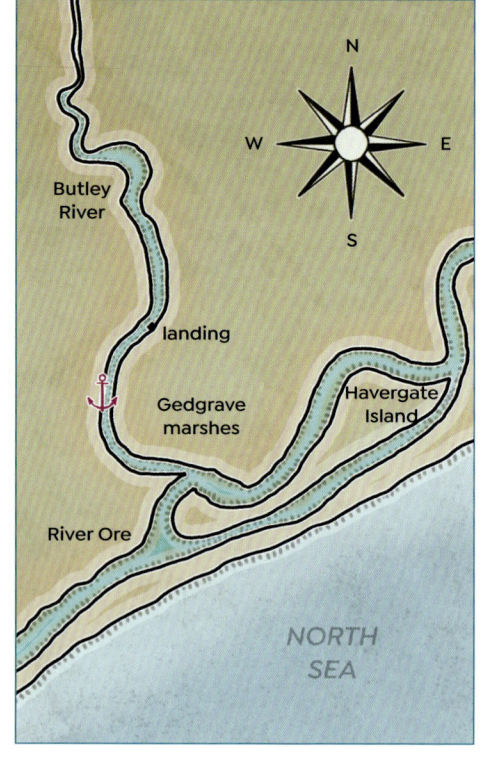

From Orford Quay you can also take a ferry across to the mysterious 10-mile (16km) long, 2,000-acre (810ha) former Ministry of Defence (MOD) shingle bar, now owned by the National Trust, where from 1913 until its closure in 1987 all manner of rockets, bombs and even nuclear devices were stress tested. Here you can access the sinister 'pagodas' – massive concrete sheds, which look like cement versions of the Acropolis and where bombs, used in atomic explosions, were dropped, heated up, cooled down, vibrated and even crushed just to see what they could endure. In the event of an uncontrolled explosion the pagodas were designed to absorb the shock: the columns would shatter, allowing the roof to collapse and seal off the blast. That they're still standing is evidence no accidents took place. Allegedly.

By the time we returned to our anchorage there were two other riding lights reflected in the creek waters besides that of *Minstrel Boy*, my Contessa 32, as the Butley River is a popular anchorage for those who seek secure holding – in mud – and with refuge from strong winds from all points of the compass.

This is an ideal anchorage for yachts preparing to leave Orford Haven, with its treacherous and ever-shifting shingle bar, as it is just a couple of miles or so downriver at Shingle Street. **– DD**

▲ A 'pagoda' on Orford Ness

▼ Sailing into the Butley River

# THE ROCKS

RIVER DEBEN, SUFFOLK

-------------

**WHEN YOUR ANCHOR** takes a grip of the seabed here it's likely to have found the same good holding ground discovered by Saxon ships in the 7th century. Here you are just 3 miles (4.8km) from the greatest archaeological find ever made in Europe: the burial of a 38-oared, 86ft long Saxon ship, a perfect imprint of which revealed her iron rivets in the sand. A body-shaped gap among the treasure is believed to have been of Raedwald, King of East Anglia. The beaten gold and iron hollow-eyed mask-helmet, sword, buckles and other treasures of Sutton Hoo are under glass in the British Museum, but you can get an atavistic sense of place as your keel hovers over the river she came up.

Shelter here is good beneath the great trees of Ramsholt Woods, except in strong winds from the north. You can land on the sandy beach that gives the anchorage its name thanks to a layer of sandstone rock further out in the stream. Much of this was dredged up and used by stonemasons to build the 12th-century Orford Castle on the River Ore to the north. Holding is mostly good but occasionally you might find

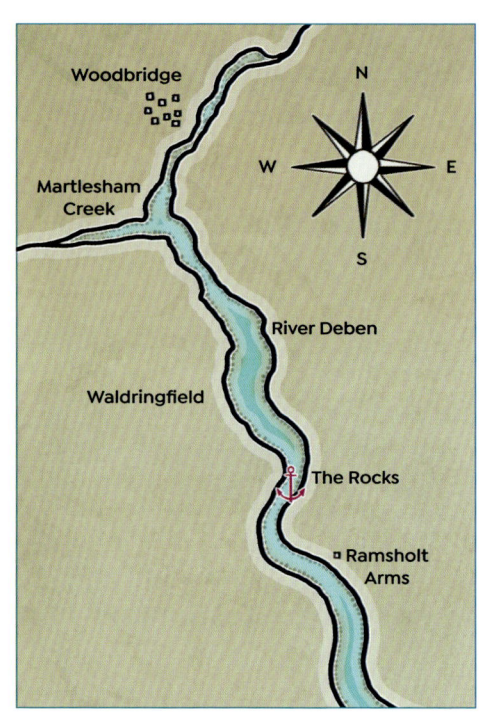

the ubiquitous 'rocks'. In a spring ebb, a strong wind against it will make the anchorage fairly uncomfortable.

My most recent visit was aboard *Betty II* and we found the beach to be the site of a couple of abandoned boats, but there was still plenty of room for our tender. Along this shoreline people hunt for fossils which litter the base of the cliff, although, personally, I'd rather make the lovely country walk to the Ramsholt Arms, 40 minutes downriver, where the ale is real enough to interfere with the return trip and the food's not bad either.

As with many East Coast rivers the Deben has a shifting bar which can move significantly, particularly in easterly gales. The Woodbridge Haven fairway buoy is frequently moved and it's best to check with the Felixstowe Ferry Harbourmaster for the latest information on the bar. It's generally best to enter HW-2hr, but never approach it in strong east or south-east winds, and entry is not feasible at night.

Once over the bar the Deben is a beautiful river and it's worth venturing up to Woodbridge to see the old mill and the Tidemill Yacht Harbour. There are now a lot of moorings all the way up the river with some classic yachts along the way. Sutton Hoo is on the opposite side of the river to Woodbridge, although there's no access from the river. The channel is marked by buoys from The Rocks up to Woodbridge; initially it is on the east side of the river then crosses to the west past Stonner Point. On the west shore is Waldringfield, which has a sailing club and Waldringfield Boatyard. **– DD**

▼ The Rocks, River Deben

# STONE HEAPS

RIVER ORWELL, SUFFOLK

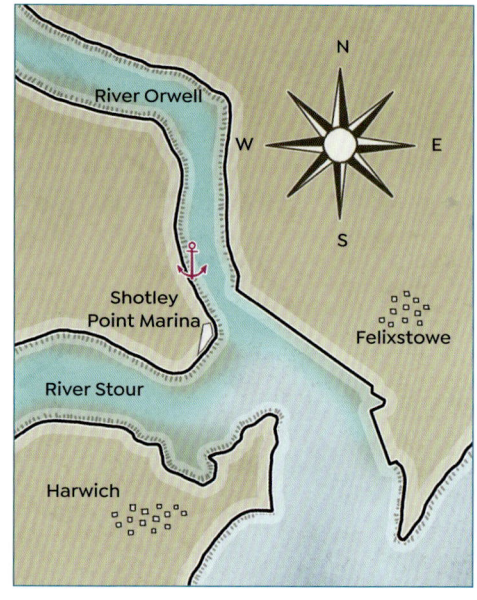

**TIME WAS WHEN** the distinctive 'triangle' of the spritsail rig could be guaranteed to be seen close in to the Shotley shoreline, just a couple of hundred metres from Shotley Point. Thames sailing barges anchored here waiting for a 'slant' (fair wind) to take the early flood up to London for their next freight, or along the coast to Great Yarmouth, The Wash or the Humber on the first of the ebb to continue their passage after sheltering from a blow. And even though marinas abound, sailors still use the anchorage today to get an early start or for a peaceful lunchtime break. The shoreline is beachy and a footpath runs either up to Pin Mill where the *Butt & Oyster* awaits or down to the *Bristol Arms* at Shotley. But both are a good stride.

Stone Heaps is a slight bay on the west shore just up from Shotley Point, with deep enough water for all craft at all stages of the tide. The holding is good and it's sheltered from all quarters. However, as you lie in your bunk at night, the throbbing of a passing coaster coming to or from Ipswich may have you thinking you are about to be run down. Sleep on – as long as your riding light twinkles – for the anchorage is well clear of the buoyed channel. These days, when I have been brought up there in preparation for an early start back to the Thames, I've found that the reversing alerts of gantries during the night shift at the Felixstowe container berth opposite may necessitate ear plugs.

Stone Heaps is so named after the septaria or 'cement stone' that was dredged up from the riverbed by smacks, loaded into barges and taken to Thames-side cement factories.

▲ Stone Heaps on the River Orwell

The River Orwell (some people call it the Ipswich River) isn't all that long because its name changes, just above Ipswich, to the River Gipping (Ipswich was originally called Gyperswick). The river is still busy with commercial traffic and the port of Ipswich runs along both banks. As you sail up here you are following in the wake of Romans, Vikings, Angles, Saxons and thousands of trading vessels, as Ipswich was one of the most important ports in England during the Middle Ages. In later centuries, the river silted up and trade dropped off until Commissioners were appointed in the 19th century and the river was deepened and widened.

The *Butt & Oyster* at Pin Mill commemorates not just the oysters that used to be found all along the river but also the butts where archery was practised. The fields around Pin Mill would have seen much activity in the weeks before the vast army boarded 300 ships to sail to the Battle of Crécy in 1346.

Pin Mill is also famous for building and repairing barges, and in July each year beautifully preserved barges gather for the Pin Mill Barge Match. It is a stunning sight to watch these amazing vessels sailing together, particularly set against the backdrop of Felixstowe container terminal. **– DD**

# ERWARTON NESS

RIVER STOUR, SUFFOLK

**IN JOHN CONSTABLE'S** *The Hay Wain* a horse and cart negotiate the top end of the River Stour in Essex. The last time I anchored at Erwarton Ness I was aboard contemporary marine artist Martyn Mackrill's yacht *Nightfall*, the 31ft gaff cutter built in 1910 and once owned by Maurice Griffiths, boat designer and past editor of *Yachting Monthly*.

Erwarton Ness is on the Suffolk side of the river that marks the border between that county and Essex. It's a great place to shelter from northerly winds, but open to both east and west. Landing can be made on the brick and stone rubble of an old farm wharf, now demolished, and walks along the Stour are isolated, rural and peaceful.

Sadly, the old *Queen's Head* at Erwarton village is now closed, and despite a public campaign to take it over as a community pub, it has become a residential property. It was probably the most inappropriate pub of that name in England, as although the ill-fated monarch Anne Boleyn lost her head at

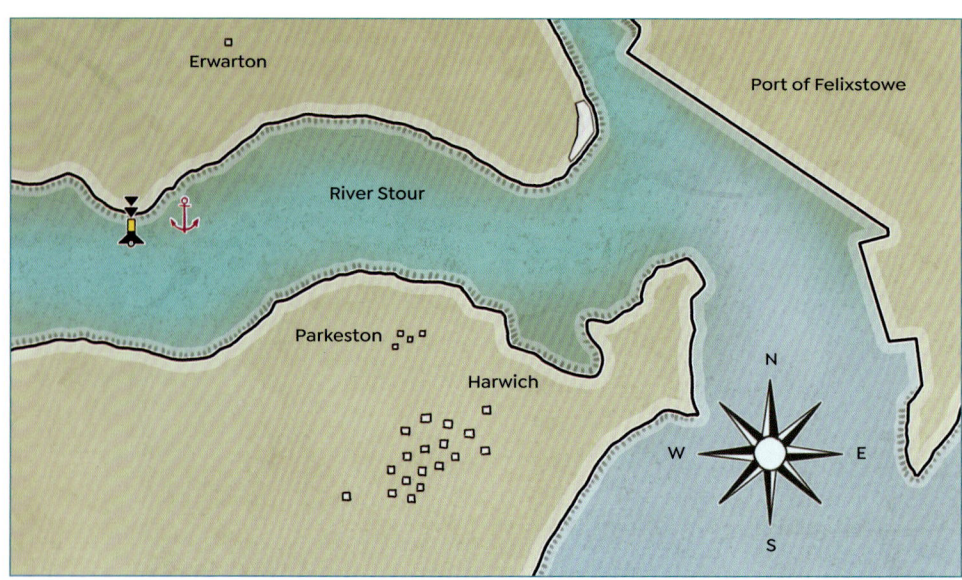

the Tower of London, some claim it's the Essex girl's heart – and not her head – that is buried in the local church.

Further upriver on the south side is Wrabness, an anchorage to choose if the wind is hard from the south and Erwarton Ness is too lively. You'll lie here in good holding, but there are several trots of moored yachts to negotiate. There's a sandy beach to land on here, but nothing ashore since the closure of the lonely local pub.

The Stour leads up to Mistley, a drying port made famous by the Horlock family who built and traded Thames sailing barges, including *Blue Mermaid*, which was blown up by a German mine in 1942 with the loss of skipper and mate. Her replacement of the same name, launched at Polruan, Cornwall in 2016, is now sailing these waters again under the aegis of the Sea Change Sailing Trust, taking youngsters to sea to make or break 'em.

Mistley Quay still receives coasters bringing in Baltic timber, so be sure to show a light if anchored overnight. If you sail up to Mistley you'll see two towers, which are all that remains of an 18th-century church designed by Robert Adam. When the church was demolished in 1870 the towers were preserved as a sea mark. **– DD**

▼ Erwarton Ness on the River Stour

# 8

# STONE POINT

WALTON BACKWATERS, ESSEX

---

**THE CHILDREN'S AUTHOR** Arthur Ransome set his 1939 novel *Secret Water* here, although the Backwaters are a secret no longer, with a 400-berth marina at Titchmarsh and trots of swinging moorings up Walton Channel.

Yachts can anchor almost within touching distance of the sandy beach at Stone Point as the channel is steep-to, which is just as well as you need to be in tight and well clear of the channel since the ebb on springs runs hard. Holding is good, although you need to check your anchor to make sure it has set before the tide comes away. The anchorage is well-sheltered from all quarters and the soft, sandy beach is a delight for sailors with young children: the landing here is popular with bathers and picnickers. That said, in stiff south-westerlies you will feel more secure further up Walton Channel if you're staying the night.

The site is managed by the old-world Walton & Frinton Yacht Club, which Ransome would recognise even after its restoration as it was founded in 1908 on concrete 'mushroom' legs, to keep it clear of big tides. The tides are getting bigger so the new club remains elevated.

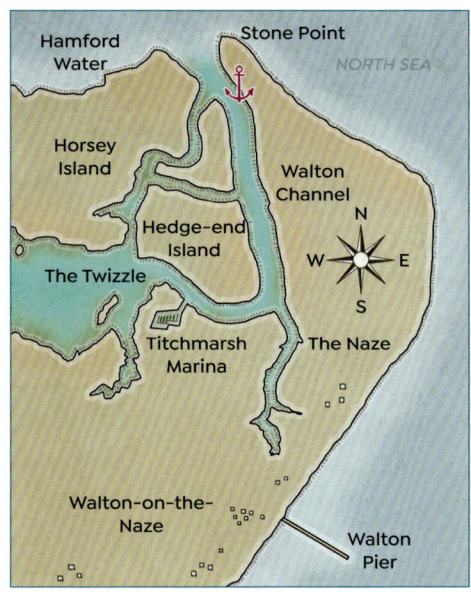

You sail up Walton Channel for Walton-on-the-Naze, a holiday resort locked into a mid-century (last century) feel. It is still served by railway train even though it is a much smaller town than nearby Maldon, which is not. Local rumour has it that during the 1960s' axing of railway lines by the late Dr Richard Beeching, chairman of the then British Railways Board, Walton-on-the-Naze was spared because he had an interest in a local holiday caravan park. Alternatively, you can sail up Hamford Water for the lost world of anchorages,

▲ Hamford Water in the Walton Backwaters

silent creeks and marshy islets ... truly away from it all.

There was a time when in and around these marshy islets you might spot a gun punt or two drifting along with her skipper lying on their stomach, finger ready on the trigger of a shotgun. This was when the winter skies of Essex were covered with 'black' geese so dense they appeared 'like the locusts of Egypt', as one old wild-fowler described the scene, and a single discharge fired at random would bring down several geese in one go. Today, the brent geese are protected and the punt-gunners are a rare sight. They still exist, however, and some set a little square sail to pull themselves into the midst of their target area.

This lost world was sought out by novelist Arnold Bennett, who moved to Thorpe-le-Soken where he spent several years away from crowds, madding or otherwise. The author, who wrote 34

▲ *Swallows and Amazons* country near Stone Point

novels, 13 plays and seven volumes of short stories, took up yachting and loved the solitude he found in the landlocked creeks of the Backwaters. **– DD**

# 9

# KIRBY CREEK

WALTON BACKWATERS, ESSEX

----------

▼ A traditional craft at Kirby-le-Soken

**A CURLEW'S-EYE VIEW** of the Walton Backwaters reveals a wader's paradise at LW, as acres of deep mud strangle two fingers of deep-water arteries: Hamford Water and the Walton Channel. At HW, six or so islands – including Skipper's, Bramble and Horsey – and several snaking ridges of training wall manage to keep their marshy profile above the tide in this inland sea.

At the heart of this Essex Venice is Kirby Creek, where an all-tide anchorage in fluke-swallowing mud can be found in

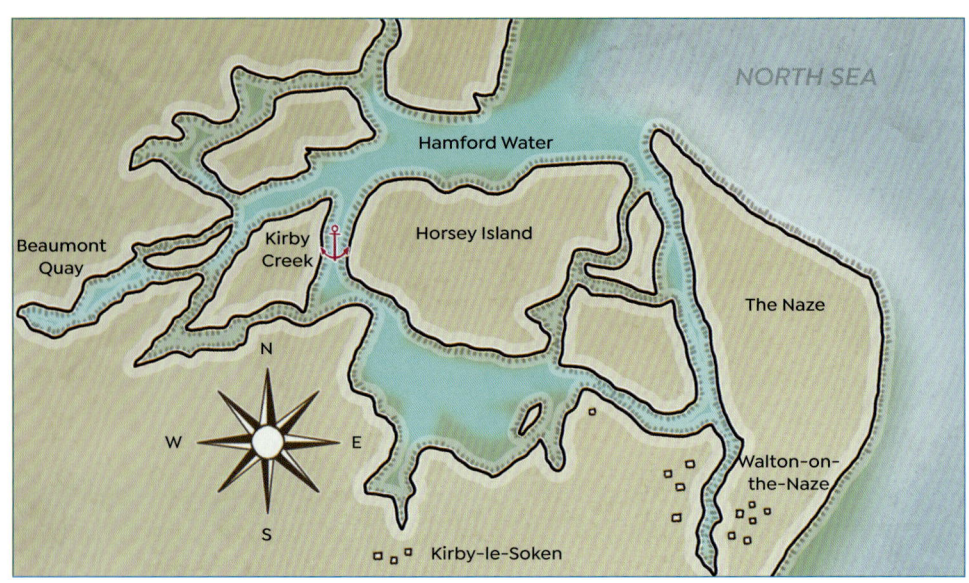

34 | ANCHORAGES OF THE BRITISH ISLES

▲ *Powder Monkey* in Kirby Creek, Walton Backwaters

the entrance above the oyster grounds. Notice boards on the marshy islets warn of the delicate bivalve layings, which must be avoided.

No gale can get you here, and your boat will ride for weeks without a wavelet to bother her topside, but to enjoy a marsh stroll or walk to *The Ship* pub in the village of Kirby-le-Soken, 1 mile (1.6km) from the old barge quay at the head of the creek, a dinghy is a must – or a gondolier, if you can find one! Kirby-le-Soken is one of several Sokens in the area, and the word probably comes from Norse and Old English and meant a special jurisdiction or immunity.

If you have a reliable outboard then a trip up to Beaumont Quay at the very head of the Backwaters is an interesting run and one we took from *Powder Monkey*, my 30ft Alan Buchanan Yeoman Junior. The old stone quay at Beaumont was built of masonry from the dismantled medieval London Bridge, and donated to the governors of Guy's Hospital, who owned farmland in the area, the produce from which was carried to supply the infirmary's needs.

Beaumont, in common with many Essex wharves, was also where sailing barges loaded haystacks for the horse-drawn traffic of London. They returned with horse manure, which farmers used to fertilise root crops. **– DD**

▼ The fascinating Walton Backwaters

# PYEFLEET CREEK

RIVER COLNE, ESSEX

-------------

**I HAVE ANCHORED** in the Pyefleet many times, and back in the 1960s it was full of motor barges denuded of their topmasts, though still sporting a mainmast and sail. Today they have all gone, but you will still find yourself anchored among moored traditional craft – usually a Colchester smack, as these lovely fishing gaffers are now used as yachts.

This anchorage is also where *Pioneer* is moored, the only craft of her kind left afloat. She is a Skillinger, a 64ft long ketch-rigged deep-sea trawler, used to dredge for oysters off the coast of North Holland from 1890 to 1930. She broke her back in 1942 in the Strood Channel – on the west side of Pyefleet Creek – and was left hulked until she was dug out of the creek in 1999 and restored.

You enter Pyefleet off the River Colne. Simply round Mersea Stone (a steep-to shingle bank), leave the first red can buoy to port (it marks a drying wreck), and steer north of west into the creek. Moorings abound, but there's plenty of anchoring room. Your anchor will not drag here in good Essex mud; there's depth enough for all craft and you have shelter from all

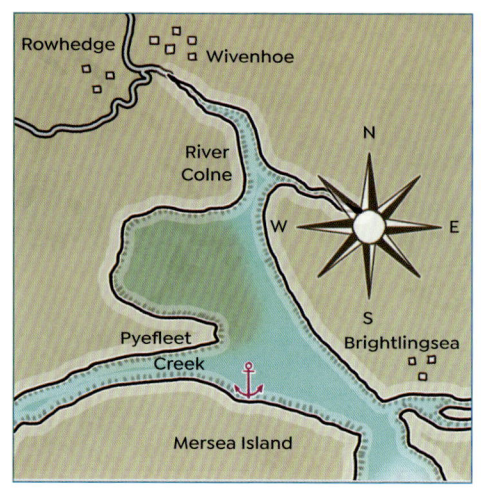

quarters, although south-easterly winds will throw up a swell.

You can sample the famous Colchester native oysters here – laid down in Roman times – and row ashore to the hard to order them.

Anchored here one year in *Powder Monkey*, my eldest daughter, Katie, was crew and – aged 13 – was unimpressed with solitude and the romance of the riding light, so I had to seek out some bright lights. The nearest are at Brightlingsea, which is a stiff row or outboard journey across the River Colne to the harbour pontoon or the Colne Yacht Club pontoon, both of which are all-tide landings. Brightlingsea Hard has a set of scrubbing posts, which are unfortunately becoming a rarity on the east coast. Here you'll find many pubs, restaurants, chip shops and grocery stores.

If you prefer a shorter dinghy passage but a longer walk, you can land on the shingle beach at East Mersea, haul your tender up the steep bank and walk to the Dog & Pheasant pub, some 3.2km (2 miles) inland.

Brightlingsea residents are now employed as crews aboard the tenders that look after the wind farms: the nearest forest of these is on the Gunfleet Sands, under an hour's passage in a high-speed launch. Time was, however, when these sands provided a different career for the town's sailors – namely searching for a wreck. A humble longshoreman could retire off the proceeds of one good shipwreck and be dubbed a hero to boot for rescuing the crew. **– DD**

▲ A traditional smack moored in Pyefleet Creek

▼ Mike Peyton, the late yachting cartoonist, getting the stove going in Pyefleet Creek

# OSEA ISLAND

RIVER BLACKWATER, ESSEX

------------

**WITH ITS MUD** and shoal waters, it comes as a surprise to learn that Essex produced a deep-keeled yacht that revolutionised racing. The 110ft *Jullanar* had a draught of 13ft 6in aft and was designed by agricultural machinery magnate EH Bentall, a builder of ploughs. With her cutaway sections, the gaff yawl looked like a giant earth-turning machine and fell onto her beam ends when launched in 1877 at Wivenhoe. But she cleaned up on the racing circuit and even the most famous yacht designer of all time, GL Watson, who drew the royal yacht *Britannia*, described himself as the 'pupil' of Bentall.

All that's left of the 'Princess of the Sea', as she was known, is her mast, which was used in the construction of the little jetty at Osea Island, itself now a ruin. Just to the east of this pier is an anchorage in 2m of water, with good holding and open only to the south and east.

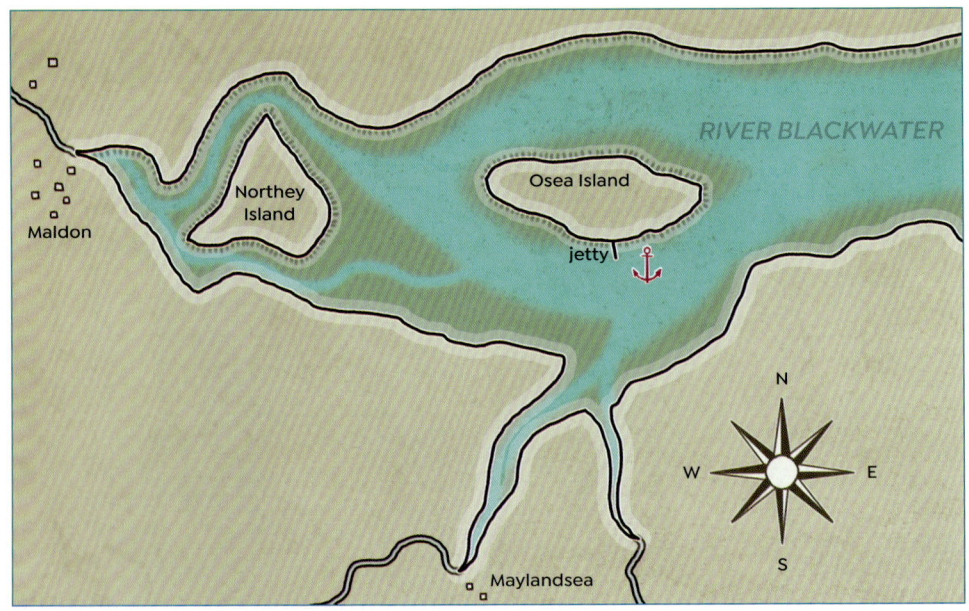

There is a beach here, and marshy walks in front of an Edwardian mansion used for wedding receptions, but which was built by Charringtons, the brewers, as a place to take 'the cure'. In other words, it was a drying out clinic, built in a fit of guilty conscience.

When I last anchored here in *Almita*, my 26ft centre-board gaff cutter built in 1906, we had run out of fresh water and so used river water to boil the potatoes. My son Richard and his schoolboy pal said they were the best spuds they'd ever had. This may have something to do with the fact that the River Blackwater is the saltiest estuary in the UK, second only to the Dee, with its own salt factory at Maldon at the head of the river. They could be right, as after dinner all I could think about was a foaming pint of Bass.

On the top of the tide you can sail up to Hythe Quay, Maldon, but the river dries out completely, so unless your boat can take the ground (soft mud here) you are best advised to take a tender and outboard up to the town if you want to spend any time there. The quay itself is home to many Thames sailing barges which run knees-ups, for wedding guests and others, downriver on the tide.

Further up the High Street are many restaurants and takeaways plus the ancient All Saints Church, which has a statue of Brythnoth – hero of the Battle of Maldon – who fought a party of raiding Vikings and lost. His head was taken back to Denmark and used as a beer mug. Fortunately, at the two pubs – the ubiquitous Jolly Sailor and the Queen's Head, both just a step ashore from the quay – more conventional drinking vessels are on offer. **– DD**

▼ *Almita* anchored off Osea Island

# 12

# CLIFF REACH

RIVER CROUCH, ESSEX

- - - - - - - - - - - - -

**WHEN YOU ENTER** the River Crouch you are still at sea. There's no sense of being embraced by the land, as on both sides of you are flat sandbanks, covered by water most of the time, but when exposed are so flat as to be imperceptible. They are the Foulness Sands to port and the Buxey to starboard: shoals which are part of the greatest mudbank in Europe.

Even at Shore Ends, when at last you get sea walls either side, there are no trees or any perpendiculars, with the

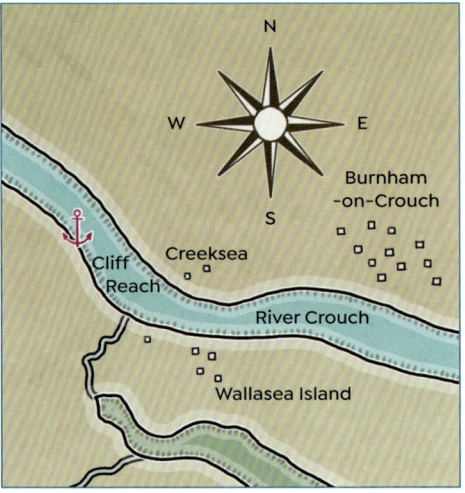

▼ Anchored in Cliff Reach, River Crouch

40 | ANCHORAGES OF THE BRITISH ISLES

▲ Second World War gun emplacement on the River Crouch

exception of a towering Second World War gun emplacement – just the bleak marshes of tidal Essex.

With the onset of Burnham-on-Crouch the river is choked with moorings. Next comes the Baltic timber wharf, visited regularly by sizeable coasters laden with Scandinavian pine, so, to find peace, shelter and a clear anchorage on the River Crouch you need to press on another 1 mile (1.8km) until Cliff Reach.

Here, in 6m at LWS, there is good holding and all-round shelter. You're just round the corner from where the Viking warrior Canute defeated our own Edmund and became King of England. The Crouch would have been a good river for Canute to explain that, even with the blessing of the Almighty, tide as well as time waits for no man, as it runs hard here, especially on the ebb.

There's no landing here, unless you want to take your dinghy into Althorne Creek just at the north end of the anchorage and moor up to the pontoons of Bridgemarsh Marina, from where you can walk along the sea wall to Burnham or westwards to North Fambridge and the *Ferryboat Inn*. But it's an hour's walk either way.

Burnham-on-Crouch is a sailor's town, with two royal yacht clubs and three more sailing clubs. Burnham Week was once a rival to Cowes Week, but although today much diminished, as boats have increased in size, it still has regattas for many different smaller sailing craft.

Burnham's Georgian architecture on the river front houses several pubs, the most famous being the White Harte, where sailors dominate the public bar.

There's also a marina dug out of the sea wall just east of Cliff Reach where there are haul out facilities, but no longer a chandlery. During the summer months a foot ferry runs from the town causeway across the river to Wallasea Bay, also with haul out facilities. **– DD**

# YOKESFLEET CREEK

RIVER ROACH, ESSEX

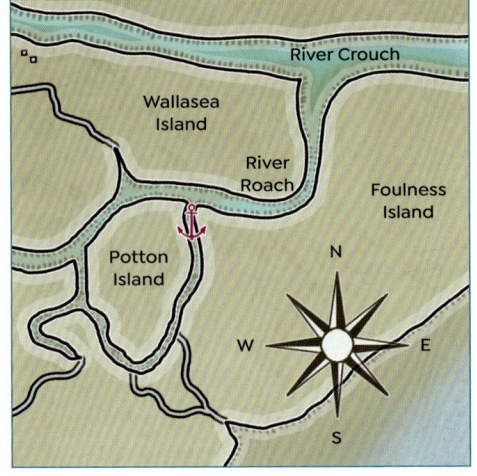

**LURED TO THE** East Coast for the first time by the 'fascinating names' of its shoal water features, circumnavigator and author Eric Hiscock and his wife, Susan, were determined to spend a night anchored in Yokesfleet Creek, as close as they could get, with *Wanderer III*'s draught, to the shallow Havengore Passage across the Maplin Sand.

Tacking up the River Crouch on a falling tide, they misjudged the depth and went hard aground on Foulness Sand. Never one to hide his navigational

▼ *Nightfall* anchored in Yokesfleet Creek

errors, Hiscock took a photo of *Wanderer* dried out, with his wife standing next to her and the RCC (Royal Cruising Club) burgee flying at a crazy angle. On the next tide they got off and sailed on up to Yokesfleet, where they were delighted to find 2m of water at low tide and good shelter from the stiff south-west wind they had been sailing against.

Yokesfleet is surrounded by marsh and is embraced by mud on three sides at LW: it dries completely to the south, and the mud spits running off Potton and Foulness Islands to the north act as a natural harbour. These islands themselves give shelter to winds from west and east.

It's a lonely spot that you'll share with seals and perhaps another yacht, and not much else but creek and sky. Landing is mostly prohibited as both islands are owned by the MOD and permission needs to be obtained from them to do so. These islands have been used to test munitions from First World War mines to modern-day explosives including shells, torpedoes and improvised explosive devices (IED). In one experiment the fuselage of an obsolete jumbo jet was filled with cases of clothes gathered from local charity shops and an IED was tested on it to discover, following the Lockerbie disaster, whether a large aircraft could be built to withstand a mid-air explosion. The results are a secret, but the clothing was spread over a wide area according to eyewitnesses.

Yokesfleet leads south to Havengore Creek, where there is a lifting bridge on to Foulness Island, which is operated by the MOD. During weekends, when the guns stop firing out over the Maplin Sand, the bridge will be opened upon request for yachts either northbound to the rivers Roach and Crouch, or southbound out over the Maplin itself, with 3 miles (4.8km) of sand to cross before reaching the deep water of the River Thames.

Just beyond the creek entrance is the most shallow part of the route, the Broomway, a submarine path that has existed since Roman times and which was used by horse-drawn traffic before the bridge was built. It is the location of the only known recorded collision between a sea-going vessel and a land-bound vehicle: a crash that occurred when a carter, having misjudged a fast-flowing spring tide, unhitched his horse to get ashore, leaving his cart behind, which was then hit by an incoming sailing barge. – DD

▼ The wide skies of Yokesfleet Creek

# RAY GUT

## RIVER THAMES, ESSEX

---

**EVERY TIME I** sail into the Ray I think of my late father, Richard Stephens Durham, who taught me to sail as a schoolboy. When he himself was a schoolboy he taught himself how to sail in *Sprite*, his Utility One Design, along this stretch of water which is entered just west of Southend Pier by the green conical Loway buoy marked Leigh. It's his 'gravestone', as he requested his ashes to be scattered here.

▲ The anchorage at Ray Gut with Southend-on-Sea in the background

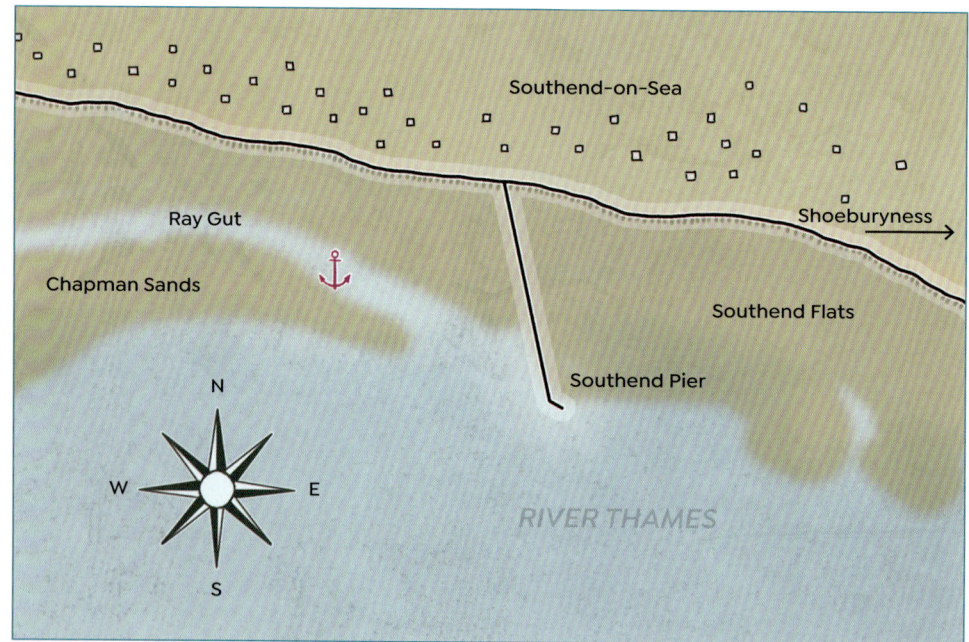

44 | ANCHORAGES OF THE BRITISH ISLES

▲ *Betty II* almost on the beach in Ray Gut

It's an open, temporary anchorage with the best shelter to the north, and this gut is regularly used by local boats coming off for a picnic, a bathe and maybe a game of Frisbee on the hard, flat mud to the south, where seals bask. It's a good jumping off place to await the next ebb down the coast towards Harwich. For yachts planning to go further upriver it's best to keep in mind that you will waste two hours of a fair tide to get through the Loway.

In settled weather you could take your tender up the drying Leigh Creek to the Old Town, where there are pubs, many named after local craft: *The Ye Olde Smack*, *The Peterboat* and also *The Mayflower*, as Leigh is possibly where the Pilgrim Fathers' ship was built. There are restaurants, too, and the Leigh-on-Sea Sailing Club's panoramic bar. If your boat can take the ground you can moor alongside Bell Wharf, although many youngsters swim here on hot days and you may find them using your decks to sunbathe.

At the heritage centre in Old Leigh you can discover the history of the bawleys, the shrimp-trawling gaff cutters, peculiar to the town, whose crew boiled their catch at sea, an operation which gave the boats their name.

At the top of the hill that overlooks the Old Town you'll find St Clement's Church and graveyard, where a brace of admirals are commemorated and several masters of Trinity House are buried. The graveyard also has a monument to the fishermen of the town whose cockleboat, *Renown*, was blown up by a mine during the Dunkirk evacuation. **– DD**

# SOUTH DEEP

THE SWALE, KENT

------------

**THE FIRST TIME** I took a cruising boat away without an adult – one with a cabin, that is – was aboard *Quartette*, a Debutante bilge keeler, owned by the father of a schoolfriend.

After an East Coast cruise, we anchored in South Deep one summer's night and sat in the cockpit, looking at the stars as the tide dropped us down behind Fowley Island, the only sound a faint trickling as the ebb rippled around the anchor chain.

Suddenly the peace was broken by a loud moaning noise and we leapt out of our oilskins. The most plausible explanation was it must have been a cow stuck in a rill. Today it is more likely sheep that will climb the sea wall seeking sweeter grass to crop. The guns to scare birds in the cherry orchards of the 'Garden of England' go off in the daylight hours, otherwise South Deep still offers peace and perfect shelter in 2m of water at LW.

An east cardinal buoy marks the entrance to The Swale as you head west past Harty Ferry, and you leave this to starboard and steer west for 1 mile

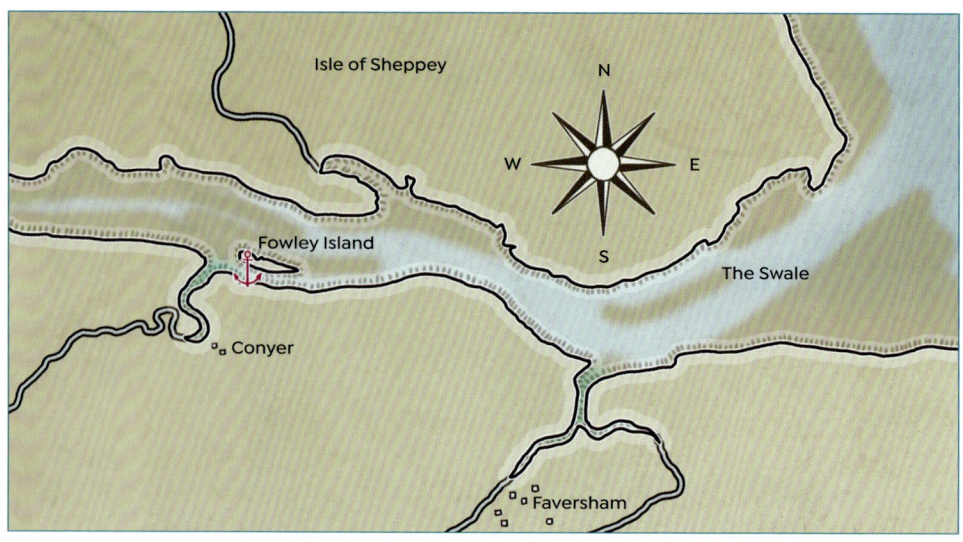

(1.8km) until you find yourself securely wedged between Fowley Island, now a bird reserve, and the mainland. You can land here on an outfall and walk across the fields and the overgrown ground of the former brickworks, to Conyer and The Ship Inn. But be sure to get back to your dinghy before LW or you'll be scrabbling over weedy rocks to get your tender afloat.

Alternatively, you can raise your anchor and motor up into Conyer Creek itself where there are two marinas at which you can lay alongside in the mud as they dry.

My father and I visited this creek back in the late sixties aboard his 20ft Belouga centre-boarder, *Mouette*. I was keen to photograph the sailing barges here which had been converted into houseboats, they included *Gold Belt*, *Percy* and the *Henry & Jabez*, all now broken up. In those days the brickworks chimney was still standing – marking one

▲ The nearest hostelry, *The Ship Inn* at Conyer

of the factories that produced the stocks for Victorian London – all the bricks were sailed upriver by fleets of barges. I made a contemporary sketch of the creek, – which hasn't changed at all – and in it looms the brickworks chimney, now long felled.

One of the fastest Thames sailing barges ever built was launched at White's Yard in Conyer in 1903. *Sara* had 16 first places and 10 second in the Thames and Medway barge races before being broken up in 1965. **– DD**

▼ *Wendy May* anchored in South Deep

# SHARFLEET CREEK

RIVER MEDWAY, KENT

------------

**IF IT'S TRUE** that the eyes of a stranger perceive a reality lost to the view of a native, then the Isle of Grain and its adjacent marsh islets appear as lilies floating in a deluge. It was my 12-year-old son Richard who, coming up on deck of *Minstrel Boy*, my Contessa 32, during his first visit to the River Medway, looked around at the flat acreage of water bordered by the low-lying land exacerbated by power station chimneys and dock cranes and said: 'Dad, is it flooded?' Through his eyes I realised what a flooded land must look like.

On the south side of the River Medway deep pools of water lurk in Sharfleet Creek, behind the mysterious and disembodied marshy islets of Burntwick Island and Slayhills Marshes. There are soundings enough for any craft here and all-round shelter, too, but because the depths differ markedly, unexpected

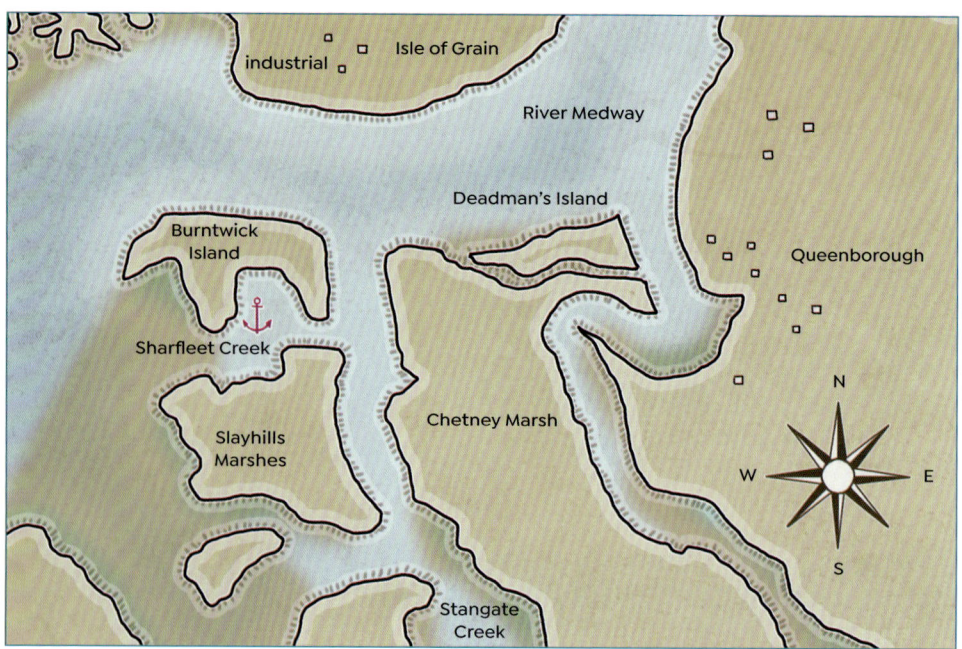

48 | ANCHORAGES OF THE BRITISH ISLES

whirlpools turn craft on their anchor as the tide pours from one submarine pool to the next. At weekends the anchorage can be quite busy.

This caught out a little gaffer not long ago and the skipper found his boat thrown up on a muddy knoll and as she canted over, he called the lifeboat. An RNLI RIB took him off and left him ashore at nearby Queenborough, but his boat still a-dry. My crew and I came to the second rescue, sailed him back to Sharfleet Creek in *Betty II*, anchored, and then with our dinghy, landed on the knoll and as the tide rose eased his boat off into deeper water. But fear not, this was a one-off event: the shallow knoll is marked with a withy and the holding is good.

At half flood you can take a shortcut through Sharfleet Creek and into the Medway, crossing Hamoaze with assistance from two beacons kept in transit to mark the best water. As kids, a pal and I cruised here in his Cadet dinghy and spent a day mud-sliding into the creek. The landing here is strictly for those satisfied with a marsh walk and no pub at the end.

The entire area has an eerie atmosphere as it is the site of great suffering and death. Attempts have been made to consecrate the adjacent Deadman's Island, the burial place of Napoleonic POWs who died aboard prison hulks – their wooden coffins with their grisly remains have been revealed in places by coastal erosion. The melancholy is compounded as the adjacent creeks are also the last berth of many a Thames sailing barge, hulked in obsolescence and left to decay in the way of all fabric. **– DD**

▼ *Wendy May* anchored in Sharfleet Creek with a transit beacon in the distance

# 17

# LYDD-ON-SEA

DUNGENESS, KENT

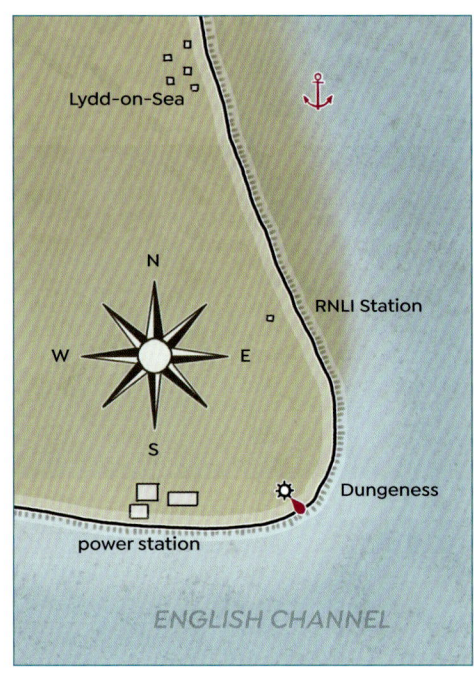

**ON THE EAST** side of the bleak and isolated Dungeness promontory is an anchorage in deep water in which any yacht can ride out a south-westerly gale. I know because I've been there. I was making my way down Channel from Ramsgate in my Contessa 32, *Minstrel Boy*, for a meet in The Solent. The wind had been from the west, enabling progress as far as Dungeness, but then it backed to the south-west – a dead-noser – and increased, and so we tucked ourselves under the shelter of the great shingle arm which supports Dungeness nuclear power station. The boat rode in almost completely flat water while the gale raged against the windward side of the point. It did not let up in time for our pre-arranged meet and so on the next flood, at night, we ran back up Channel to Dover. However, we could have remained in the anchorage until the wind eased or changed direction without any problem.

As Sir Alker Tripp, yachtsman and author, noted: 'This ... flat shingle bank, which at its highest part is only some four feet above the level of high-water ... this bank of loose pebbles resists the full force of the south-westerly gales that come roaring up the Channel'.

The steep-to shingle bank offers deep water 1 mile (1.8km) or so north of the 43m (140ft) high black and white striped lighthouse, which marks the Dungeness nose. For extra reassurance and just to the north of here is the white shed of the Dungeness RNLI station, visible from your cockpit!

▲ Clinker cottage, clinker boat, nuclear power station!

In settled weather you can anchor here and land on the shingle bank by dinghy for a beer at the Britannia, or the Pilot pub, or a visit to the garden of the late filmmaker and gay rights activist Derek Jarman's Prospect Cottage.

You would need to follow the example of the fishing boats, though. These craft are hauled bodily by tractors or power winches up the shingle and clear of the tideline. Many of the old wooden potting boats have been left to rot on the shingle and their abandoned carcasses dot the peninsula.

Sailing up Channel, Dungeness is the last great peninsula to double and the disembodied chimneys of its power station are the first daymarks you pick up having left Beachy Head astern. But because the promontory is so low and the chimneys so high it takes several more hours before you round Dungeness and head for Dover and the East Coast. **– DD**

▽ The surprising anchorage at Lydd-on-Sea, east of Dungeness

# WEST ITCHENOR

CHICHESTER HARBOUR, WEST SUSSEX

- - - - - - - - - - - - -

**ON MY FIRST** visit to Chichester Harbour I was amazed at the number of boats shoe-horned into such a small area. This beautiful, enclosed estuary bestrides Hampshire and West Sussex and sports 15 sailing clubs, six marinas and eight boatyards: a lot to cram into four narrow muddy channels. Directing traffic is the harbour conservancy's eight-strong team, headed up at time of writing

△ The ferry across from West Itchenor to Bosham; it's also a water taxi back to your boat

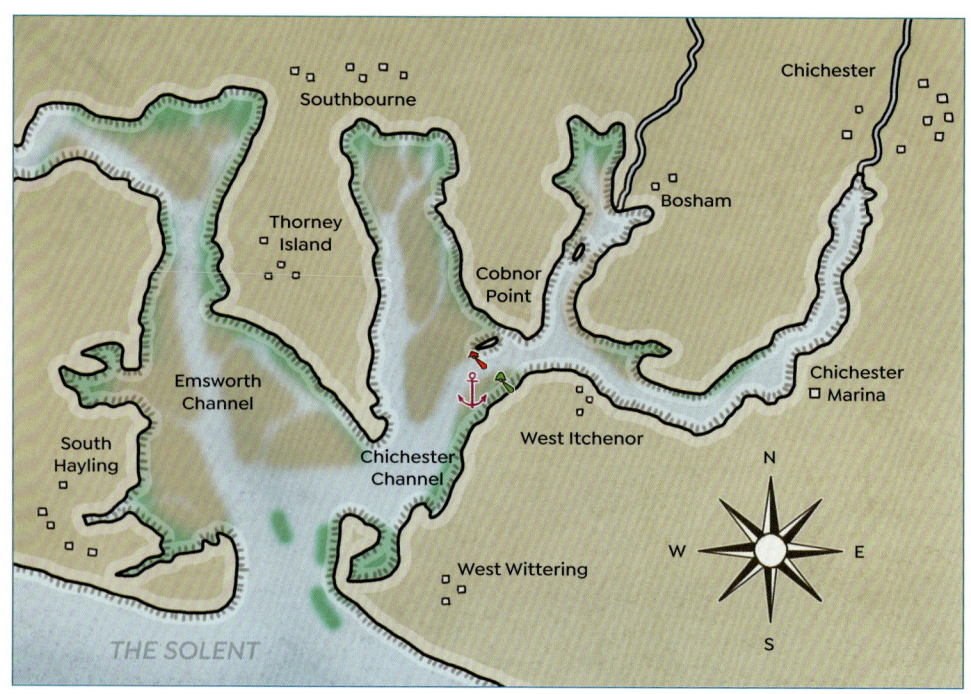

by harbourmaster Jo Cox, who poses proudly in the mariner's handbook with her dog, Finn. This guide has an emphasis on protecting the environment and local wildlife and is strictly adhered to.

Chichester Harbour, a National Landscape, has had its own conservation body since 1971, which was set up for 'landscape protection'. Although it is the smallest AONB in the South East, it has up to 50 employees as more than 1.5 million people arrive each summer for sailing, angling, birdwatching, walking, wildfowling, painting and photography.

You enter the harbour over a bar between Hayling Island to the west and the wonderful beach of West Wittering to the east. The bar is dredged to provide 2m depth at LWS, but an ebb tide and southerly wind can cause confused seas, so it's best to cross the bar between three hours before and one hour after HW. The deepest water is on the west side.

Because of concerns over seagrass there are only three anchorages in the entire 28.5sq km (11sq miles) of Chichester Harbour's water. Of these, the most protected is West Itchenor, where you can lie sheltered from winds from all quarters in anchor-grasping mud just inside the green spherical channel buoy off Itchenor itself and opposite Cobnac Point on the Chidham peninsula. Once across the bar you follow the buoys and head east as you reach Fishery S-cardinal, leave Camber S-cardinal to port and anchor before you reach Fairway S-cardinal. There is a charge ranging from £7.50 to £14 depending on your LOA.

▲ The anchorage at West Itchenor, Chichester Harbour

By dinghy you can land at Itchenor Hard at all states of the tide. At HW you could land on the grassy sea wall next to the anchorage, always taking care to give a wide berth to seals and birds who, according to the mariner's guide, need space for time to digest their food. From the sea wall there is an arcadian walk through a tunnel of old Spanish oaks 0.8km (0.5 miles) to the local pub, *The Ship*.

One of the world's greatest yachtsmen, the late Sir Peter Blake, the New Zealander who took his country to victory in the America's Cup, made his home in Emsworth on the north shore of the harbour. As an old Fleet Street hand, I'm used to covering tragedies, but I never expected I would have to do the same as features and news editor for *Yachting Monthly*. However, it was here in 2001 that I interviewed Sir Peter's widow, Pippa, after he was shot dead by pirates while monitoring another part of the world's ecosystem – the Amazon in Brazil. **– DD**

# BEAULIEU RIVER

HAMPSHIRE

**THE OAKS OF** the New Forest were felled to construct Nelson's fleet of warships at Buckler's Hard on this privately owned scenic river. Whether the shallow bar at the entrance provided a hazard for these newly launched men-of-war back in the day, history does not record, or if it does it's in a book I've not read. But suffice to say you'll need to allow two hours flood before leaving the Solent and lining up the leading marks: Number 2 port beacon in transit with Lepe House on 324°T, passing the red dolphin about 40m (130ft) to port, which marks the entrance. Red and green piles mark – and mar the beauty of – both sides of the channel and take you round on a dogleg from north to west by south.

It appears there is plenty of room in the river for anchoring and there is, were it not for new restrictions applied by the Beaulieu Estate, whose harbourmaster came speeding down in his dory to tell us we had anchored in the wrong place.

*Peregrine*, the 40ft Fife I was sailing in, had brought up between port-hand piles

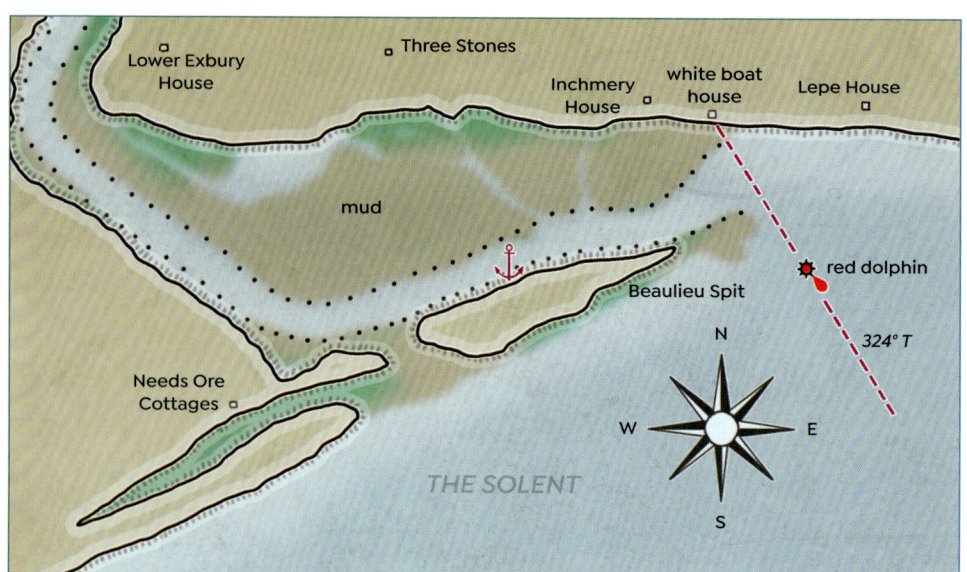

▲ Anchored in the Beaulieu River

numbers 22 and 24. This meant her 20kg (45lb) CQR was nestling atop the diver-planted seagrass meadow, where seeds have been directly injected into the sediment. Solent seagrass, I am reliably informed, provides a sort of carbon sponge that removes the equivalent of 242,000 car exhaust fumes annually.

Being in the wrong place meant we had to fire up our own engine, weigh anchor and drop the hook instead between piles 22 and 20, which is now the only permitted anchoring zone. There is an overnight charge – £10 in 2025. The holding is excellent, in mud, hopefully free of any environmentally useful flora. Shelter here is nigh on perfect with a high shingle bank to seaward, where no human is allowed to tread as gulls nest here. To northward the woodland of the New Forest provides a lee from northerly winds.

It is a truly beautiful and peaceful anchorage, but because of the Reducing and Mitigating Erosion and Disturbance impacts affecting the Seabed (ReMEDIES) restrictions there is not much room. You can take a tender upriver about 0.5 miles (0.8km) and land at the pontoon of Gin's Farm, where the Royal Southampton Yacht Club has a clubhouse with a first-floor bar and restaurant that enjoys panoramic views of the river.

I once drove down through the New Forest one night to join a Little Ship Club cruise at Gin's Farm and I stopped at the *Master Builder's House Hotel* at Buckler's Hard to get directions. When I got back to the car it was surrounded by creatures in the dark: a herd of New Forest ponies crowded round the bonnet to enjoy the radiated heat from the still hot engine. Perhaps horse power, too, can ingest exhaust fumes! **– DD**

# NEWTOWN RIVER

## ISLE OF WIGHT

------------

**IT WAS BLOWING** a good force 4 as *Peregrine* surged through the narrow entrance to Newtown River, or Creek as it is often called. The entrance is easy to find and marked by a west cardinal, after which there are leading marks to take you in on a bearing of 130°T.

Just south of the shallow bank of mud to port, where the channel splits behind Fish House Point, is a mud knoll, marked with an isolated danger buoy. You round this and head north-east up Clamerkin Lake, a narrow creek that has good holding in mud and 2m depth at

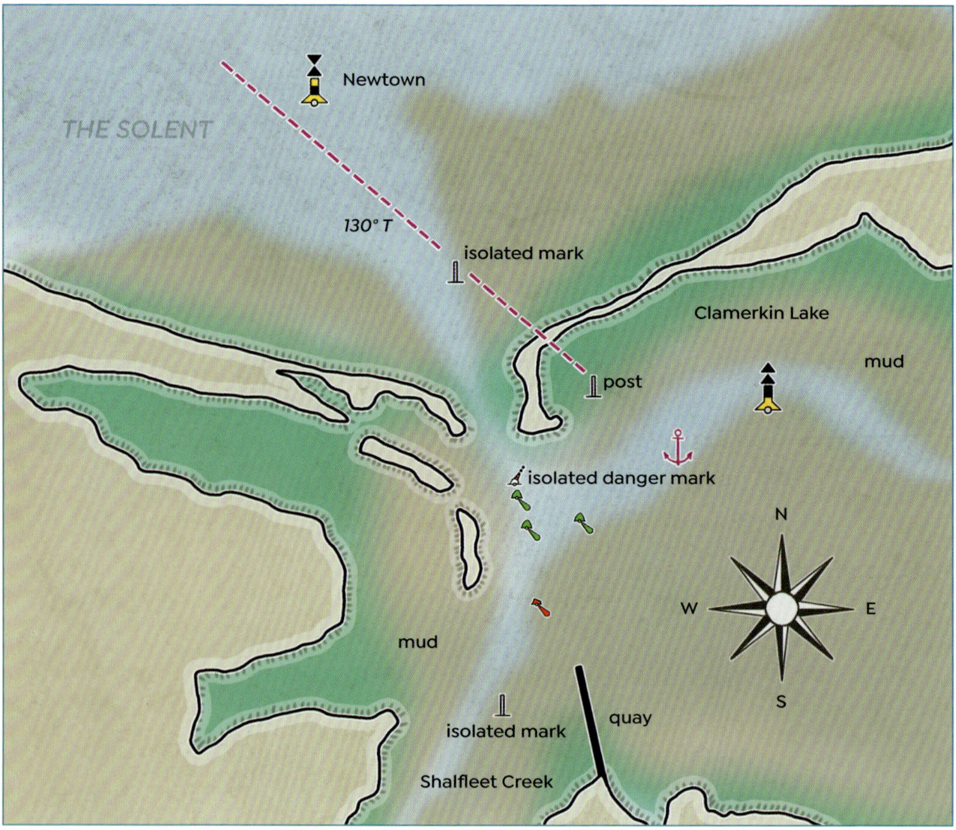

▲ A breezy day in Newtown Creek on the Isle of Wight

LW. The whole area is sheltered from all directions – although at the top of the tide in a northerly blow the marshy arms at the entrance can cover and this results in a bit of a chop.

The other arm of Newtown River is Shalfleet Lake, although this even narrower, even muddier creek, which has a limited area for anchoring and dries out further from the quay than its neighbour, must have been named by the local tourist board. Both arms have oyster layings marked by boards warning you not to drop your ground tackle on the crusty bivalves; it is said that the Romans thought the oysters here were particularly good.

The tide runs fiercely into the mini estuary and care must be taken to set the anchor properly; we were using a 20kg (45lb) CQR, but it dragged even though we were on neap tides – as we had not bedded it down at the outset.

Newtown River is a beautiful area of marsh, creeks and ancient woodland copses owned by the National Trust, and there is a charming walk ashore with landing via dinghy at Newtown Quay, although this staging dries at LW and you will need two hours flood to get back without muddy boots. The whole area is a haven for wildlife with sea lavender and thrift, terns, dunlins and oystercatchers to name but a few. It has been a nature reserve for nearly 60 years. In a dinghy you can explore Western Haven and its creeks – if you're very adventurous up as far as Ningwood Bridge. You need to feel your way to find the deepest water, so it's best to take it gently and remember to ship a pair of oars.

The 17th-century *New Inn* pub, renowned in the past for its food and real ale, has been struggling with various management issues in recent years and at time of writing is closed. Even the Newtown Old Town Hall is currently closed. So, for now, enjoy the moral high ground: go for a walk without having a drink. **– DD**

# CHANNEL ISLANDS

------------------------------------

You can cruise the Channel Islands every season for years and still find new and interesting anchorages. With such a massive tidal range, off-lying rocks and reefs become breakwaters at low tide and the possibilities change dramatically at springs and neaps. Each of the main islands has its own charms and the differences of Sark's steep cliffs, Alderney's sweeping tides, Herm's drying acres, Jersey's sandy bays or Guernsey's rugged south coast all add to the enjoyment of a summer cruise around the islands.

Further off from the main islands are the extensive reefs and tiny above-water islands that make up the Plateau des Minquiers to the west, *Wreck of the Mary Deare* country, and Les Ecrehous to the north-east, both belonging to Jersey.

Don't be put off by the huge areas of drying rocks on the charts as they can offer protection from swell and wind.

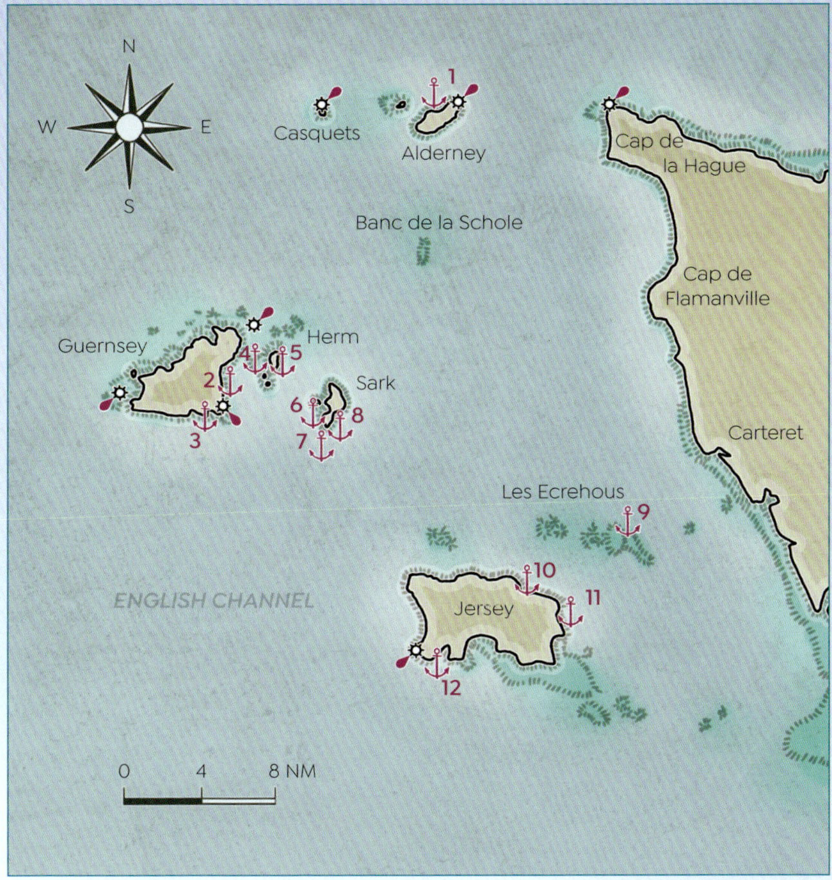

▽ A quiet anchorage in Puffin Bay

# SAYE BAY

ALDERNEY

-------------

**ON THE NORTH-EAST** edge of Braye Harbour is Saye Bay, which offers a charming anchorage in settled weather. Facing just west of north the bay has a gorgeous beach of almost-white sand, and the sea can look a Caribbean turquoise, which cries out for you to plunge in.

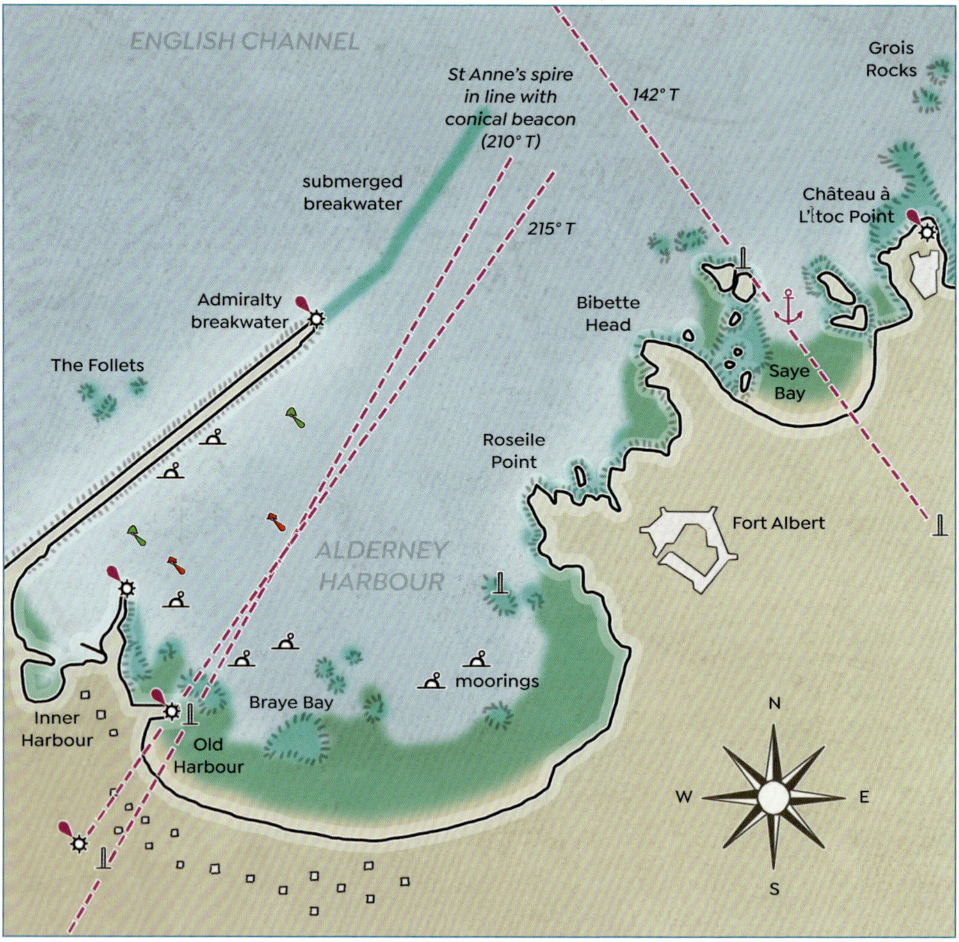

▲ Saye Bay, just east of Braye Harbour

The best time to enter Saye anchorage is about an hour or two after HW St Helier. If you're coming from across the Channel, follow the St Anne Church leading line – 210°T – until Homet des Pies white beacon on the rocks on the west side of the bay is just open to the west of the beacon behind the beach on the shore. Turn into the bay on this line – about 142°T – leaving Homet des Pies rocks around 50m (164ft) to starboard.

The tidal range here can be up to 5.5m so you need to put out enough chain – at springs you should be careful, as there isn't lots of swinging room if several boats are anchored. The holding is fairly good in sand with some rocks, and you're protected in winds from just north of west, through south to just north of east, but it is exposed to anything with much north in it.

On the eastern headland is Château à l'Étoc, one of 18 forts built on the island, or improved, during Queen Victoria's reign as defence against the French. The château is an imposing building and is now privately owned and used for events; it makes a very romantic wedding venue. Slightly south-east of the bay is Fort Albert, originally called Fort Touraille but renamed in 1861 after Prince Albert died. This was the last one to be built, and was intended to be used as the main defence if the island was overrun. In June 1940 the residents of Alderney were evacuated to the UK before German Forces occupied the island. Once established, the Germans heavily reinforced all the forts and used the island for concentration and forced labour camps. The defences were built by East European slave labour who lived in unspeakable conditions.

Saye is a lovely bay for a family day at the beach; the sand is soft and the rock pools offer lots of interest. Just in from the beach is the Saye Bay campsite, which has a shop and a café, and you can even use their shower block if you ask at the office. There are easy walks around the north end of the island and it isn't far to the distinctive black and white lighthouse on Quénard Point.

Within Braye Harbour itself there is room to anchor away from the mooring buoys, though it does have a reputation for persistent swell, even in fairly benign weather. A water taxi runs in the main harbour during the season and you are nearer to restaurants and better facilities.
– JC

# FERMAIN BAY

GUERNSEY

-------------

**ABOUT 1.5 MILES** (2.7km) south of St Peter Port entrance is Fermain Bay, a sheltered anchorage in westerly weather facing across the Russel to Herm and Sark. This is a popular beach for holidaymakers, and from the late 1920s to the early 1990s a ferry service ran from St Peter Port round to Fermain, where you would land on a fairly rickety wheeled jetty that moved up and down the beach to suit the tide. Sadly this route is no longer available, but Fermain is on the coast path, about an hour's walk from town, which attracts lots of people in good weather.

Leaving St Peter Port in your own boat don't turn south too soon, continue for about 0.25 miles (0.45km) eastward then leave three spars, the Oyster beacon, Moulinet and Anfré, to starboard. The sweep of Fermain's shingly beach is clear as you round Fermain Point and turn in towards the anchorage. The holding is generally good in sand, with between 2m and 5m at LAT. It can get a bit rolly, with swell coming in with winds from the south or south-west. The anchorage can get busy on summer weekends as it is a favourite spot with locals coming out for lunch and a swim.

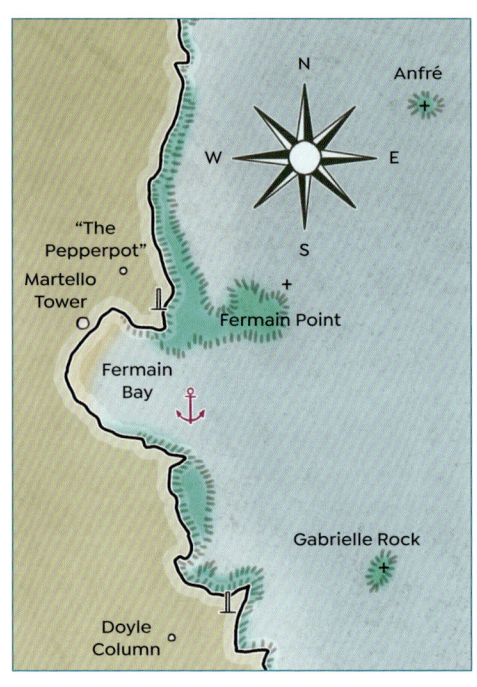

▼ Looking down on Fermain from the coast path

▲ Fermain Bay with its distinctive Martello Tower

If you're approaching Fermain from the south having come along the south coast, you need to be sure to clear Gabrielle Rock, about 370m (1,200ft) east of Bec du Nez. To the north of Fermain Bay the white 'Pepperpot' on the hill and the red and white beacon below it are a striking line for Gabrielle Rock, not a leading line into the bay.

There is a distinctive Martello tower behind the wall at the top of the beach which is now owned by the National Trust of Guernsey and can be rented as self-catering accommodation. Close to the tower is the *Fermain Beach Café*, which is well worth a run ashore. There are tables along the wall that have wonderful views out over the bay and the menu, though not extensive, is good. For more substantial fare you can walk up the hill to the *Fermain Bay Hotel*, which has lovely terraces for eating al fresco.

With the steep cliffs behind it, Fermain Bay does tend to lose the sun fairly early in the evening – even in high summer – but if you are here overnight sunrise can be spectacular. **– JC**

▲ Fermain Bay is a popular anchorage

# PETIT PORT

GUERNSEY

------

**THE SOUTH COAST** of Guernsey is rugged with high cliffs, very different to the low-lying north, and it is often this south end that lifts first as you approach the island from the West Country. Tucked into the south-east corner, the bay between Icart Point and Jerbourg Point is a wonderful location for a day trip from St Peter Port. In its north-east corner, below

▼ Petit Port on Guernsey's south coast

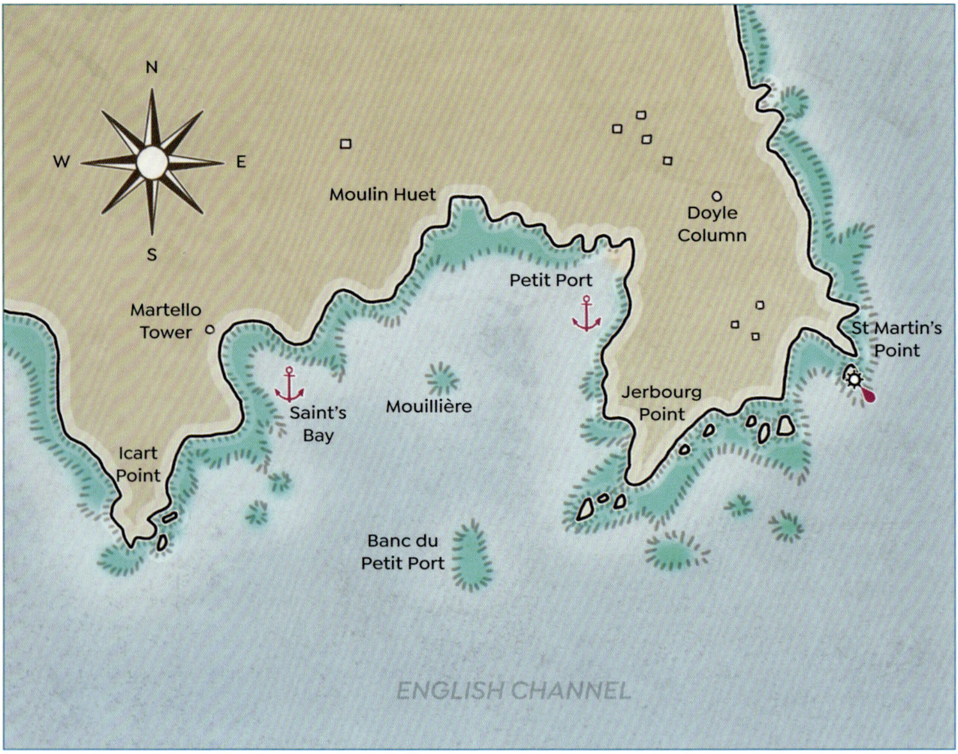

64 | ANCHORAGES OF THE BRITISH ISLES

▽ The steep cliffs of Petit Port

the conspicuous Doyle Column, Petit Port is a glorious anchorage in quiet summer weather, or in winds from between north and east. Coming from St Peter Port you just have to round St Martin's Point and Jerbourg Point a safe distance off, setting clearing waypoints 0.5 miles (0.8km) east and seven cables, (1,300m, 4,260ft) south of St Martin's lighthouse, then four cables (750m, 2,430ft) south of the seaward tip of Jerbourg Point.

Roughly in the middle of the bay, Mouillière rock dries 8.5m; you can usually see it. Continue on a westerly heading until the rock is east of north before turning in towards a waypoint about midway between Jerbourg Point to starboard and Mouillière to port. This will leave a small rocky shoal, Banc du Petit Port (2.8m datum depth), which lies to the south-west of Jerbourg Point, a cable (185m, 600ft) to starboard, then head in towards the beach and anchor.

This anchorage feels wild and remote, and would have looked much the same centuries ago, though it's popular with local boats and can get quite busy at weekends. Steps lead up to Doyle Column, high up behind Jerbourg Point. It's a bit of a hike up to the monument, but you can reward yourself with a trip to the Jerbourg cliff kiosk or a meal at the *Jerbourg Hotel*. The views from the point are spectacular down to Jersey or to Sark and Herm, and on a clear day you can see the French coast.

Round the bay to the west you reach Moulin Huet. This is a lovely beach but easier to approach by dinghy. A short walk up from the beach is the Moulin Huet tearoom – their Guernsey crab sandwiches are legendary, or why not try a cream tea and home-made cake. The views across the bay are fabulous and at LW, Mouillière really stands out in the centre. The high cliffs feel slightly Mediterranean, especially when the sea is a deep summer blue, and the tearoom is on the Renoir Trail. Renoir visited Guernsey in 1883 and painted several bold landscapes along the south coast that echo the south of France.

Close east of Icart Point, the narrow inlet known as Saint's Bay lies just opposite Petit Port, easily identified by its Martello tower. There's also a handy kiosk here. From a stone quay on the west side there are several small boats on running moorings. If you do choose Saint's Bay, you need to anchor towards the east side near the mouth to avoid the moorings and allow local fishermen to come and go so as they can catch those mouth-watering crabs. **– JC**

# ROSAIRE

HERM

**LOOKING AT A** chart of Herm may be a little daunting if you have never visited the island by boat before, but all that off-putting green will be nicely covered by sea at HW. Once you have chosen your anchorage and the tide has fallen away, the rocks provide perfect shelter.

Heading over to Herm from St Peter Port it's best to leave about two hours before HW, or once you can get over the marina sill, and the stream will be starting to set north up the Little Russel. It's only 3 miles (5.4km) across to Herm and you should approach using the Alligande Passage, the west end of which is a short 0.5 miles (0.9km) SSE of Bréhon Fort. You should be on a heading of 074°T, leaving the green Alligande beacon with its A topmark to starboard. When you are abeam Alligande, line up Vermerette, a yellow pole with a V topmark, with the white patch on the harbour wall to clear the dangers north of Godfrey, a green beacon with GB topmark. As you pass abeam of Épec – green with an E topmark – you should edge north to line up two white barrels on the shore on 078°T. Boats that can take the ground can continue into the tiny drying harbour, but be aware that above half-tide the ferries from St Peter Port use this quay. When Vermerette rock is awash there's about 1m of water at the harbour breakwater. The harbour is well protected and only open to the north-west and north.

To reach the Rosaire anchorage turn to starboard into the Percée Passage between Vermerette and Épec on a heading of 128°T until you have passed Gate Rock W-cardinal about 50m (165ft) to port. Gradually curve round to port, giving Mouette islet a wide berth, and anchor between the islet and the Rosaire Steps, avoiding the local moorings. The anchorage is open to the south, south-south-east to south-south-west – but protected from the east, north and west at LW. Be aware of the strong south-going stream for about an hour before HW until a couple of hours after, particularly if you are moving between the boat and the shore.

Herm Island is owned by the States of Guernsey but is leased and run by a charitable company. Once ashore, it is only a five-minute saunter up to the *White House Hotel*, which offers a restaurant, or the more casual *Ship Inn*. There's also the *Mermaid Tavern*, where you can start your island visit with breakfast. There's a small shop here for fairly basic needs. In your stroll around the island it is a courtesy to call in at the administrative office, which has showers, to register your arrival and make a contribution, as there is no fixed fee for visiting yachts.

At only 1.25 miles (2km) long and 0.5 miles (0.8km) wide, you can have an easy walk right round the island, visiting beautiful Shell Beach and Belvoir Bay on the east side and look across to Sark. At low water springs, Herm seems to double in size. The low-lying Humps at the north-east are breeding grounds for puffins and terns, and these little islands are out of bounds from 1 January to 15 July. You are also quite likely to see seals and dolphins. When the day trippers have gone home Herm is a magical place. **– JC**

# EAST COAST

## HERM

**ON HERM'S EAST** coast are three tempting anchorages – in Puffin Bay, Belvoir Bay and Shell Bay – any of which is an enjoyable day trip for all the family.

A couple of days after the top of springs gives the best access times for Victoria Marina, with HW about 1000 or 1030, so you can leave after breakfast on a rising tide and come back in the evening. On the north tip of Herm, at low water springs, you can experience the dramatic rock scapes, azure lagoons and sandbanks in and around the Humps.

For a first visit to any of these anchorages tidal streams will be quieter and you can nudge a bit further in at neaps.

Having crossed the Little Russel from St Peter Port, follow the Alligande Passage to the north of Épec Beacon, then turn south-east through the Percée Passage, keeping midway between Herm and Jethou. Avoiding Meulettes rock off the south tip of Herm, simply follow the east coast of the island northwards about 0.25 miles (0.45km) off.

▼ A quiet anchorage in Puffin Bay

▲ Looking north across Belvoir Bay

The first bay you reach is Puffin Bay. You need to clear Boue au Port and Selle Roque (9m), ensuring you avoid the drying spur to its north before turning west into the bay. On the north side is Putrainez, also 9m, which is much larger and joined to the island for most of the time. Puffin Bay is virtually impossible to access from the coast path round the island, so the beach is likely to be less crowded than the other two, although there are no facilities here. The wide, sandy sweep is perfect for swimming and a picnic ashore, provided you come with a well-provisioned boat.

After rounding Putrainez you approach Belvoir Bay with Caquorobert (15m) on its south side and Moulière rock (2m) to the north. Backed by cliffs, Belvoir Bay is sheltered in westerlies and the sandy beach is very popular. During the season there's a lovely beach café here.

The greatest expanse of beach on Herm is Shell Beach on the north-east side, snug in westerlies. As its name implies, it is made up of millions of tiny shells brought here by the Gulf Stream – they sparkle in the sun against the clear turquoise water. Although this long, low beach is popular with Herm's visitors it never feels crowded, and at LW there are dozens of fabulous rock pools to explore. The beach has that carefree, toe-scrunching quality of childhood, and beyond the dunes, Herm's lush green slopes tempt you to explore.

If you're approaching Shell Beach from the Big Russel you should watch out for Noire Pute rock (only 2m high with a small light beacon) and the drying tail extending up to 1.5 cables (280m, 910ft) north of it. These dangers lie nearly 1 mile (1.8km) off the east coast of Herm. Also avoid the Aiguillons reef (dries 3.1m) lurking about 0.5 miles (0.9km) east of Shell Beach. When entering or leaving this bay, keep well south to avoid the various drying rocks, which are the south-east outliers of the extensive dangers fringing the north end of Herm. **– JC**

# LA GRANDE GRÈVE

## SARK

▼ La Grande Grève

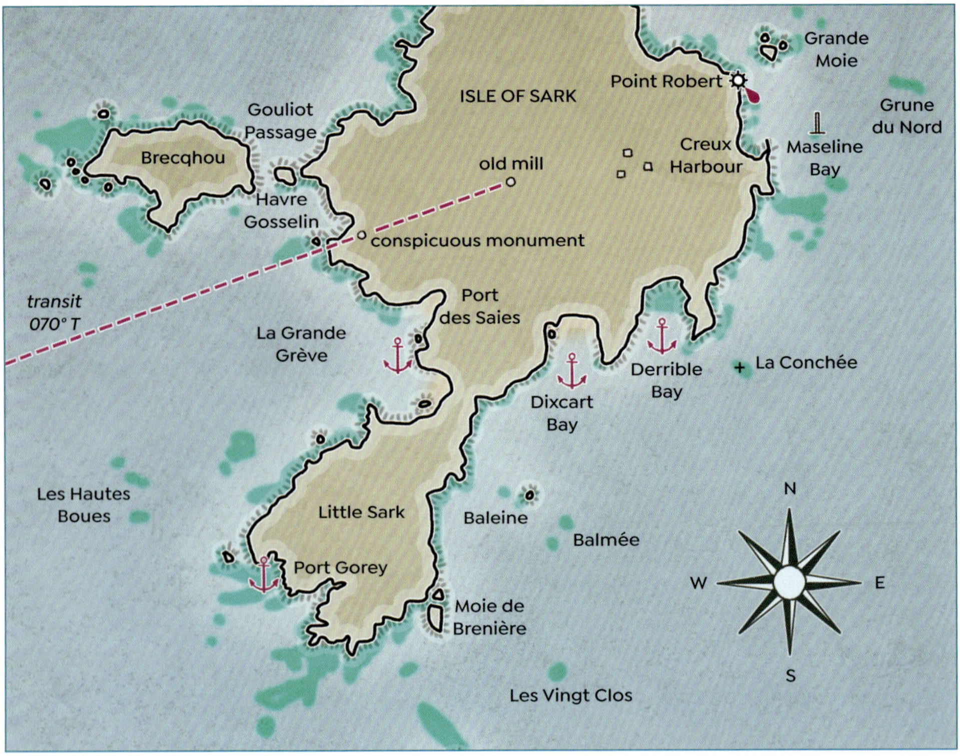

**LOOKING ACROSS AT** Sark from Guernsey, the island can appear a bit intimidating on a grey day, but when you venture over the Big Russel from Herm the bays on the west coast are very alluring. Havre Gosselin is just to the south of the Gouliot Passage, which separates Sark from Brecqhou. You can still anchor here, although there are now quite a few moorings, including several visitor buoys.

Around 0.5 miles (0.9km) south of Havre Gosselin is the wider sweep of La Grande Grève, in the bay below La Coupée, which joins Sark and Little Sark. The cliffs are nearly 100m (330ft) high, but this doesn't deter visitors who scramble down the track to one of Sark's best beaches. The approach is quite straightforward from due west – stay fairly close south of Les Dents rocks to ensure you pass Boue de la Baie rock and a drying head just north of it. When Pilcher's Monument is due north true, you will have passed the dangers and can nudge into the bay to choose your spot. The holding in sand is generally good and you are protected from north-east through east to south-west.

This is a lovely swimming beach, but if you're going ashore in the dinghy be careful as you land or you may find yourself in the water sooner than anticipated – a sneaky swell can flip a dinghy at the last minute. There are no facilities at the beach.

It is worth the fairly strenuous climb up to La Coupée, from where you can walk to the centre of the island and the Avenue – the commercial hub of Sark – where you can pick up a map at the visitor centre. If you need some shopping there's the Food Stop or Mon Plaisir Stores, both of which stock local produce including seafood. You can't visit Sark and miss the Seigneurie, the historic home of the Seigneur, and its beautiful gardens. In the old Island Hall is an exhibition telling

▲ La Grande Grève from La Coupée between Sark and Little Sark

the story of life on the island during the German occupation; it wasn't fun. In the visitor centre is the Heritage Room, which has lots of information about the island and its natural history as well as its dark skies.

If you don't fancy walking then take a carriage ride. It's the perfect way to visit the island. Horse-drawn carriages wait at the top of Harbour Hill. Alternatively you can hire a bike from one of several hire companies, and this way you can explore the island and meet some of Sark's many creative people in their studios or shops.

There's a choice of good eating places – in the grounds of the Seigneurie is Hathaways, or down at Dixcart is Hugo's Bar and Brasserie. Next to the visitor centre and the prison is the Fleur du Jardin.

Finally, what better way to round off your day than to buy a local lobster and take it back to the boat to eat in the cockpit while you watch a fantastic sunset over Guernsey. **– JC**

# PORT GOREY

SARK

-------------

**ON THE SOUTH-WEST** edge of Little Sark is a fascinating, hidden anchorage in Port Gorey. A port was developed here in the early 19th century to service a silver mine, the remains of which you can see on the top of the cliff where the ruins of two ventilation shafts still stand. This was a slightly hare-brained scheme of the 17th Seigneur, Pierre Le Pelley III, and ended up bankrupting his family, eventually causing the sale of the fiefdom of Sark.

Mining started in 1835 and initially a

▽ Port Gorey is an unspoilt anchorage

▽ Reefs off Port Gorey

▲ A local fishermen threading the reef, with Guernsey in the background

rich seam was struck, but it proved to be very short-lived and the money that had been used to sink shafts and build a jetty was not recovered. The shafts went down to a depth of 700ft, and it is thought the galleries extended to 2,000ft. The jetty was used to bring in coal to keep the steam pumps running as well as ship out the ore; though it's possible that only one shipment of silver ever left Port Gorey, and according to local history the ship and its cargo sank. Pierre drowned at sea in 1839 and his brother, Ernest, became Seigneur. After a ceiling collapse in 1845, when 10 miners drowned, the mine was closed.

This is a quiet anchorage, slightly off the beaten track between two long tails of reefs jutting out from the cliffs. It's best to choose a quiet day and approach from the south-west at about half-ebb; the tidal stream should be slack at this time and the reefs clearly visible. Off the south-west edge is Boue Tirlipois, a dangerous rock that dries 1.1m; approaching from the west or south-west you must ensure you have rounded this safely before turning into the anchorage. You then leave Sercul rock (5m) and Grande Bretagne (18m) to starboard, the latter is quite steep-to so you can keep over to the east side of the entrance. Once anchored in the fjord, the rocks outside will give increasing shelter from any swell as the tide falls away. The holding is generally good in sand, though as you nudge further in there are also some rocks. Anchor in the centre of the bay to avoid two drying rocks on the edge, one on the north side and the other in the south corner.

The sea is beautifully clear so it's a great location for a swim off the boat and keen swimmers walk here. At low water there is a small beach at the head of the inlet but to go ashore you would need to use a dinghy and land at the, slightly precarious, ladder.

It is well protected from north-west round to north-east but a big swell can run in from anything with south in it. If you are planning to venture in here you need a good forecast of settled weather, preferably a nice high pressure. It is probably best as a lunch-time stop as there are no lights and leaving in the dark, if the weather changed suddenly, could be tricky. Make sure you have an exit plan if you do decide to stay overnight. – **JC**

# DIXCART AND DERRIBLE BAYS

SARK

-------------

**THERE ARE SEVERAL** anchorages around Sark but two of the most delightful are Dixcart and Derrible Bays on the south-east side. These lie either side of Point Château, just 0.5 miles (0.9km) south-west down the coast from Creux Harbour. The simplest route is probably approaching direct from St Peter Port, south about Little Sark, and it's roughly 10 miles (18km) from Guernsey via the Lower Heads buoy.

▽ Dixcart Bay in the foreground with Derrible Bay to the east

△ The lovely gardens at La Seigneurie are well-worth visiting

Coming from Guernsey you need to keep a good 0.5 miles (0.9km) south of L'Étac, as drying ledges straggle up to four cables (750m, 2,430ft) south-west of Little Sark. Continue on an easterly course until Point Château is west of north. The old leading line of Sark Mill is now obscured by trees, but if you make for a point just over 1 mile (1.8km) 290°T from L'Étac and then turn towards Point Château on 340°T, you will clear the drying patches of Balmée and Demie de Balmée, which lie east of Little Sark. Near half-tide is a good time to approach, when the streams around the island are fairly slack.

When you're about three cables 550m (1,800ft) off Point Château, you can either edge to port into Dixcart Bay or to starboard into Derrible. Except near low springs, when the ebb runs well away from the beaches, you can tuck fairly close into either of these sandy coves to escape the strong tidal streams that set along the east side of Sark. Both these bays are perfect in north-westerlies, when it's safe to stay at anchor overnight; if the wind is south-westerly a swell tends to roll in.

Paths lead up to the top of the island from either of the beaches, although the walk from Dixcart Bay is probably less steep. This will lead you up the valley to *Stock's Hotel*, which has a good restaurant and bar. Turning left when you join the lane at the top will take you to the dramatic Coupée, which joins the main island with Little Sark. Looking westward from La Coupée is the anchorage of La Grande Grève then across the Big

▲ Dixcart Bay is a popular anchorage

Russel to Herm and Guernsey. If you walk across Little Sark you can see the remains of the Sark silver mine, a sorry tale of an enterprise that bankrupted a 19th-century Seigneur.

It is a marginally shorter walk from Derrible Bay up to the Avenue – the commercial hub of Sark. As there are no cars here, a carriage ride is the traditional way to tour the island. A visit to the Seigneurie Gardens makes the climb well worthwhile, and *Hathaways Restaurant* can satisfy any hunger pangs. If you can time your visit for mid-July you'll see the sheep racing – great fun for everyone, not least the sheep. Sark is a dark sky island and organised stargazing events are held throughout the year. Contact the Sark Astronomy Society or enquire at the visitor centre. **– JC**

# MARMOTIÈRE

## LES ECREHOUS

**VISITING LES ECREHOUS** should really be a day trip from Jersey, as there are no facilities here and the streams running through the islets can reach 6–7 knots at springs. Although neaps offer slightly easier navigation, spring tides are more dramatic and interesting and you can take the dinghy and explore the rocks and banks, which will be under tons of water a couple of hours later. You can land at the slip on the west side of La Marmotière and climb up to the highest point by the flagstaff, from where you can see Jersey, Sark and the Cotentin peninsula. The stone cottages on the island were once used by fishermen but are now the summer retreats of a few select Jersey sailors.

Les Ecrehous are technically part of the parish of St Martin on Jersey and

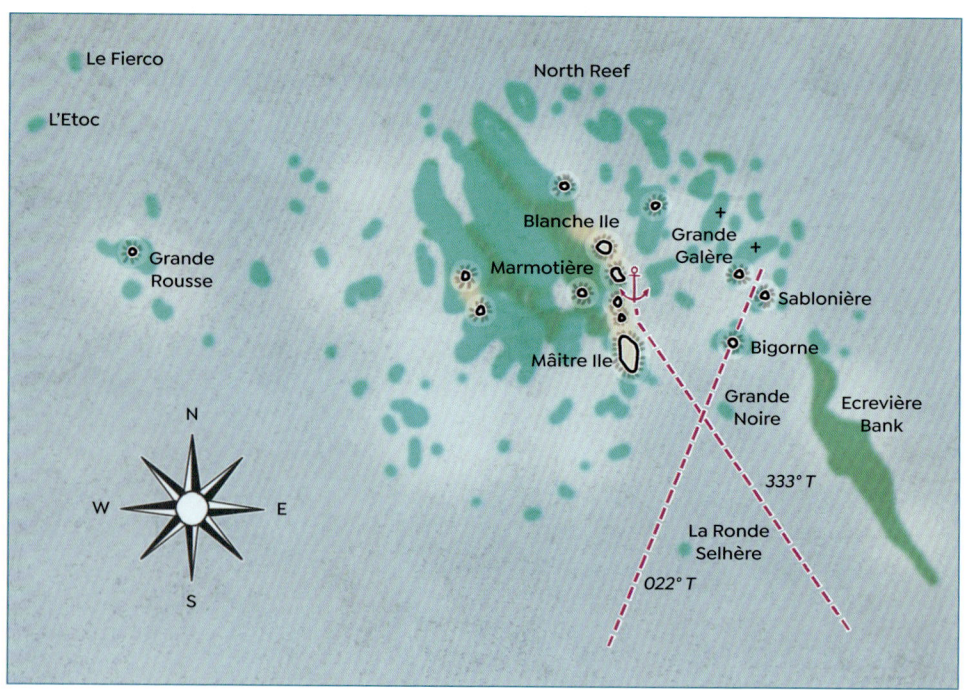

▲ Low water springs in Les Ecrehous

lie about halfway between Jersey and Carteret. The largest island, Maître Ile, is about a quarter of a mile (0.45km) south of Marmotière and is essentially a seabird colony. North of La Marmotière is Blanche Ile, which is joined by a low-water causeway but detached at HW. A couple of small properties cling to it.

The anchorage lies to the south of Marmotière, and arriving near HW, the terra doesn't look very firm. Gradually, as the water ebbs away, rocks and islets merge and you can explore rock pools while your boat lies perfectly sheltered in a landlocked lagoon. About an hour-and-a-half after LW the tide starts to creep in again between the reefs, gradually spreading and joining up as the pools fill and channels widen. Time to get back on board.

The tidal range at Les Ecrehous is about 9.5m at springs and 4.5m at neaps. Marmotière offers little protection at HW, which is why it's best just to come on a day trip, having chosen your day with

▲ Anchored in Les Ecrehous

care – quiet weather with no swell. Gorey harbour in Jersey is a good jumping-off point. You should aim to arrive about 1.5 miles (2.7km) south by west of Maître Ile near to half ebb, when there should be plenty of water in the channel but the key rocks will be exposed.

As you draw near to Maître Ile, with a stone beacon on its highest point, Marmotière with its flagstaff will become less distinct. About 0.5 miles (0.9km) east-north-east of Maître Ile, three above-water rocks – Bigorne (5m high), Sablonière (2m) and Grande Galère (4m) – provide the first leading line into the plateau. The first transit is Bigorne rock, looking like a large inverted tooth, four cables (740m, 2,430ft) east of Maître Ile, brought between Grande Galère and Sablonière behind it bearing 022°T or a shade over. Grande Galère and Sablonière have flatter profiles and appear as a matching pair at half-tide. Follow this transit NNE, allowing for cross-tide. Don't stray east of a line with Bigorne midway between Grande Galère and Sablonière, since this will bring you very close to La Ronde Selhère (dries 2.7m) and La Petite Noire (dries 4.8m). You can err to port until Bigorne touches the west edge of Sablonière.

When 0.5 miles (0.9km) from Bigorne, come onto the inner marks – Marmotière flagstaff in line with a vertical black board behind it bearing 330°T. A white-painted rock below the flagstaff makes the transit easy to pick out. Stay exactly on these marks until within two cables (370m, 1,210ft) of Marmotière and then borrow slightly to the east (not too much) to clear the drying ledges that fringe the shore of Maître Ile. You can anchor and stay afloat just south of La Marmotière.

You can leave this outer anchorage at any state of tide, but most yachts will want to be here over LW and leave again around half-flood. However, you must clear out of Les Ecrehous in good time with any hint of deteriorating weather. Even on a fine summer day, keep an eye on visibility and get to sea post-haste if mist or fog looks likely. Gorey is easy to reach on the flood and well protected in any winds from the west. If you are forced to leave while the ebb is still running hard, the anchorage off Rozel harbour, on the north-east corner of Jersey, may be easier to fetch than Gorey. It's not safe to leave (or enter) Les Ecrehous at night, since there are no lights anywhere on the plateau. – JC

▼ Les Ecrehous can feel very peaceful

# 10

# ROZEL AND BOULEY BAY

JERSEY

-------------

**JERSEY'S NORTH COAST** has a rugged grandeur, with the off-lying reefs of the Paternosters and Les Dirouilles providing a hint of menace in rough weather. On the north-east corner are two delightful fair-weather anchorages, Rozel Bay and Bouley Bay. The tidal streams are strong at springs so a first visit may be best at neaps.

▼ The charming harbour at Rozel

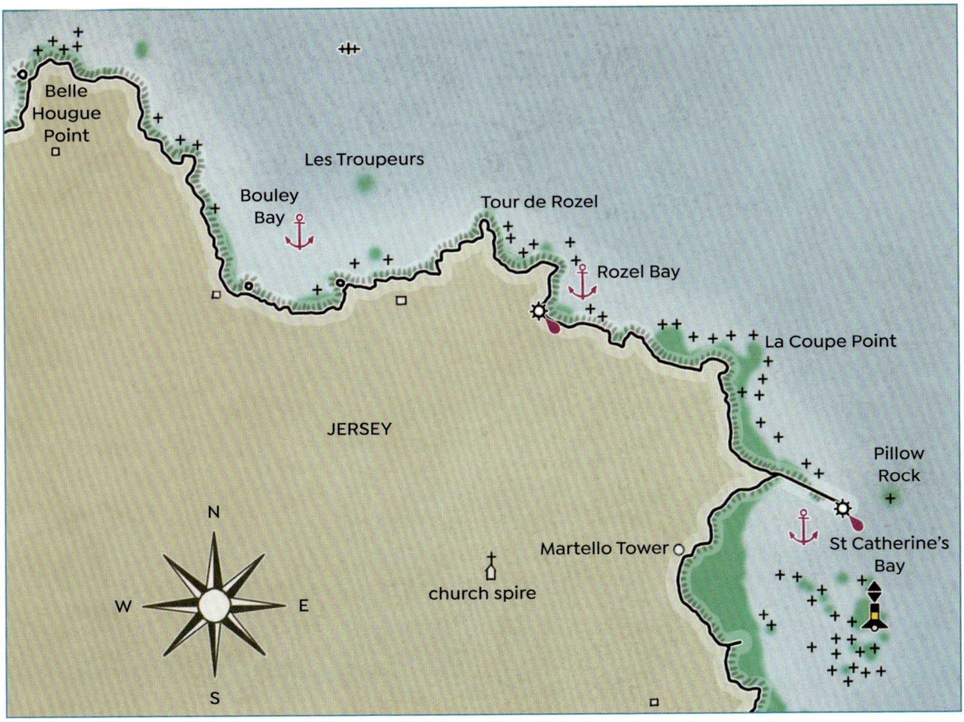

JERSEY | CHANNEL ISLANDS | 79

The picture-book village of Rozel overlooks a tiny drying harbour used by local fishing boats. In quiet weather this is one of the most charming parts of Jersey's varied coastline and well worth a visit. From 0.5 miles (0.9km) offshore, bring Rozel pier head to bear 245°T and head in on this line towards the fishing boat moorings until you pick up the small red and green buoys marking the final approach. The entrance is narrow, leaving the pier head close to starboard and a west-cardinal spar beacon to port. Bilge keelers or yachts with legs can dry out on firm sand in Rozel if there is no swell, anchoring fore-and-aft a little to the west of the local boats and facing the quay as they do.

You can stay afloat outside Rozel, clear of the fishing boat moorings, although an uneasy scend usually finds its way in near HW. The anchorage is sheltered from south-south-east through south to west.

One good reason for stopping overnight is to sample the cooking at the *Hotel Château La Chaire*. There's a choice of restaurants but all use excellent locally sourced meat, fish, dairy products and vegetables. Under the same management but with a rather less formal atmosphere, the *Rozel Bay Inn* offers good bar food. Down next to the pier is the brilliant Hungry Man kiosk, which does wonderful snacks and home made cakes.

Just 1.5 miles (2.7km) west of Rozel, the wider sweep of Bouley Bay opens up. Be careful to avoid Les Troupeurs shoal, which lies about 0.5 miles (0.9km) just east of north of L'Étaquerel headland, which has a fort on it. The bay has a stunning sense of scale tempered by a hint of discrete civilisation. Up on the high cliffs, some desirable houses have extensive views out towards Les Ecrehous and the long coast of Normandy. You tend to lose the sun quite early as the cliffs are about 120m (400ft) high.

At the head of the bay is a short stone pier and in calm or south-westerly weather you can anchor a little way east-south-east of the pier head, opposite grassy cliff slopes and a large hotel. The pier shelters a few local fishing boats which take the ground at LW. The anchorage off the pier head is snug in any winds from the south and west but somewhat prone to swell from the north-west.

Ashore is *Mad Mary's Beach Café*, which is popular for local crab sandwiches or a Bouley burger. Bouley Bay is also the headquarters of Jersey's diving community. – **JC**

▼ Bouley Bay on the north-east of Jersey

# ST CATHERINE'S BAY

JERSEY

-------------

**NOT FAR NORTH** of Gorey on Jersey's east coast, you can't miss the enormous breakwater at St Catherine's Bay. There's good shelter in westerlies, but usually a roll near HW even in calm weather, and this spot should be avoided in southerlies or south-easterlies. Approach from due east, leaving the breakwater close to starboard. There are a lot of moorings here but there's also room to anchor. South of the main mooring area the bay is littered with drying rocks.

The massive breakwater was started in Victorian times with the intention of creating a naval base to defend against the French, but the water was too shallow and the works moved to Alderney where Braye Harbour was built. At the head of the breakwater is a landing slip, which is the best location for getting ashore.

There are no facilities at St Catherine's but you can catch a bus to Gorey or St Helier. On the west side of the bay, the *Driftwood Café* is close to the prominent red and white Archirondel Tower, which is now self-catering accommodation.

From St Catherine's you can join a RIB trip around the island or out to Les Ecrehous or the Minquiers. You might enjoy a visit to the French islands of Chausey or across to Carteret. If you haven't been into some of these more tricky places before, the experienced RIB skippers can give you pointers for navigation when you decide to do it yourself. **– JC**

▼ There's usually plenty of room in St Catherine's Bay

# 12

# BEAUPORT BAY

JERSEY

------------

**ON THE WEST** edge of St Brelade's Bay and just a few kilometres east of La Corbière lighthouse is Beauport, a delightful cove for a lunchtime stop. The approach to this anchorage on the south-west coast of Jersey is straightforward, and it's perfectly sheltered with any north in the wind. To the south you'll see a steady stream of traffic heading to and from St Helier, including yachts, fishing boats, coasters, the inter-island and UK ferries, which can send a rolling wash into the bay.

When coming into Beauport, make for a point a little over 1.5 miles (2.7km) west of Noirmont Point tower then head due north into the bay. This line will leave the impressive rock of Grosse Tête about 250m (820ft) to port and a smaller above-water rock east of Grosse Tête 150m (490ft) to port. Fournier Rock, which dries 0.9m, will be a cable (185m, 600ft)

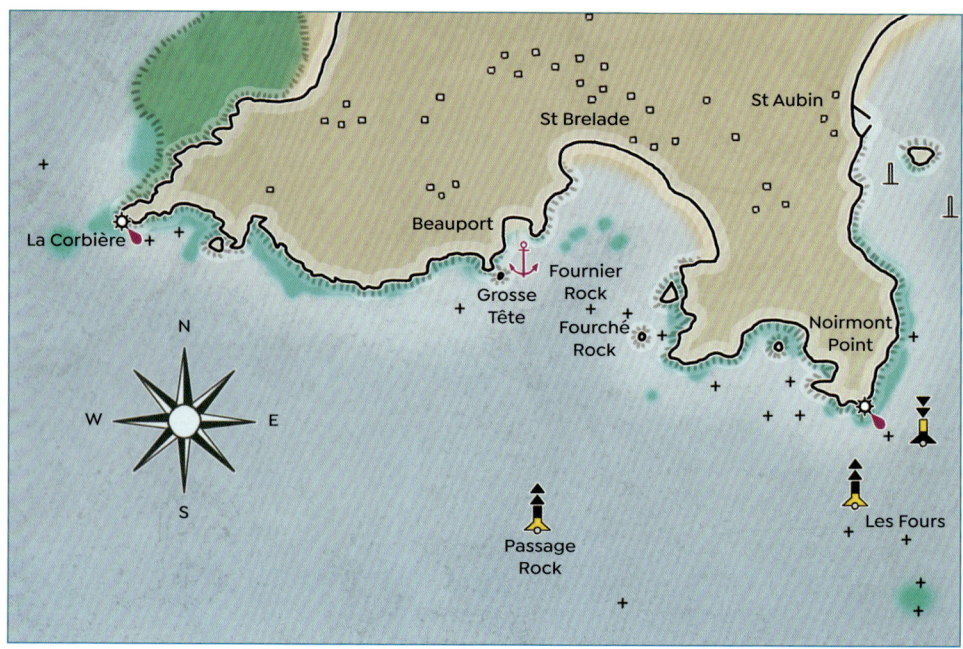

▼ Beauport on Jersey's south-west corner

to starboard. If you approach near HW, Fournier will be well covered. Continue on this course for about 0.6 miles (1.1km) at springs then drop your anchor in this perfect haven. You can probably nudge in a bit further at neaps.

Beauport is rightly regarded as one of Jersey's most attractive beaches. It is completely unspoilt and surrounded by steep cliffs, which makes access by land more challenging, so it's mostly locals who come here. The beach is golden sand and the water always seems to be warmer than in other places. In north-westerly weather the offshore wind passes over Mont Fiquet to leave the cove quiet and still, and with its south-facing aspect it is a real suntrap. Anchored here in the turquoise water, who could resist a swim before lunch?

There are no facilities ashore, which adds to its appeal as an anchorage. The cliffs, shoreline and land immediately up from the beach are a nature reserve, so this magical place will remain undeveloped. The cliffs are part of the 45ha (110 acre) Les Creux Millennium Park and the area is an important heathland habitat and part of the coastal heath that runs to La Corbière on the south-west tip of Jersey. If you land on the beach and climb to the top of the path you can experience the wonderful views east to St Brelade's Bay and Portelet Common.

By the cliff path and lanes it's about 2 miles (3.2km) to *Corbière Phare* restaurant, which has spectacular views and a tempting menu. The walk back will help to work off any overindulgence you may have succumbed to. On the way you can take a short detour to see the remains of a Second World War German bunker, and close to the restaurant is an austere concrete lookout tower, which you will probably have seen from seaward after rounding La Corbière. **– JC**

▼ Approaching the anchorage at Beauport

JERSEY | **CHANNEL ISLANDS** | 83

▼ Hope Cove anchorage is just round Bolt Tail and open to the west

# WEST COUNTRY

POOLE TO NORTH SOMERSET

------

The West Country coast, from Poole via the Isles of Scilly to North Somerset, is wonderfully served with anchoring possibilities, but some have become so popular that numerous buoys have been laid and anchoring may no longer be feasible. There are no anchoring spots now in Fowey – you have to pick up a visitors' buoy, and it's fairly difficult in Newton Ferrers, too. Many parts of Salcombe Harbour and the Helford River are also restricted for anchoring.

Despite this, there are still plenty of secluded and peaceful places you can drop the hook, with snug coves, enticing rivers and attractive bays. From a lunchtime stop for a swim to a remote overnight location with no other boat in sight, the West Country has so many alternatives that you're almost guaranteed to find something, whatever the wind direction. The south coast and the islands have more possibilities for short coastal hops, but once round Land's End and into the sweeping tides of the Bristol Channel, distances between safe havens are rather longer. There are still lots of places to explore, and for the self-sufficient cruising boat you can really get away from the modern world.

# STUDLAND BAY

### DORSET

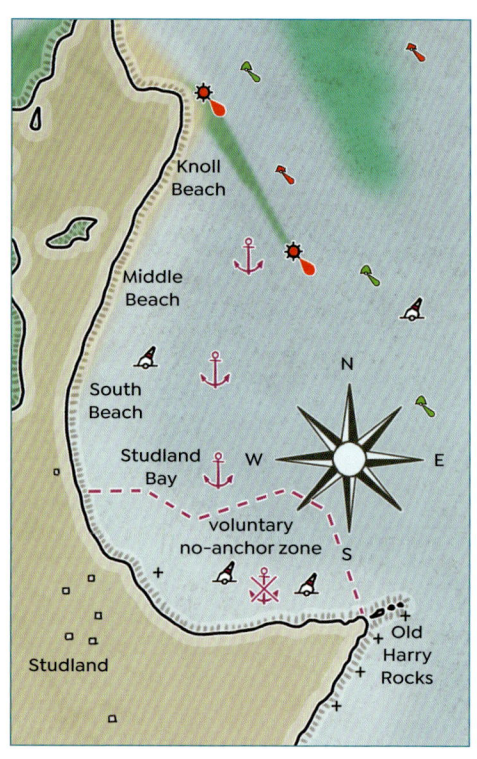

**BLOWING FORCE 6** from the west and with a spring ebb heading directly towards it we were 'shipping it green', as they say aboard *Peregrine*, Martyn and Bryony Mackrill's 40ft Fife-built Bermudian cutter. The seas were steep enough for a pod of dolphins to emerge whole-bodied from their sides as we passed Christchurch Ledge.

As the shelter of the Purbeck Hills rose to greet us, the seas eased and we looked forward to anchoring in Studland Bay while Bryony's home-cooked cod mornay heated below in the oven. But then she came on deck and announced: 'I've just got the forecast; the wind's going south and increasing to force 7,' so instead, we sailed into Poole Harbour and anchored behind Brownsea Island.

In fact, Studland Bay – if you snuck in as far as depth will allow – would be sheltered from the south right round to north if you allow for a little swell. In anything from north-east through to south-east the bay would be a lee shore and, in such winds, empty of all craft with prudent skippers.

There is good holding to be had in sand, but because of the ongoing protection of seagrass and the on-off fears for the safety of seahorses, the anchorage is under the regulation of Marine Management Organisation (MMO) strictures, which currently request that sailors observe a no-anchor zone in the southern part of the bay. The restriction is voluntary, but as *Yachting Monthly* magazine's intrepid cruising correspondent, Ken Endean, reports, there is a threat that it will become compulsory if too many boats ignore the request.

The bay is marked up in sectors from Old Harry Rocks in the south to the headland beyond Knoll Beach to the north, including Middle Beach and South Beach, which is where the voluntary no-anchoring request is in operation.

However, there is still plenty of room if you're happy to make a 0.25 miles (0.45km) dinghy trek ashore. On the day I visited there were many craft, mostly motorboats but plenty of yachts, too, anchored as well as moored, off both South and Middle Beach.

Landing is on soft, sandy beaches and then you face a stiff walk, up eroding cliffs to woodland walks, a pub – the *Bankes Arms* in Studland village – and abandoned concrete gun emplacements left over from a feared Nazi invasion.

▲ Studland Bay

I went for a swim off Middle Beach and certainly within 50m (164ft) or so of the shore there was no seagrass, weed or any other flora growing on the seabed, which I could clearly see was bald sand. One 25ft sloop was anchored just 100m (330ft) off the beach, but most craft, including several bigger yachts, were anchored further out. The wind was west and the sea perfectly flat. **– DD**

▽ Studland Bay

# CHAPMAN'S POOL

ISLE OF PURBECK, DORSET

-------------

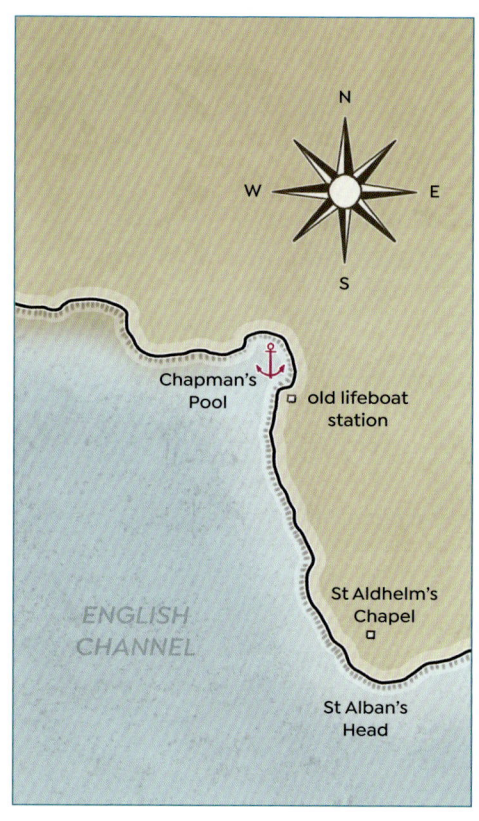

**WHEN YOU LOOK** at the chart, Chapman's Pool appears to be the perfect anchorage – the one you dream about finding if you're cruising to get away from it all. It's a semi-circular bay with steep sides for protection and little sign of human habitation to spoil the delights of isolation. Located on the south coast between Poole and Weymouth, the anchorage is often bypassed by yachts cruising this stretch of coastline, but it can be a popular spot for day-trippers on a hot, sunny day.

Chapman's Pool looks like one of those places that should have been developed as a small resort or even as a port, but it has one fatal flaw: it's wide open to the south and south-west, which is where the prevailing winds come from. If you plan to spend the night then you need to take a close look at the weather forecast and only use this anchorage in settled conditions when the wind has a strong northerly element.

Chapman's Pool is tucked in just to the west of the striking St Alban's Head and to reach it coming from the east, you head close in round the headland and then follow the coast, keeping 0.25 miles (0.45km) off. This should keep you out of the lively seas of St Alban's Race, which stretch offshore, where you'll usually find about three standing waves as the tide pours over the shallow ridge. Coming from the west there are no off-lying dangers to worry about and again, St Alban's Head will provide your guide for entering. There is 2m or more of depth

▲ Beached rowing boats at Chapman's Pool

quite close up to the shore except on the west side, where a shallower patch stretches out towards the centre. There are no guiding marks so the sounder is your guide coming in to anchor and you can judge your position quite easily by eye. With the high land all round, you may find the GPS erratic, as satellites disappear below the raised horizon.

The only buildings here are those around the old lifeboat station that was established about 150 years ago. Sadly, it only lasted a few years due to problems recruiting volunteer crew from nearby villages. Today, the lifeboat house is a boat store mainly used by local anglers.

The villages of Worth Matravers and Kingston have pubs that might make the hike over the hills worthwhile. Worth Matravers is the nearest at just under 2 miles (3.2km), and the *Square & Compass* offers traditional pub fare and has a fossil museum. The peace and quiet of Chapman's Pool is likely to disappear on a fine summer's day when boats from both Poole and Weymouth make the trip along the coast to find this wonderful oasis. However, the chances are that, come nightfall, you will have this spot to yourself, with the only disturbance coming from the gentle breaking of the waves on the shore and the sound of the gulls. **– DP**

▽ Chapman's Pool, looking NE towards Poole Harbour

DORSET | WEST COUNTRY | 89

# LULWORTH COVE

## JURASSIC COAST, DORSET

**LOOKING AT AN** aerial photo of Lulworth Cove it's almost a perfect hoof-print shape with a bite taken out, and this is your entrance from the English Channel. Renowned for its amazing geology, Lulworth can be a bit overwhelming when ashore owing to the crowds that visit (there is an enormous, very unattractive car park), so arriving by boat is the best possible way to go there. Any foray ashore can be brief if you don't want to partake of the mêlée and then you can quickly scuttle back aboard.

The entrance to the cove can prove elusive to the naked eye and traditional forms of navigation, but a carefully positioned waypoint south and a touch to the east of the centre of the entrance will bring you in without any problem. Below-water rocky ledges nudge out on both sides but those on the west are more pronounced, so keep slightly to the east side. Once inside head towards the centre, probably dodging among the many boats already there, then ease towards the north-east to find somewhere to drop your hook. The south-east quarter is shallow and rocky, and all around the beach rises quite steeply, so don't go too far in.

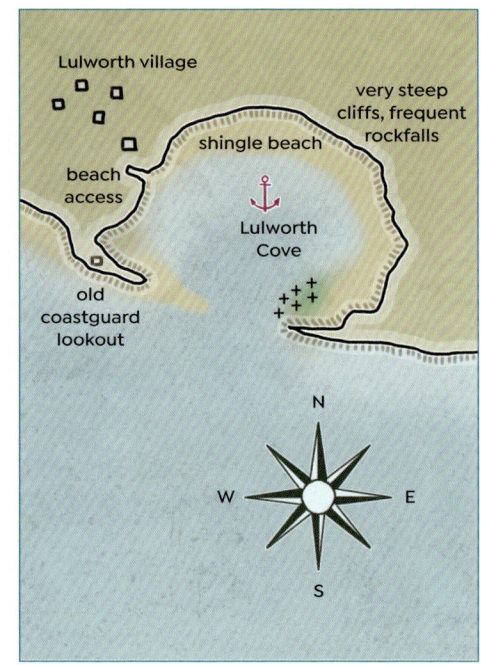

▽ Entering Lulworth Cove

As with so many popular places there are now far more local moorings than there used to be, and a weekend of favourable conditions will attract lots of boats – great if you enjoy a bun fight. If you prefer a calmer atmosphere try to visit midweek with a fairly gentle northerly breeze, when the Cove offers perfect shelter. Stronger northerlies tend to cause nasty downdraughts, and any significant wind from the south will bring in a swell, so head out before things become exciting.

Ashore there is a pub and a couple of cafés if you're in need of refreshment. The visitor centre has lots of information about geology and fossils. The nearest village, West Lulworth, is about 0.5 miles (0.8km) walk away. Lulworth is on the South West Coast Path, but several sections have been closed – hopefully only temporarily – due to cliff falls.

▲ Lulworth Cove

An interesting excursion in the dingy is round to Stairhole, a shallow rocky pool just west of Lulworth. Here you can see the crumpled Purbeck rock strata particularly easily and there are a couple of rock arches you can navigate. Rock falls around the high cliffs of Lulworth Cove are a fairly regular occurrence with two quite serious ones in 2024, so you're safer out on a boat than on the beach. **– JC**

▼ The perfect horseshoe shape of Lulworth Cove

# BEER

## JURASSIC COAST, DEVON

**HOW CAN YOU** resist anchoring for the night in a place called Beer? Not only is it a delightful anchorage but when you land on the beach, virtually the first building you come to is a pub. Beer is also well located to break the long voyage across Lyme Bay, especially in a westerly wind when tacking is likely.

The white chalk cliffs of Beer Head are a good guide when approaching from the east. As you get closer the rather large caravan park on the hills just inside the headland should appear and then you'll see the village, with its square church tower. The seabed slopes inshore quite gently although it gets steeper near the headland, but you can use your echo sounder to feel your way into the anchorage just to the west of the open beach area, and there are no off-lying dangers.

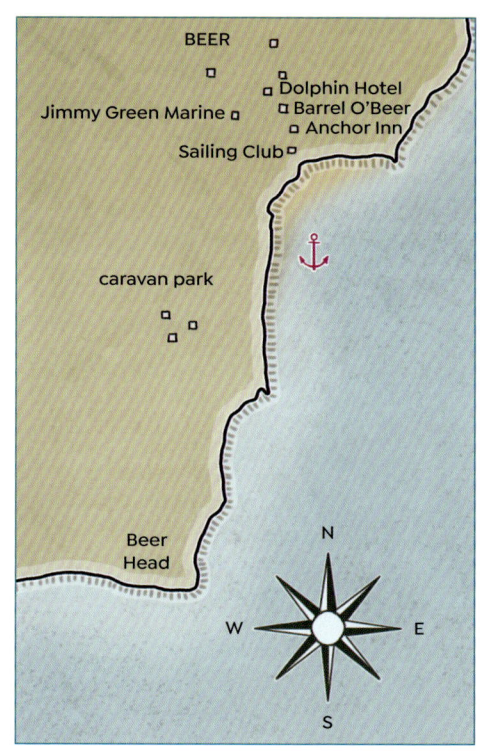

This location is probably the best spot to drop the hook as you'll be well clear of the working boats, which are common in the summer months. You'll also be better protected from any westerly winds, although if these are fresh you might experience some turbulence. Any wind from the south-west could bring a bit of swell into the anchorage when the waves are refracted around the headland. Winds from the south and the east will leave you quite exposed. This really is a fine-weather anchorage and you'll need to keep a watch on the weather forecast, but as winds tend to veer around towards the north after a fresh sou'wester you should get reasonable shelter. The holding ground is good.

▲ The White Chalk Cliffs at Beer Head

If you decide to head ashore, you're probably best to land on the shingle beach to the west of the main boat landing place, which is clearly visible. The Beer Sailing Club clubhouse is perched on the low cliffs above a good landing point and you'll see their dinghies parked on the beach below. The club offers a warm welcome to visitors and could be a good starting point on a trip ashore. It is advisable to check with the club about opening times.

On the beach itself is *Ducky's*, a café with outside seating and an extensive menu. If you walk up the road to the village you'll find the *Anchor Inn* and its welcoming beer pumps and food. Further up the road there's the *Barrel O' Beer* and the *Dolphin Hotel* plus a fish and chip shop, so there are plenty of choices for drinking and eating. If you need any chandlery then *Jimmy Green Marine* is further up the hill.

Beer is on the edge of the South West Coast Path, the route from the village to Seaton is particularly stunning with its dramatic views across the coastline. Beer comes close to being the perfect place to anchor, but as a popular, small, traditional seaside resort it can get busy in the summer. **– DP**

▽ Colourful beach huts at Beer

# BABBACOMBE BAY

TORQUAY, DEVON

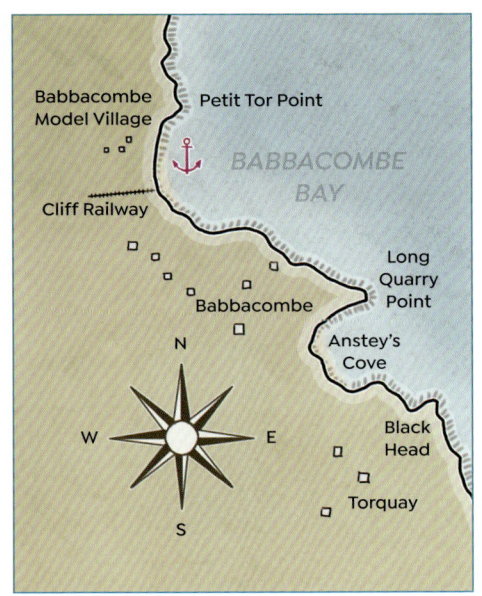

**TORBAY HAS BEEN** an anchorage for shipping for hundreds of years, not least for the Channel fleet during the Napoleonic wars. Even today, you often see ships anchored off, waiting for instruction if they're between cargoes or coming in to pick up a Channel pilot. Although you can anchor in the main part of Torbay it isn't the most peaceful location, particularly in the summer with water-skiers, shore lights, trip boats and floating discos.

About 5 miles (9km) north, around Hope's Nose, you come to the east-facing anchorage of Babbacombe Bay. Say the name Babbacombe to most

▼ The funicular railway and a land slip on the north side of Babbacombe Bay

94 | ANCHORAGES OF THE BRITISH ISLES

△ Babbacombe village and pier

people and they will probably think of the model village on the northern edge of Torquay. This is certainly one attraction, but at the bottom of the cliff railway, an anchorage snuggles in between Petit Tor Point and Long Quarry Point. It's also known as Oddicombe Beach and is now popular for the waterside boutique pub and hotel, the *Cary Arms*.

Babbacombe, a former fishing village, is at the bottom of the cliffs on the south side of the bay. The concrete pier at this end is often busy with fishermen, just to carry on the tradition. There are some visitors' buoys during the season but these are owned by the *Cary Arms*. It's best to anchor towards the north side of the bay, though possibly not too close in, as there have been major cliff falls over the years. The holding is good and in westerly winds this is a comfortable location, although it can get busy on warm summer weekends with big motorboats coming round from the Torbay marinas.

Babbacombe Corinthian Sailing Club has a summer clubhouse down at the beach and an active race calendar from April to the end of September. The main clubhouse is up in St Marychurch on top of the hill, where they welcome visitors.

A trip up the cliff railway shouldn't be missed. The idea was originally proposed in 1890 by Sir George Newnes, who had built the funicular at Lynton. Unfortunately, he died before he could pursue Torquay's railway, which was built in the 1920s. It finally opened on 1 April 1926. The Torquay Corporation took over the cliff railway in 1935 and that year, 192,000 people used it. It remained in local government ownership until 2009 and is now owned and run by a Charitable Incorporated Company (CIO). The views out into the English Channel as you travel in the carriages are absolutely stunning.

Just to the south, round Long Quarry Point, is Anstey's Cove. This is another good anchorage, especially for those who want more peace and quiet, as there is no land access to the cove, so arriving by boat is the only way to reach it. **– JC**

# BLACKPOOL SANDS

## DARTMOUTH, DEVON

-------------

**TWO MILES WEST** of Dartmouth, this magnificent crescent beach is enclosed by soft hillsides of fir trees, luxuriant shrubs and the lush meadows of a family estate. Approaching Blackpool is straightforward and there are no off-lying dangers in the immediate vicinity. The anchorage is protected from north-east through north to south-west, but open to the east and is subject to swell from the south.

Blackpool Sands is one of the rare private beaches along the south coast, which does mean it is beautifully maintained. In summer you anchor outside the yellow swimming buoys in the west crook of the bay, where you can while away your day in Côte d'Azur style. After a night at anchor you can row ashore for a full English breakfast at the café, or just buy coffee and croissants and take them down to eat on the beach. There's also a beach sauna, so why not swim ashore, have a sauna then indulge in breakfast? You could always buy something to take back on board.

Across the road from the beach is the fascinating garden, started by the present owner's grandfather at the end of the 19th century, although the land

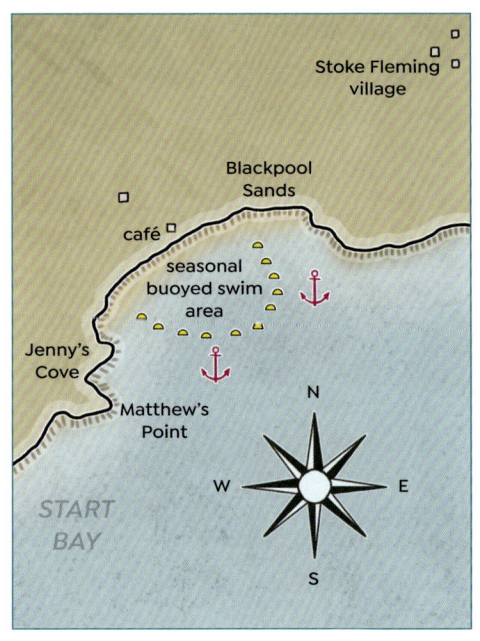

▼ Anchored in beautiful Blackpool Sands

▲ Blackpool Sands is a popular beach in the summer

had been owned by the Newman family for many years before. Up until the 1970s flowers and vegetables from the garden were sent to markets in London. Sir Ralph Newman extended the garden during the 20th century and planted many of the exotic species that are now growing here.

At the turn of this century, Sir Geoffrey Newman set about restoring the garden. New winding paths were created which lead on a magical tour up the side of the hill until you are way above the beach. This is not a garden of ordered flower beds and regimented planting but an organic landscape with different species helping each other; there's an amazing wisteria popping out of the trees at the top of the garden, although it is planted far down the slope.

After your walk in the woods, head back to the café for lunch. All the produce is locally sourced: Dartmouth crab, Start Bay scallops, Salcombe ice cream, Salcombe gin or Torbay beer or cider.

After a siesta on the beach you can hire paddleboards or kayaks to work up an appetite for supper. If you are experienced you can head off on your own; for learners, there's tuition or guided explorations along the shore.

During the season there are major events here, such as Tunes on the Sands, a weekend of music and fun in July. Also there's often live music at the café.

Many years ago some friends had taken their boat round from Dartmouth to anchor off Blackpool for the day. The beach was pretty packed and cars were queuing up the hill to get into the car park. Their ten-year-old son was sulking down in the cabin and when asked what was wrong he said, 'Why can't we come in the car, like normal people?' **– JC**

# ELENDER COVE

PRAWLE POINT, DEVON

- - - - - - - - - - - -

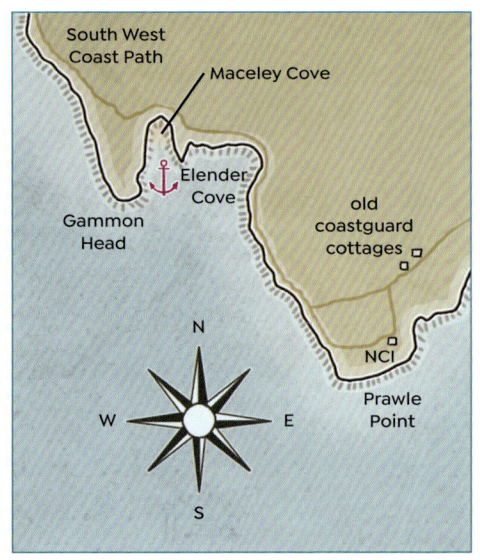

**TUCKED IN BETWEEN** Prawle Point and Gammon Head, Elender Cove is an anchorage for the self-sufficient cruising boat. There are absolutely no facilities ashore here – just two lovely sandy beaches. Elender Cove itself is on the east side of the bay and access is only really possible from a boat, as a cliff fall a few years ago made the path down unsafe. Closer to Gammon Head is Maceley Cove, which is accessible from the South West Coast Path for intrepid walkers.

This is a popular lunchtime stop for boats out from Salcombe or those

▼ The steep cliffs around Elender Cove

en route along the coast heading east or west. The holding in sand is good, with plenty of water as the cliffs are steep-to. There is good protection from all winds from the north but you're pretty comfortable from easterlies through north round to south-west. You're exposed to the south, so if the wind heads in that direction it's best to nudge into Salcombe. Coming from Start Point and the east you'll see the National Coast Watch lookout on the top of Prawle Point and a row of old coastguard cottages, now holiday homes. It's comforting to know there's someone keeping an eye on things.

Elender Cove has a wider, more gently shelving profile with Maceley in a narrower cut into the cliffs and a gorgeous sandy beach at its head. From offshore it's not so easy to spot the entrance until you're fairly close, but during the summer the Prawle buoy is about 650m (2,130ft) due west of Prawle Point and a short 3 cables (550m 1,800ft) a smidgen to the west of south from Gammon Head. You may also see quite a few boats already at anchor, soaking up the atmosphere. In fine, settled weather this is a perfect location for a night or two away from it all. **– JC**

▽ Elender Cove is wider than Maceley, which is right under Gammon Head

# HOPE COVE

SALCOMBE, DEVON

**THERE'S HOPE COVE** just north of Torquay, and Hope's Nose, but this nestles into the coast round Bolt Tail, west of Salcombe. It's just off the village of Hope, which was once a fishing and smuggling community but became a popular holiday destination in the 1920s and 1930s – some would say it hasn't changed much, except for the influx of cars down the very narrow Devon lanes.

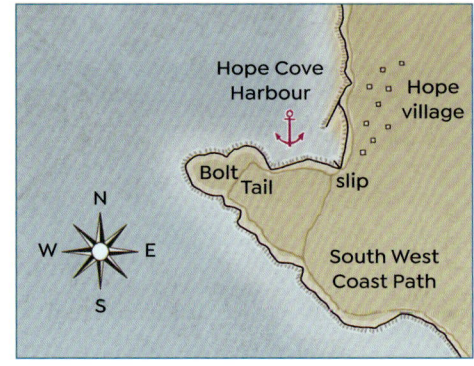

▼ The breakwaters link up rocks around the drying harbour

On a calm summer Saturday, Hope Cove can get fairly busy with boats out for the day from Plymouth or Salcombe and also with trailed boats being launched at the slip by the old lifeboat house. There will be lots of people on the beach and paddleboards and kayaks scooting about.

In winds from the south through east to north-east you're quite sheltered, but the cove is exposed to the north and west, even south-westerlies tend to get swell running in round Bolt Tail. A breakwater joins various rocks close under the village, but this little harbour dries, so is only suitable if you can take the ground – most cruising boats will need to anchor over towards the cliffs. With its westerly aspect you can have some amazing sunsets here. Be careful as you come in to anchor, as Goody Rock is near the centre of the cove and you need to pass to the north of it.

In the village, the *Hope & Anchor* pub is a popular place for a drink or a meal. Sadly, the post office in Hope Cove has now closed, but there's a general shop as well as a gallery, which offers a range of arts and crafts made by about 30 local artists. The restaurant of the *Cottage Hotel* has absolutely stunning views across Bigbury Bay, or you can eat local lobster – although there are other things on the menu – at the *Lobster Pod Bistro*. Don't miss *The Kiln* for your ice cream, drink or snack.

Hope village is divided into Outer Hope, slightly to the north, and Inner Hope further south. The anchorage is closer to Inner Hope, which may well have been the original village. If you walk up from the slip, a short way along on your right is a charming square with old, thatched cottages, and from here you can join the South West Coast Path. It's definitely worth walking up to Bolberry Down for the amazing views. Bolt Tail is now owned by the National Trust but during the Second World War there was an aerodrome on Bolberry Down and a Ground Control Interceptor Radar Station. Many of the WAAFs (Women's Auxiliary Air Force) stationed here were billeted in hotels in Hope Cove.

As you round Bolt Tail when approaching Hope Cove, the first bay you pass is Pilchard Cove, which probably harks back to the days when pilchard fishing was an important part of village life. The fishing fleet was disbanded when the pilchard shoals stopped coming. Today, local fishermen mostly catch crab and lobster. – **JC**

▲ Hope Cove anchorage is just round Bolt Tail and open to the west

# CAWSAND BAY

PLYMOUTH SOUND, CORNWALL

**ON THE WEST** side of Plymouth Sound is this delightful bay. Whether you drop the hook here just as a pleasant lunchtime stop or for the night, this is a classic anchorage. Cawsand and Kingsand are at their most relaxing midweek at either end of the season, as the bay is very popular with local boats. The approach is straightforward, it's perfectly sheltered with any west in the wind and makes a good stopover when on a West Country cruise if you don't want to go into a marina. To the east you can watch all sorts of vessels negotiating the channel around Plymouth's historic breakwater: fishing boats, naval ships, Brittany Ferries and scores of yachts.

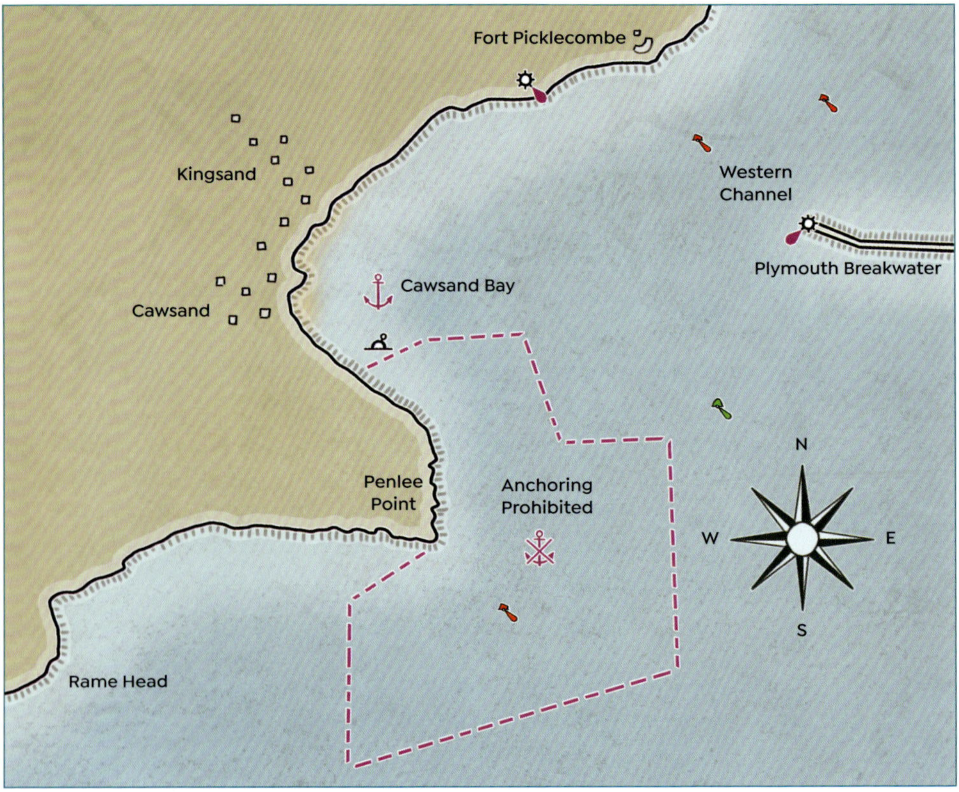

▼ Cawsand and Kingsand share the bay

Approaching up Channel, from Falmouth or Fowey, Rame Head is a distinctive mark, with its little chapel on the summit. Draystone red buoy lies just off Penlee Point, around which is an area where anchoring is prohibited, clearly marked on the Admiralty chart. Coming from the east you should head for the west end of the breakwater and in towards the pretty village waterfront. You can anchor anywhere clear of the local moorings, nudging in as close as your draught allows. The holding is good, but it's worth attaching an anchor buoy.

Dividing the two beaches is the Maker with Rame Institute, the third building on this site, both of the earlier two having been destroyed by storms. In 2014 it was again severely damaged, but swift action saved it and it has been beautifully restored and the sea wall below it strengthened. The clock tower was built in 1920 to commemorate the coronation of George V, which took place in 1911 – the same day the foundation stone of the institute was laid.

From the beginning of April to the end of October a ferry runs from Cawsand beach to the Barbican in the centre of Plymouth. It's a good way to visit the city, but be sure to leave someone on board as a shift of the wind into the east would necessitate moving pretty quickly. There are pubs and cafés in the villages and Kingsand has a Spar mini-market for supplies. The *Halfway House Inn* is a good choice for a meal ashore as they use local produce and offer a selection of West Country ales.

You can join the South West Coast Path here, with lovely walks either west to Rame Head or east towards Cremyll. The Bay forms the east boundary of Mount Edgcumbe Country Park with its folly, formal gardens, deer park, ancient barrows and the house that was originally built in the mid-1500s. There are shops and a choice of cafés if you need fortifying before you follow one of the walks around the estate.

Until 1844 Kingsand was in Devon and Cawsand in Cornwall and you can still see the house with the dividing line marked on it. Historically the inhabitants of the two villages would have made their livings through pilchard fishing and smuggling. There was a network of tunnels under the cottages to store contraband, though it has now been sealed up. **– JC**

# POLPERRO

CORNWALL

---

▼ The fishing village Polperro

**THE CHARM AND** picturesque beauty of Polperro has been something of its undoing, as it has become such a tourist attraction that arriving by sea is probably the best way to get there. The inner harbour dries and it is a very narrow entrance, so even if you can take the ground or nab one of the two moorings against the wall it's questionable whether it's worth it. Outside the east pier there

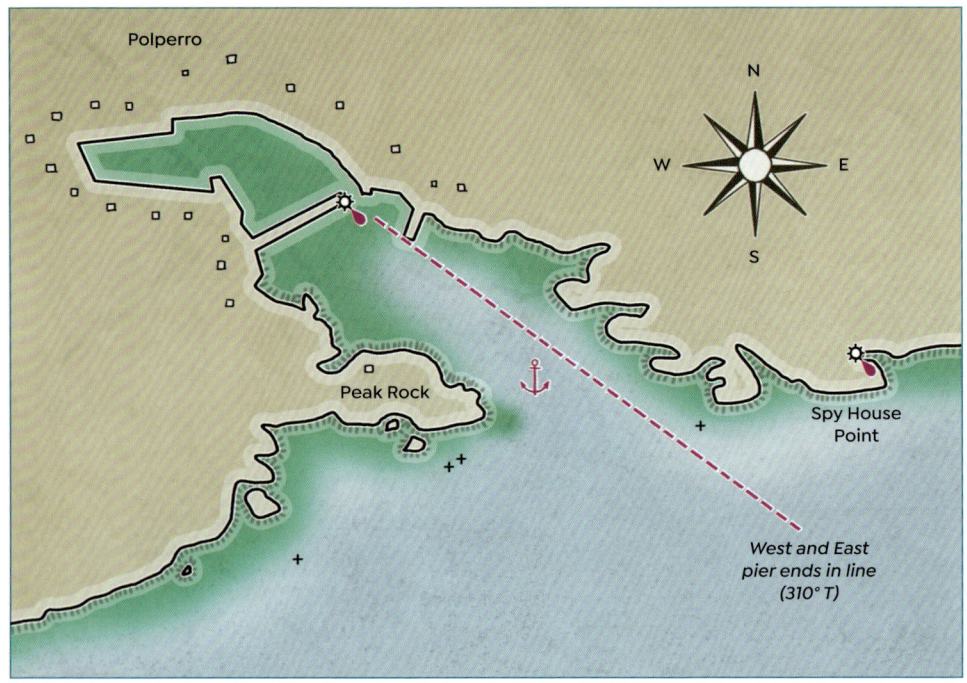

Polperro

Peak Rock

Spy House Point

West and East pier ends in line (310° T)

▲ The anchorage at Polperro

are now some visitor mooring buoys, which have taken up quite a bit of the anchorage.

From the east you round Spy House Point and then, as the ends of the east and west piers just align, come onto the leading line of 310°T, which keeps you clear of the rocks off the east side and the Raney reef on the western point. The Polca is a rock (least depth about 1m) roughly 200m (660ft) south and a shade west of Spy House Point, and this should be left to port as you come in on the line. Coming from the west you go between Polca rock and Raney Reef before turning to port on the leading line. The anchorage is open to the south-east and any strong winds from this direction make it dangerous – in severe weather the inner harbour is shut off with a steel gate. The anchorage is well protected by high cliffs from the north and round to the west.

Ashore, the village is a jumble of narrow lanes and alleyways with pretty cottages. There are a number of shops for tourists plus a newsagent, small supermarket and bakery. Some fishing boats still work out of the harbour, though not quite like in the days when pilchards were numerous. The pilchards were landed at the harbour then taken to factories where the oil was pressed out. They were then gutted, salted and packed in barrels ready to be sent around the country. Don't miss a visit to the Polperro Heritage Museum of Smuggling and Fishing; it gives you an insight into life here in the 18th and 19th centuries.

In settled weather this is a great place to spend a night or two and there are lovely walks along the cliffs, with a figure-of-eight walk around the harbour and the headlands each side of the entrance. For the energetic it's about 5 miles (8km) to Fowey or 3 miles (4.8km) to Looe along the South West Coast Path.

On the Quay you can call in at *The Three Pilchards* for a pint and a meal, or there's *The Blue Peter Inn* or *The Ship Inn* in Fore Street, all suitably nautical hostelries. Further into the village there's a good choice of restaurants for a meal ashore. **– JC**

# 11

# PERCUIL RIVER

## FALMOUTH, CORNWALL

**ROUNDING ST ANTHONY** Head into the famous Carrick Roads there are several places you could choose to anchor. The River Fal estuary could easily keep you entertained for the whole of a summer cruise, so if a dodgy forecast keeps you here for a while enjoy the variety of places to visit.

Throughout the summer the Falmouth racing calendar is pretty active but there are creeks and corners you can find to get away from the throng. In a fairly shallow-draught boat

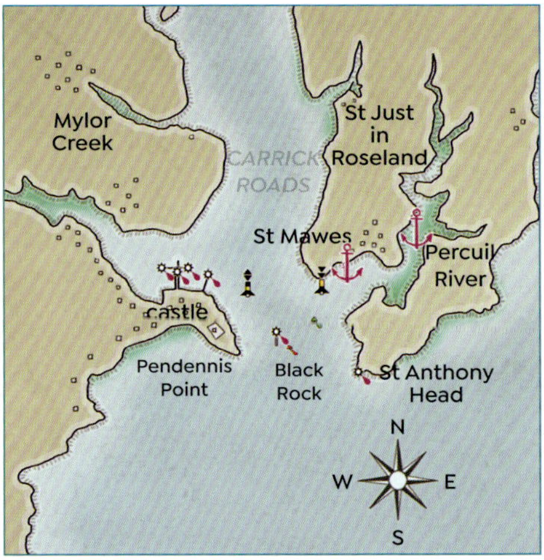


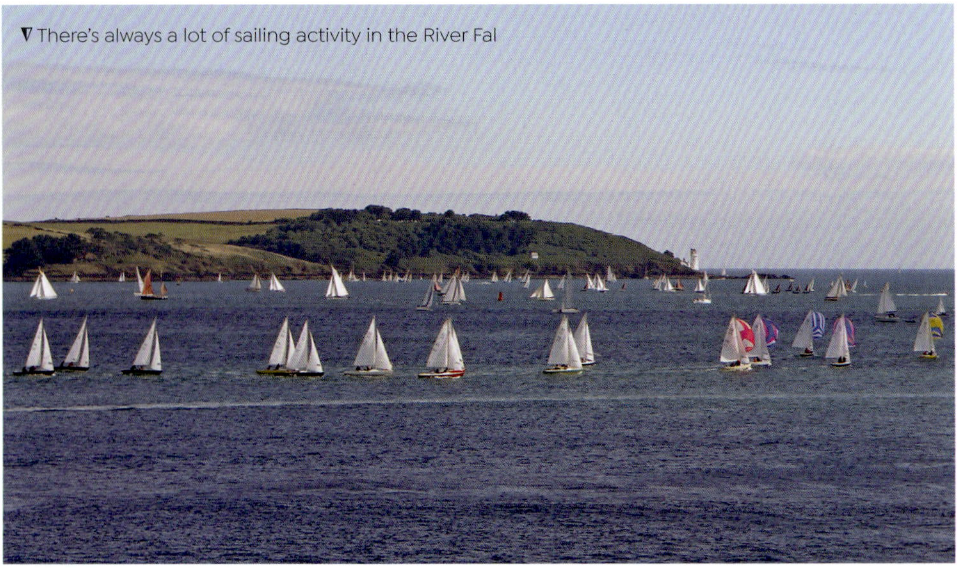

▼ There's always a lot of sailing activity in the River Fal

you can nudge right up to Truro and dry out alongside the quay to explore this fascinating city. At the other end, Falmouth obviously has lots going on, with the Falmouth Classics regatta in June and the famous Sea Shanty Festival running at the same time. It is wonderful to see the Falmouth working boat races, which are very competitive, and don't miss a visit to the fascinating Maritime Museum and Pendennis Castle on its point overlooking the entrance.

On the opposite side of the estuary is St Mawes, with its own castle, and a great place to drop the hook off Tavern Beach, just to the east of the castle. This is fine in easterly or northerly conditions but you definitely don't want to be here if the wind goes round to the south or south-west. If that happens, round Amsterdam Point and edge up into the Percuil River. There are now quite a lot of moorings up here and the upper reaches of the river dry out, so if you can take the ground this is a practical alternative. Up as far as North Hill Point, on the starboard hand, there's a minimum of 2m of water and you can usually anchor on the edge of the channel as the river bends away to the north-west. Depending on your draught you might just nudge the bottom at low water springs. Be careful where you moor, as inshore above Polvarth Point, there are oyster beds on both sides of the river. There's a boatyard at Percuil village on the east shore, past Pelyn Creek.

▲ The St Mawes approaches

St Mawes castle is a perfect example of Tudor defensive works. It was built on a cloverleaf pattern and was intended to share the defence of the Fal entrance and Carrick Roads with Pendennis Castle. During the civil war it was unable to hold out for the king against the Parliamentarians, as it could not be easily defended on its landward side. Consequently, the governor of the day surrendered without a fight, which is why it is such a fine building today.

There are lots of good restaurants and pubs in St Mawes if you're looking to eat ashore – *The Idle Rocks* is popular, as is *The Watch House*. There's also a good bakery and several takeaways.

A ferry runs across the Percuil River between St Mawes and Place, which links up with the South West Coast Path. You can also take a ferry across to Falmouth if you want to enjoy all the town has to offer, but come back to the peace of the Percuil River. – **JC**

# HELFORD RIVER

CORNWALL

------------

**WHO CAN CONTEMPLATE** visiting the Helford River without conjuring up images from Daphne du Maurier's novel *Frenchman's Creek*? Coming from the north, the entrance to the Helford River is a little short of 4 miles (7.2km) from Pendennis Point and the River Fal. Off Rosemullion Head is August Rock, marked by a green buoy that you leave to starboard. Having passed this there are no further hazards, as the river runs westward and is sheltered in most winds except easterlies.

The Helford River now has a lot of moorings from Helford Passage onwards and anchoring is not allowed in the upper reaches above Porth Navas Creek. On both sides of the river from Frenchman's

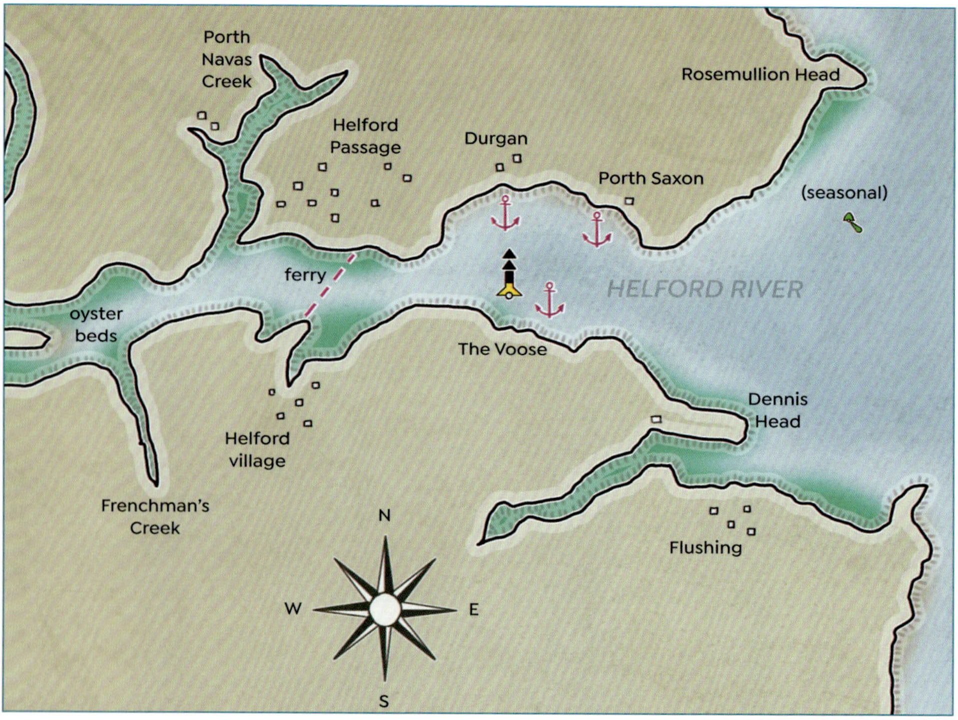

▼ Helford River looking east towards Rosemullion Head

Creek onwards are the Duchy of Cornwall oyster beds, said to date back to long before the Duchy existed, possibly to Roman times. Porth Navas Creek is a possibility for boats that can take the ground, but it dries completely.

As you enter the river and round Toll Point on the starboard hand there's an area of eel grass with a voluntary no-anchoring policy, so if you choose to anchor between Toll Point and Porth Saxon it should be outside the marker buoys. Slightly further on you can anchor off the hamlet of Durgan in Polgwidden Cove on the north shore which is sheltered in northerly and westerly winds. If the winds are southerly there is more shelter on the south side at Bosahan Cove or Ponsense Cove east of Voose Rocks, which are easily identifiable as they're marked by a north cardinal.

With the huge Fal Estuary so close there was really no need for the Helford to develop and it remains one of the least spoilt harbours along the south coast. In the 18th and 19th centuries coasters and sailing barges used to go right up to the village of Gweek, but the coming of the railways and silting in the river saw this trade fall off. It's still fascinating to explore up the river, either in the dinghy or on the tide if your boat doesn't draw too much.

As you pass Frenchman's Creek you can spot the beach where du Maurier's Lady Dona was captured, and the stone quay where she and the eponymous Frenchman, Jean-Benoît Aubery, cooked their fish supper. You can almost imagine his pirate ship, *La Mouette*, riding at anchor, awaiting her next adventure.

Helford Passage is on the north side and is linked by a ferry to the village of Helford on the south shore. A ferry has existed here for over 300 years. Not surprisingly there's *Ferryboat Inn* at Helford Passage, overlooking the landing, or you can find the Shipwright's Arms in Helford village.

Just to the north-east of Durgan beach is the Bosveal Nature Reserve, owned by the National Trust. A slightly longer walk from Durgan takes you to Trebah Gardens with an amazing range of subtropical trees and shrubs growing in the perfect climate here. The gardens run right down to the edge of the river and after working up an appetite walking around, you can satisfy your hunger pangs at the Trebah Kitchen. **– JC**

# LAMORNA COVE

PENZANCE, CORNWALL

---

**ON ANY CRUISE** heading west along the Channel, Land's End is always something of a milestone. It is the point where you turn the corner into the Irish Sea and where you can get exposed to the full force of the Atlantic. It is also a place where you will be watching the forecast carefully, particularly if the wind is in the north-west.

Lamorna Cove offers a great spot to wait for the wind to ease before rounding Land's End. The cove offers good protection in any winds from the north-west right around to the north-east. When you look at the chart you might think that there is good protection from the west, but any winds from that direction can generate quite a swell coming into the cove that might spell a disturbed night at anchor. If you want shelter from the west then it is best to head a bit further into Penzance Bay, and find calmer waters off Mousehole or Newlyn.

The white lighthouse a mile (1.6km) along the coast from Mousehole is a good indication that you are approaching Lamorna. Look for the scattered buildings on the shore and

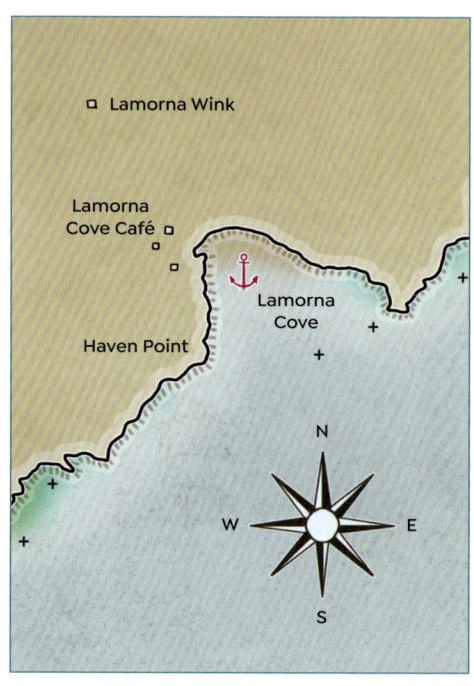

the spoil heaps of granite rocks on the eastern side of the cove, which are the remains of the quarries where high-quality granite was excavated. It was this quality granite that led to the tiny harbour being built at Lamorna. It's tucked into the north-west corner of the cove but the granite breakwater is in poor condition. The last time I visited it looked as though a whole section of the breakwater had collapsed under the battering of winter storms, leaving a trail of rocks close to the dinghy landing site. This means you'll need to land on the beach if you plan to go ashore, which can be pretty stony.

Entering the cove is straightforward enough with no off-lying dangers. The depths gradually decrease, so it is easy to head straight in with the sounder operating until you find the depth you're comfortable with. Depending on the wind direction, you'll probably want to choose an anchorage towards the western shore, although the depths here can shoal quickly.

At lowish water you might want to head ashore for the pretty curved sandy beach that becomes exposed. A café is built into the harbour wall under the cliffs, but the gem of Lamorna is the pub, the *Lamorna Wink*, a 0.5-mile (0.8km) walk along the main road in and out of the cove. The last time I was there they did fabulous fish and chips plus excellent beer. Lamorna has a long heritage of smuggling and the name of the pub reflects this, an indication of what you might get if you got the 'wink'. Much of Lamorna is privately owned, including the harbour, and it has changed hands several times over the last few years. As an anchorage, let's hope Lamorna remains unspoilt for everyone. **– DP**

▲▼ Lamorna Cove

# GREEN BAY

BRYHER, ISLES OF SCILLY

------------

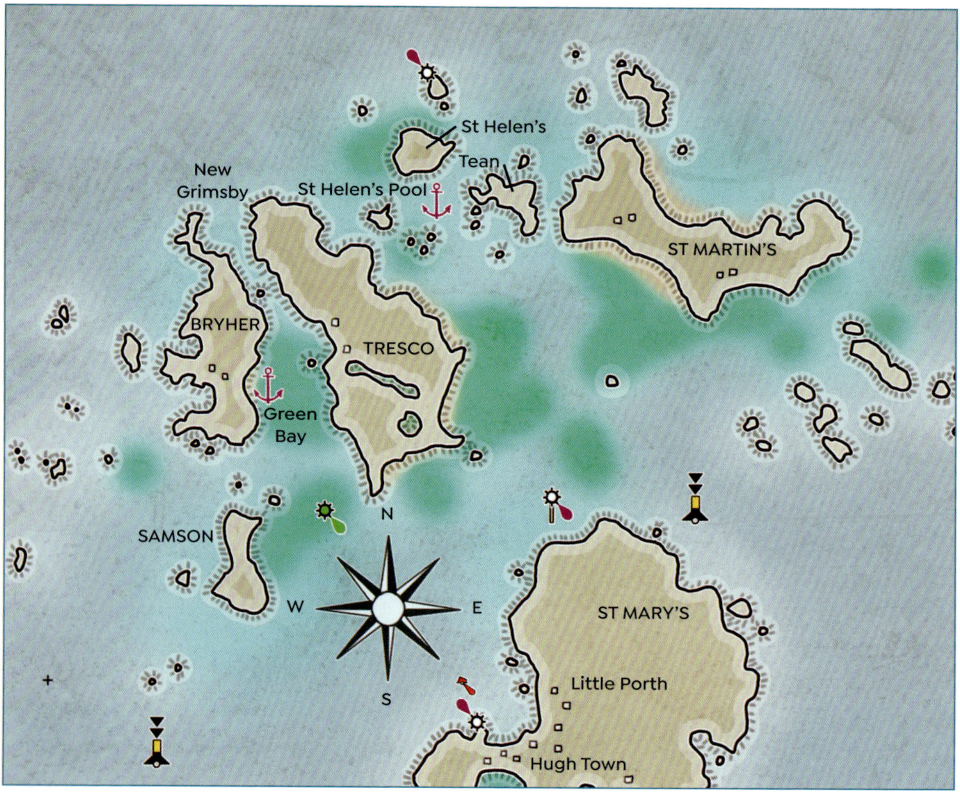

**THE MAIN NAUTICAL** shortcoming of the Isles of Scilly archipelago is its paucity of all-weather havens. Green Bay comes close to fulfilling this need, albeit only for those able to take the ground. This idyllic drying bay is just off the Tresco Flats between the islands of Bryher and Tresco and enjoys near all-round shelter on firm, drying sand. On our last visit a neighbouring boat had been there all summer soaking up the Scillonian sun, safe and secure in the knowledge that both he and his spaniel would be well protected should the weather turn inclement. For those yachts constrained to deep water, the moorings and anchorage of adjacent New Grimsby Sound are the next best bet, albeit for a token fee paid to the Tresco Harbourmaster.

Sleepy Bryher is the smallest inhabited island in the Isles of Scilly and contrasts with its popular neighbour Tresco across the flats. While Tresco is renowned for its lush exotic Abbey Gardens and upmarket accommodation, Bryher is more informal, although the *Hell Bay Hotel* does cater for the luxury market. It's an island of raw beauty and peace – my bedroom wall is adorned by two lovely prints from artist Richard Pearce (no relation), who works from an old gig shed on the shore. They're the second thing I see each morning and get my day underway with a sense of Bryher tranquillity. A walk past the *Hell Bay Hotel* takes you to Hell Bay itself; although allegedly the venue for 18th-century wrecking tales, the teeth of the rocks lining the Atlantic-facing shore look sharp enough to need no assistance. Returning to the east over the high point of the well-named Watch Hill and it could be time to slake your thirst in the *Fraggle Rock Bar*, set in a peaceful beachside position looking out at Tresco past Hangman Island (don't ask). The return to Green Bay first passes Anneka's Quay before reaching All Saint's Church. We attended a Sunday morning service here, unexpectedly taken by a senior clergyman on vacation from Canterbury Cathedral, who was accompanied on the shipwrecked harmonium by his son-in-law who had been more accustomed to playing at St David's Cathedral!

Bennett's boatyard occupies a corner of Green Bay and offers boat and canoe hire, showers, a chandlery and water. Steve Hulands at Bryher Marine Engineering produced us a replacement outboard, which still does good service. Bryher Boatyard provides care and repair of leisure craft and is situated just down the lane from the Bryher general supply shop.

Green Bay is best approached from New Grimsby Sound. Pass just north of Merrick Island on a course of 245°T to clear The Three Brothers Rocks and Brow Ledge, which occupy the southern section of the bay. The water is clear, permitting a scan of the sandy bottom that dries to 2.2m before dropping the hook.

Bryher entrances us and we can't wait to visit again – I too could spend a whole summer there. **– JP**

▼ Green Bay looking south

# 15

# ST HELEN'S POOL

## ISLES OF SCILLY

**ENSCONCED BETWEEN THE** northern islands of the Isles of Scilly, St Helen's Pool enjoys near all-round shelter, a rare attribute in these parts. With Tresco to the west, St Martin's to the east, and the islands of St Helen's and Tean to the north, only the south is open, although distant St Mary's acts as a weak windbreak. This picturesque expanse of water provides several small nooks and crannies to explore, as well as a spacious deep-water anchorage.

Historically this was one of the best Scillonian havens for large craft seeking a roomy sheltered refuge when St Mary's Road became too exposed. With good holding in sand and a depth of 5m in the centre, the islands ringing the anchorage keep it free of swell except at high tide. The pool can be accessed from Tean Sound, Old Grimsby Sound or from the Crow Sound area to the south. Pilotage through the channels does need care, especially from the south or Old Grimsby, and for your first visit it is wisest to choose a rising tide and avoid LW. My own preference is to navigate through Tean Sound or use St Helen's Gap, a narrow channel to the north of the pool between

▲ *Aurial* dried out in Green Bay, between Bryer and Tresco

St Helen's and Tean Islands, through which entrance can be gained from Round Island, marked by its magnificent lighthouse. Start a cable (185m, 600ft) off the east side of Round Island and head due south to leave the rocks off Didley's Point, the easternmost part of St Helen's Island, well to starboard until you identify the gateway between West Gap Rock and East Gap Rock ahead, altering course to 190°T to pass through the centre of the gap. Continue 1 cable (185m, 600ft) until you pass the bar (least depth 1m). Pick your spot, check the depth and drop the hook – you've arrived!

As for shoreside facilities – well, forget it. This is a haven of peace and quiet for family picnics and beach barbecues rather than the revelry of hostelries. The neighbouring islands of Tresco and St Martin's host local facilities like shops and pubs; both these islands are easily reachable by a moderate dinghy ride should you choose. The best place for fuel and water is St Mary's, so it is wise to be self-sufficient for your stay here. Both St Helen's and Tean islands offer a chance to stretch your legs: you can explore the old seaweed farm on Tean or the chapel and old isolation hospital on St Helen's; the vista from the top of each is magnificent. We celebrated the end of an idyllic Scillonian fortnight with sundowners on Tean's highest point – a truly peaceful spot.

We love it here – there are few pleasures greater than being surrounded by nothing but sleepy islands and the sound of undisturbed nature while watching the sun sink into the west. And then, as dusk fades into dark, the stars shine brightly overhead while the loom of Round Island's lighthouse sweeps around. **– JP**

▼ Round Island lighthouse

▼ A panoramic view of St Helen's Pool and the surrounding islands

# CARBIS BAY

ST IVES, CORNWALL

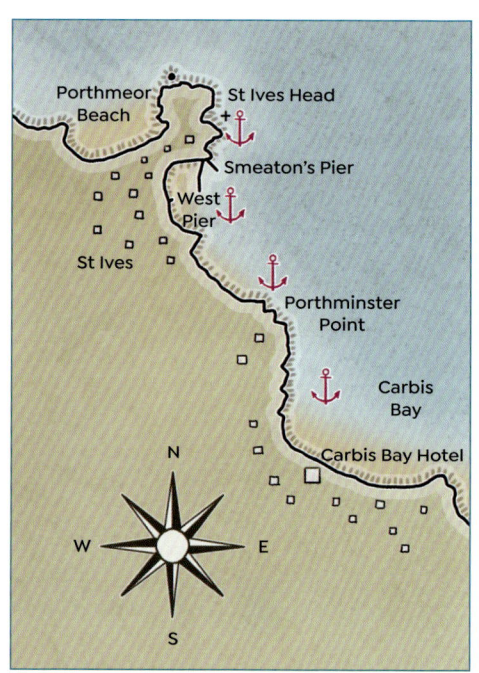

**COMING FROM THE** north or from the Bristol Channel, you might want a break before tackling the challenging seas and tides off Land's End. Arriving from the south after rounding Land's End, the first chance to stop is in the deep waters of Carbis Bay.

If your plans include a run ashore for food and drink then anchoring off St Ives is probably your best bet because this popular seaside town has more than its fair share of hostelries. If a quiet night at anchor is top of your list of priorities, then it's best to head a bit further south for the anchorage in Carbis Bay. St Ives is a busy port used by several fishing boats along with a considerable number of tripper boats in the summer months. The whole

▼ The expanse of St Ives at LW

▼ St Ives has a lot of local drying moorings

harbour dries out at LW; to find a spot, your boat will need to be a bilge keeler and you'll probably have to pick up a mooring. Cruising yachts are much more likely to find an anchorage outside the harbour than a drying berth inside.

In a fresh westerly the swell coming in from the Atlantic can be refracted around the St Ives headland. However, you can find reasonable shelter in anything from the prevailing south-westerlies. Just south of the rock off Bamaluz Point is a good spot, but it can get crowded. I would tend to head south of the harbour and tuck in just north of Porthminster Point. Beware of the rocks lying off the point. It's a bit further to get ashore from here, but it should be a more peaceful and more sheltered option.

Landing in St Ives with a tender can be a challenge in the summer months because the beach inside the harbour is usually full of holidaymakers. The best spot is either at the slipway or by the pier adjacent to the lifeboat slip. On the ebb you may have to carry your tender a fair way along the sand in order to get back to the water.

I much prefer to escape the crowds and anchor further south in Carbis Bay. You probably won't want to go as far south as the *Carbis Bay Hotel*, unless you want the wide sandy beaches here, but 0.25 miles (0.45km) south of Porthminster should be about right, where the only disturbance is likely to come from the passing trains along the clifftop. South of here you're likely to find the waters very busy on a summer's day, with the beaches and the shelter from the wind being the main attractions for visitors, but the evenings should be tranquil, with only the sounds of the sea and the ever-present cries of the seagulls. **– DP**

# PORT GAVERNE

CORNWALL

---

**IN THE LAST** 20 years since the television series *Doc Martin* was filmed here, Port Isaac has become so popular that the village is overrun with tourists, and yachts aren't exactly welcome. There's also a problem with sand being washed away, so more rocks are being exposed in the harbour and the breakwater is deteriorating.

The next cove to the east is Port Gaverne, which is a lovely, away-from-it-all sort of place. The entrance is narrower than at Port Isaac and at more of an angle. Off the eastern headland at Main Head, there are two above-water rocks, the outer one being Castle Rock, but the approach is straightforward with no

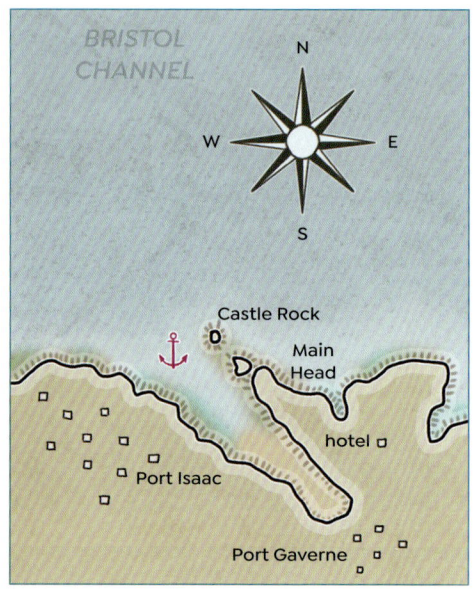

▽ The beach at Port Gaverne is popular with families

dangers. Nudge in as far as your draught allows and anchor. The holding is good and you're protected from north-east round to south-south-west, but exposed to the west and north.

The beach here is well protected and perfectly safe for young children. The village now has few full-time residents but there is a choice of a pub or a hotel for a meal ashore. The spread of Port Isaac on the top of the hill has all but incorporated Port Gaverne, but in its deep cleft it feels quite cut off. You can walk into Port Isaac, and along the road on the way back there's a good deli, *The DeliBox*, and a bit further on the *Angry Anchovy* is great for takeaway pizza.

Port Gaverne has always been a fishing port with local boatbuilding, and during the 15th and 16th centuries inevitably smuggling was fairly rife. For much of the 18th and 19th centuries the harbour developed to export serpentine and slate mined locally, the latter from Delabole Quarry, about 5 miles (8km) away. Once the railways were developed, the slate and minerals were no longer transported by sea, so Port Gaverne became a more active fishing port, particularly for pilchards, herring and mackerel, through the 19th century. The pilchard shoals would arrive in late summer or early autumn to spawn, and vast quantities were caught and exported. At times there was oversupply, and the market fell away in the 1930s.

Today the village relies mostly on tourism, with lovely walks through beautiful countryside and along the dramatic North Cornwall coast. **– JC**

▽ Port Gaverne is sheltered except from the west and north-west

# LUNDY

BRISTOL CHANNEL

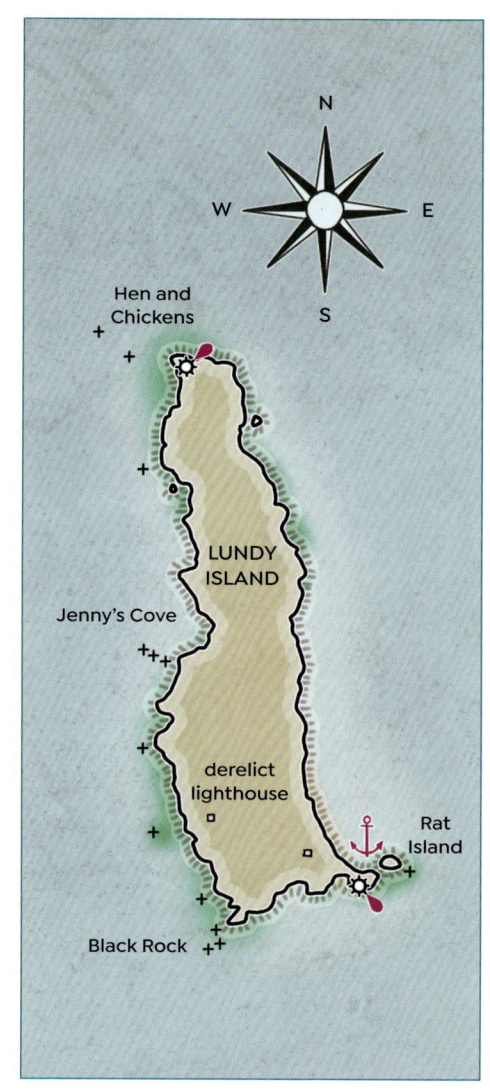

**PERCHED IN THE** middle of the Bristol Channel, Lundy offers a welcome bulwark of shelter in the exposed and highly tidal waters of the Severn Estuary. The north coasts of Cornwall and Devon create a funnel in conjunction with the south coasts of Ireland and Wales; the result is that prevailing south-westerlies can concentrate serious seas around the island. These are compounded both by the White Horses race, whipped up by the Stanley Bank shoal to the island's north-west, and the tidal rips that cut round Lundy's southern tip. The whole area deserves treating with a great deal of caution in adverse conditions.

When the weather is settled, the main anchorage on the south-east side is well sheltered from the west and, in the absence of swell, a comfortable and secure overnight stay can be enjoyed. A visitors' buoy and the warden's buoy can sometimes be used, but other buoys are private and in regular use by fishing vessels 24/7. My preference is to anchor on the shingle seabed in about 6m, with enough scope for the large tidal range. I admit that Lundy is not my favourite anchorage, nicknamed 'Lumpy' in view of the swell that may sweep round the island before hitting broadsides any boat lying head-to-wind. Use of a 'flopper stopper' might be considered. Lundy is untenable in bad swell and in any strong wind from the north round to the south-east, so have an alternative up your sleeve.

The eastern approach is free from hazards, although care should be taken with the tidal streams and overfalls if coming round the north or south of the island. Both extremities are marked by lighthouses, and the church tower provides a useful reference point. Watch out for the MS *Oldenburg*, Lundy's own ship, bringing visitors and stores from the mainland to the quay. A Marine Conservation Zone and Special Area of Conservation extend round the whole island so respect the environment – in particular, fishing is forbidden on the east coast.

Lundy is owned by the National Trust and administered by the Landmark Trust, which rents out the 23 holiday properties and manages the farm and campsite. The landing jetty should be kept clear at all times, but it is possible to land on the shingle beach. The village is up the cliff road, where the Marisco Tavern offers the chance of refreshment while you pay the landing fee before looking into the well-stocked shop. At just under 3 miles (4.8km) long and around 0.5 miles (0.8km) wide, the island offers a wealth of walks, fantastic views, and great birdwatching. It is especially associated with the puffin – Lundy derives its name from the Norse word for this charming bird. Over 140 different bird species are recorded each year, so there's always something to catch your interest.

Whether visited as a passage halt or as a destination in its own right, Lundy remains an attractive option, bathing in its own particular character whose contrasts offer something for all. **– JP**

▽ The anchorage on the south-east corner of Lundy

# 19

# BUCK'S MILLS

BIDEFORD BAY, DEVON

---

**BUCK'S MILLS, JUST** a short distance east of Clovelly, is one of those strange places that can be found around the British coastline that has a very interesting history but today is little more than a backwater. It can, however, offer a quiet night at anchor along the south side of the Bristol Channel, and it could certainly be a worthwhile anchorage if you're waiting for the tide or the right conditions to enter Bideford Harbour. Tucked in behind the dip in the coastline after exposed Hartland Point, the coast here offers protection from winds from

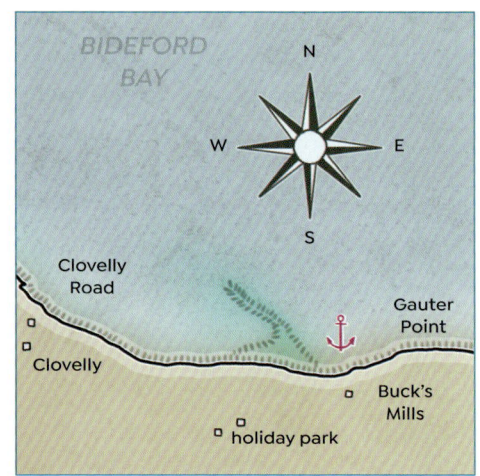

▽ The village of Clovelly

122 | ANCHORAGES OF THE BRITISH ISLES

▲ Buck's Mills

the south-west, but there is also a spit of shallow water extending seawards that breaks up any Atlantic swell running up-channel.

The history of Buck's Mills is particularly interesting as it's an example of trying to create a harbour on a very inhospitable coastline. In the 15th century there were attempts to build a harbour here, partly due to the shelter available from a naturally occurring spit of rocks – The Gore, which runs out from the coast just to the west of the hamlet. The harbour was built to the east, but it did not last long and succumbed to the ravages of the sea so that Buck's Mills then relied on the cargo boats beaching in a gut that was blasted out from the foreshore rocks. This gut can be seen today at LW, and both coal and limestone were landed on the beach during summer months to be burnt in two lime kilns built under the cliffs, which can still be seen. Fishing boats also operated off the beach and a few still do today. Buck's Mills got its name from the water mill driven by the stream that ran down the valley that was used to grind corn.

Finding your way in to anchor at Buck's Mills is pretty straightforward, but come in from the north, as The Gore runs out to seaward for close on 0.75 miles (1.35km) in a north-westerly direction. Run in with the echo sounder going and you can still get 3m of depth fairly close inshore at LW.

The bottom is quite rocky, so you'll need to choose your spot carefully in order to find substantial holding ground. The inner section of The Gore dries out at LW, so if you come in when the tide is low this can be a good guide; otherwise, use the cleft in the steeply sloping land with white houses.

You can land ashore by tender, and a slipway built into the stone walls will guide you as to the best spot to land. Be warned that at high tides this is a very stony beach and not hospitable.

There are no facilities ashore unless you're prepared for a long walk up to the main road, but it is interesting to land and climb up the hill to look at the remains of the hamlet's industrial past. **– DP**

# ILFRACOMBE

DEVON

**ILFRACOMBE, ON THE** north coast of Devon, can be a useful anchorage on your way up the Bristol Channel or as one of the last places you might stop over on your way to Land's End. It's a significant port for both fishing boats and yachts but it does dry out at LW, so this is really bilge-keeler country. For yachts with a fin keel, you might be able to dry

▲ The inner harbour dries completely

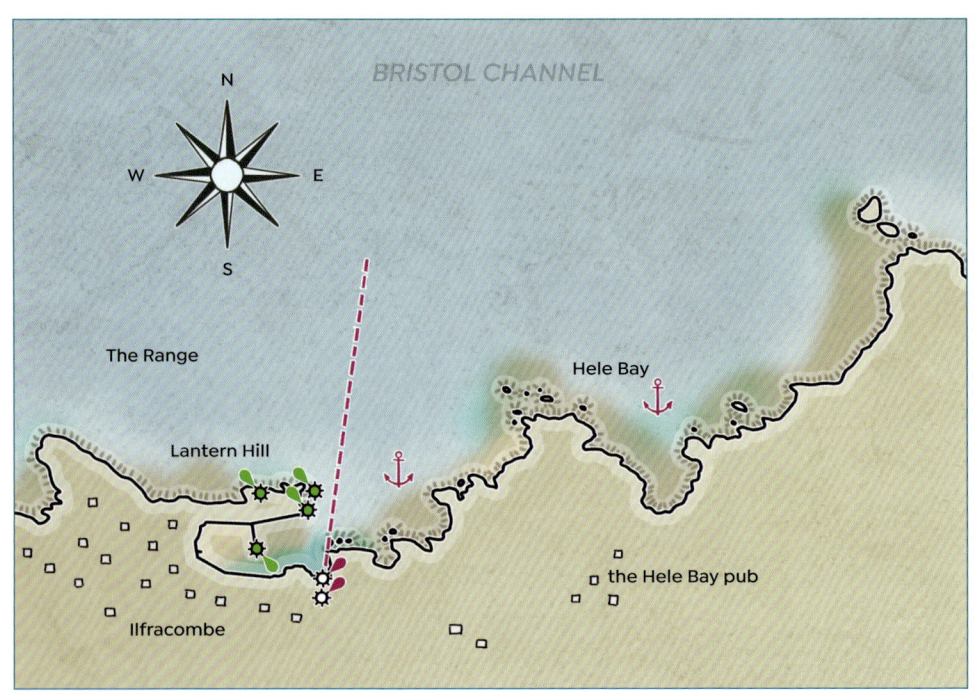

▼ Looking north across the outer harbour

out alongside the harbour wall if there's space but anchoring off is also a viable alternative, particularly in the summer when the harbour is very crowded.

There are two possibilities for anchoring here. One is just off the entrance, tucked in close to the rocks on the east side, although you do need to choose your spot very carefully. The ferry out to Lundy often berths alongside in the outer harbour and the fishing boats come and go regularly, so you need to leave room for these activities. Make sure you're to the east of the line of the leading lights into the harbour and you'll find enough space to drop your hook.

The alternative is to head a short distance to the east into Hele Bay where there will be a bit more shelter from a westerly and it will certainly be quieter. Here, you can find an anchorage in about 5m roughly 300m (980ft) from the shore. There's also a slipway for landing your tender.

Unless the conditions are very quiet and settled, this coastline is no place to stop in any winds from the north. Neither of these anchorages is viable in anything over a fresh breeze from the west but should work reasonably well in a south-westerly and, of course, anything from the south. The high cliffs offer good shelter and the bottom of the bay is sand, which should give good holding. A white house high up on the headland to the east of Hele Bay gives a reliable guide for where to head in.

The *Hele Bay* pub is just a short walk from the slipway and offers good-quality pub food and a wide selection of beers. It's roughly 0.5 miles (0.8km) walk into Ilfracombe, where you're spoilt for choice for pubs and restaurants as the town is making a name for itself as a foodie destination. I recommend *Lynbay Fish & Chips Shop* on the harbour, or for something a bit more upmarket seek out *The Antidote Restaurant* in St James Place. Don't miss the *S & P Fish Shop* on the south quay, either, where you can get the best crab or lobster sandwiches at lunchtime.

Finally, the town has the most amazing stainless steel and bronze statue of a pregnant woman as a sea mark to welcome you into its harbour. Damien Hirst's *Verity* was erected here in 2012 and stands just over 20m (66ft) tall. Ilfracombe is well worth a visit if the wind direction favours you anchoring off. **– DP**

# IRELAND

-----

Ireland is a veritable heaven for the cruising sailor, and to narrow down a selection of anchorages to a mere 20 is not an easy task. The south-west corner of the island offers many times this number, so those we have chosen are just a taster to set you off on your own voyage of exploration.

From Cork harbour westward you enter an area of rias that cut deep into the land with islands, sounds and rivers, where you can find yourself in complete isolation. Working up the west coast you are obviously more exposed to the full force of the Atlantic with striking headlands, deep bays and river mouths that can offer protection and a quiet night. The east coast is rather more challenging to find anchorages, and marinas and moorings are more prevalent. In the north-west and on the north coast you need to be well equipped and self-sufficient, but that is much of the joy of cruising.

# DRAKE'S POOL

CROSSHAVEN, CO. CORK

------------

**HISTORY RECORDS THAT** in 1589 Sir Francis Drake's small squadron of five warships was chased into Cork Harbour by an overpoweringly strong Spanish fleet. Turning swiftly to port after rounding Rams Head, Drake entered the River *Owenboy* and continued upriver past Crosshaven, until he found secluded anchorage in a pool set deep in cloaking woodland and hills. This safe basin is now called Drake's Pool; the Spaniards sailed up into Cork Harbour but were perplexed not to trap their prey, eventually returning to sea empty-handed.

Though still a picturesque refuge, the pool is not as deserted as in Drake's day; as with most well-sheltered havens, moorings have multiplied to the point that visitors have to use all their whiles to find enough space to drop their

Anchored in Drake's Pool ▷

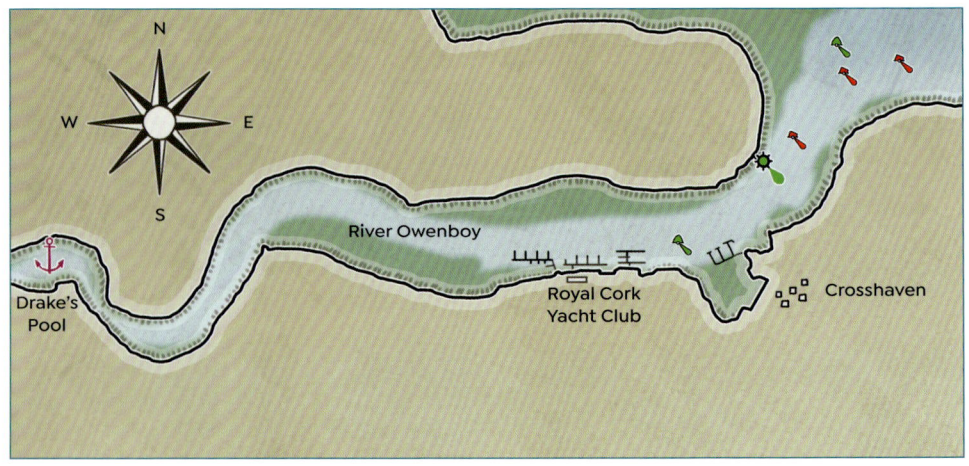

128 | ANCHORAGES OF THE BRITISH ISLES

anchor. A useful ploy is to look for vacant moorings and occupy the space between them, trusting that their owners will not return to render your chosen spot untenable. For this reason, I cannot realistically recommend this anchorage as one where you can leave your boat unattended when going ashore. So why suggest it as an anchorage, I hear you say? The best reason is that the upriver trip is worth it simply to relish the beauty and tranquillity of this historic pool; while just motoring around may be enough for you, finding room to stop either for a memorable meal or overnight has to be viewed as an added bonus.

The approach is quite straightforward; anything Sir Francis Drake could do in his engine-less warship squadron should be easily possible for modern auxiliary powered yachts. From seaward, leave Roche's Point 2 cables (370m, 1,200ft) to starboard to enter Cork outer harbour sound, obeying the navigation marks. Leaving Rams Head a cable (185m, 600ft) to port, identify the first River Owenboy buoys, starting with the port-hand C2A and the starboard-hand C1, and keep midway between these and the following channel buoys – the bottom shoals outside the marked route. Crosshaven Boatyard Marina occupies the south shore before the C3 starboard-hand mark (which seems to be overly south); ensure you leave C3 to starboard to avoid the shallow area it protects. Thereafter the buoyage is straightforward past Salve Marina and the Royal Cork Yacht Club marina.

▲ The wooded banks either side of Drake's Pool

Drake's Pool lies 1 mile (1.8km) upriver from Royal Cork Yacht Club; continue between the moorings lining the channel, erring to the outside north bank for the first bend but remaining midstream for the second bend and the entrance to the pool. With a muddy bottom the river's least channel depth is 2m, while the pool reportedly offers 4m, although I found it shoals to the south-west.

Drake's Pool is sheltered by a protecting kink in the river; fortunately, given the strong currents, the holding is outstanding, but with bygone debris littering the bottom it's wise to deploy a tripping line. There are no facilities, though a rocky outcrop can be used as a makeshift slipway and, across the Carrigaline Road, a useful open 'barbecue area' can be found behind the trees.

This ancient river anchorage is a treat for coastal sailors, hidden in the serene wooded valley that saved the day for Sir Francis Drake over 430 years ago. Relax, and imbibe the historic atmosphere. **– JP**

# COURTMACSHERRY

## CO. CORK

**THE NATIONAL INSTITUTION** for the Preservation of Life from Shipwreck, later to become the RNLI, was founded in London in 1824. Its first two stations in Ireland, in the same year, were at Arklow, south of Dublin, and Courtmacsherry in West Cork. For ships heading for the port of Cork and beyond, Courtmacsherry Bay, with its reefs and the cliff-bound Old Head of Kinsale beyond, was a place to be avoided, and many were embayed and lost there. For two centuries the lifeboat has been central to the village's culture, and has responded to many disasters, including the sinking of the *Lusitania* in 1915 and the Fastnet Race of 1979, probably the worst UK sailing disaster, when an unforecast storm caused 25 yachts to sink and 15 people lost their lives. Today it remains one of the busiest in Ireland. In recent times the crew has included as many as eight qualified coxswains, and Courtmacsherry has provided relief personnel to stations all over the British Isles.

The charming and unspoiled village sits on the estuary of the Argideen River, one of the most sheltered harbours on the south coast. The approach from the

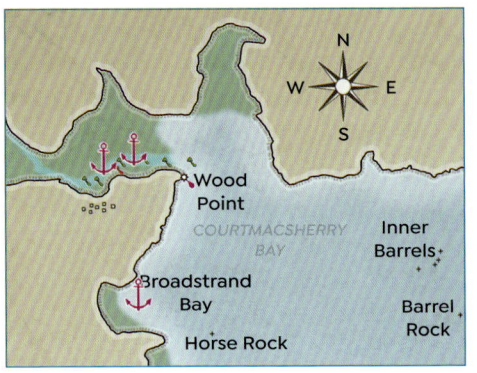

Old Head is marked by a starboard-hand buoy on Black Tom rock and a derelict but substantial perch on the drying Barrel Rock, while to port, the conspicuous Horse Rock seldom covers. A sectored light on Wood Point marks the entrance. The bar has 1m of water at LAT, and a narrow but well-marked dogleg channel between drying sandbanks leads to the deep-water pier and 36m (120ft) pontoon. Good anchorage on a sand bottom is available in the wider parts of the channel. The tree-clad slopes behind the village give perfect shelter from south and south-west, and the sandbanks dissipate the swell, even in heavy onshore weather. The shallow river channel winds on for a few kilometres to the village of Timoleague, which has the imposing ruins of a 14th-century Franciscan abbey.

Courtmacsherry has a community shop, restaurants and pubs, and is a centre for inshore fishing, whale watching and sea angling. It has a lively buzz in summer, when it's thronged with its second-home owners from Cork and Dublin, and it has a busy programme of events, including an annual community festival in early August and a storytelling festival in September. There are walks out through the bluebell wood to Wood Point and beyond to Broadstrand (which is also a good anchorage), and – in the other direction – to Timoleague, along the line of the old narrow-gauge railway. In times past, barges used to be grounded on the banks at low tide and sand was shovelled into them, to be shovelled again at the pier and taken away by train to sweeten the sour fields of clay in less fertile places. Today, Courtmacsherry's sailors may wish it still happened, but the estuary is now a Special Area of Conservation (SAC), noted for its seabirds and waders. Courtmacsherry is an unpretentious and friendly place, and visitors invariably relish its ambience. **– NK**

▽ The drying sandbanks bordering the channel into Courtmacsherry provide additional shelter

▽ Moorings dot the channel into Courtmacsherry, the Old Head of Kinsale in the distance

# CASTLE HAVEN

CASTLETOWNSHEND, CO. CORK

------------

**CASTLE HAVEN LIES** on the south coast of County Cork between Glandore and Baltimore, and is a charming, popular and very sheltered anchorage. The village of Castletownshend is centred on one long, narrow and steep street, lined with old terraced buildings. Two mature sycamore trees in a circular plot almost block the street, forming a narrow 'roundabout'. The village is named after Richard Townsend, a Cromwellian soldier who was granted the estate in the 1650s. The first 17th-century castle of the Townsend family was essentially rebuilt during two centuries and is now a boutique hotel – the castellated mansion sits on the seafront, but the eponymous castle, to the south of the village, is much older and now in ruins. The form 'Townshend' was adopted in the late 19th century.

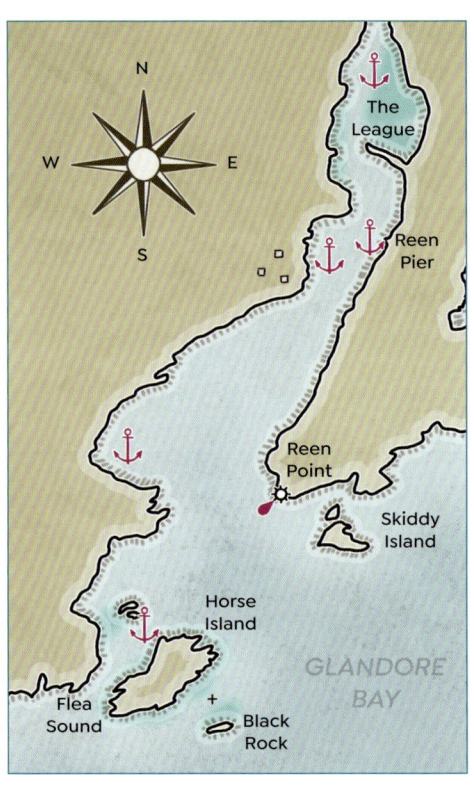

The approach to Castle Haven is straightforward but the entrance can be difficult to discern from seaward. It lies between Horse Island and Reen Point, which has a small light beacon. The shores on each side are generally clean and steep-to, and the anchorage, sheltered from all winds, is off the village. Further in, a gravel spit called The League extends halfway across, and while this provides a natural breakwater, the area immediately beyond it is mostly taken up by moorings. Further in, it is possible to moor to two anchors, and a dinghy trip to the head of the inlet at high tide is worthwhile. The quays at the village dry, but are convenient for landing.

Castletownshend has a small shop and pubs, and restaurants including the renowned Mary Ann's, which has been in the same family since 1947. The village was the home of Edith Somerville, author (with her cousin Violet Martin, who wrote as Martin Ross) of the 'Irish RM' stories, serialised for television in 1983. Edith Somerville was also an accomplished painter, a campaigner for women's rights, a Master of Foxhounds and for 70 years the organist of St Barrahane's church; she died, aged 91, in 1949.

The little Anglican church, dating from 1826, on an elevated site overlooking the sea, rewards a visit. Its walls are lined with memorials to the Somervilles, Townshends and Coghills who owned the local 'big houses', and served the Empire with distinction as soldiers, sailors and judges. The church hosts classical music concerts throughout the year, and the West Cork Chamber Music festival takes place here every year at the end of June. Whale-watching and sea-angling boats sail from Reen Pier, on the east shore, in summer.

Most of the houses are now second homes, but the peaceful old-world ambience of Castletownshend is unchanged. The coastal scenery in the approaches to the inlet is spectacular, and there are many walks offering breathtaking views. The hilltop fort of Knockdrum, 0.6 miles (1km) from the village, is believed to date from the 1st century AD. – **NK**

▼ St Barrahane's Church overlooks the jetty at Castletownshend

# BARLOGE

CO. CORK

-------------

*I know a lake where cool waves break,*
*And softly fall on a sylvan sand.*
*No steps intrude on that solitude,*
*And no voice save mine disturbs the strand.*

FITZ-JAMES O'BRIEN

**THE WORDS OF** the 19th-century poet Fitz-James O'Brien refer to Lough Hyne, a remarkable lake 4 miles (6.4km) east of Baltimore in West Cork. Its water is salt, because at half-tide, the sea pours in over what is essentially a natural sill. On the ebb, the water streams out again, creating rapids. These connect the Lough to Barloge Creek, a sea inlet of which visitors by road are usually unaware; but it's a favourite anchorage of all who love this coast. South-east facing, it is nevertheless surprisingly sheltered from the south.

The entrance to Barloge is hard to discern from seaward, but a stand of trees on the summit of Bullock Island shows the way, and the transit of the Stag Rocks offshore with Gokane Point on the mainland leads to it. The channel is narrow but deep and steep-to, and the basin shallows from 3m to less than 2m towards the rapids. The bottom is sand, and areas clear of weed are easily visible

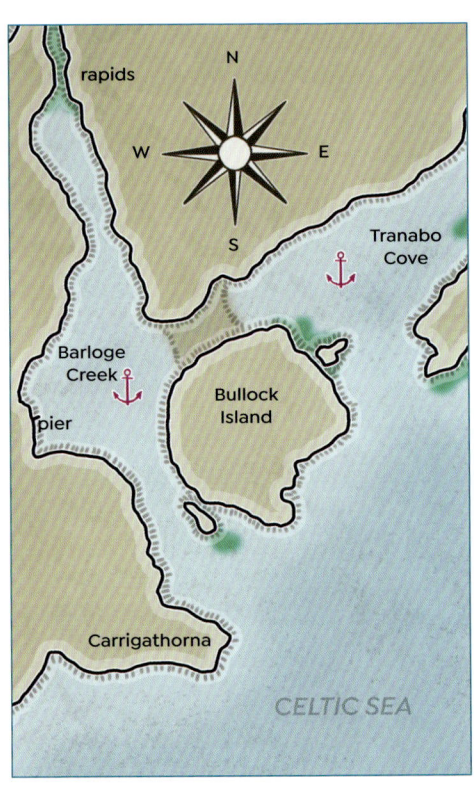

for anchoring. There is a pier on the west side, with a steep and winding single-track road leading up the hill. Opposite is Bullock Island, joined to the mainland by a drying sand bar. Tranabo Cove, beyond the sand bar, is also a pleasant anchorage, but is more exposed to the south. Barloge benefits from a projecting

▲ Barloge Creek

bluff, ending in the rock Carrigathorna, which forms a breakwater on the west side of the entrance.

Near HW it is possible to take a dinghy into Lough Hyne when the rapids are well covered – but beware the ebb tide! The Lough, 44m (144ft) deep, became Ireland's first Marine Nature Reserve in 1981. Its almost unique habitat is home to a huge range of creatures – 100 species of sponge, 72 species of fish and 28 of crab, and many more. At night, its bioluminescence is spectacular. It is believed to have begun as a freshwater lake, becoming salt as sea levels rose 4,000 years ago. The words of the poet must be taken with caution today because the Lough attracts many visitors, and is intensively studied by ecologists and marine biologists from all over the world. But for all that, its natural peace still prevails.

On the rising tide, the current over the rapids can change very suddenly, from 1 knot ebb to 1 knot flood in five minutes. When the ebb gets going, a popular pursuit is to body-surf the rapids – with care, and preferably wearing a wetsuit! The ingoing stream there starts at -0320 Cobh and the outgoing at +0115 Cobh.

The walk to the top of nearby Knockomagh provides splendid views over Barloge, Lough Hyne and the adjacent coasts. – **NK**

▼ Lough Hyne and the Rapids at low tide

# CROOKHAVEN

MIZEN PENINSULA, CO. CORK

------------

**THE PRETTY VILLAGE** of Crookhaven lies on a fine natural harbour 4 miles (7.2km) east of Mizen Head. Thronged with visitors in summer by land and sea, Crookhaven is at the western end of the magnificent sailing area of Carbery's Hundred Isles, between Baltimore, Cape Clear, Schull and the Mizen.

The history of the village has been defined by its strategic position and its proximity to the Fastnet Rock, 6 miles (10.8km) offshore. In the 19th century, Crookhaven was a landfall and victualling port for transatlantic shipping – there were even grand plans for an oceanic passenger port. Today it's a thriving holiday village, but the winter population, once 700 or so, is now no more than 50. The extensive lighthouse precincts – now largely converted to private houses – reflect the fact that this was the shore base from which the Fastnet lighthouse, the tallest and widest in the British Isles, was built 125 years ago, and until 1989 this

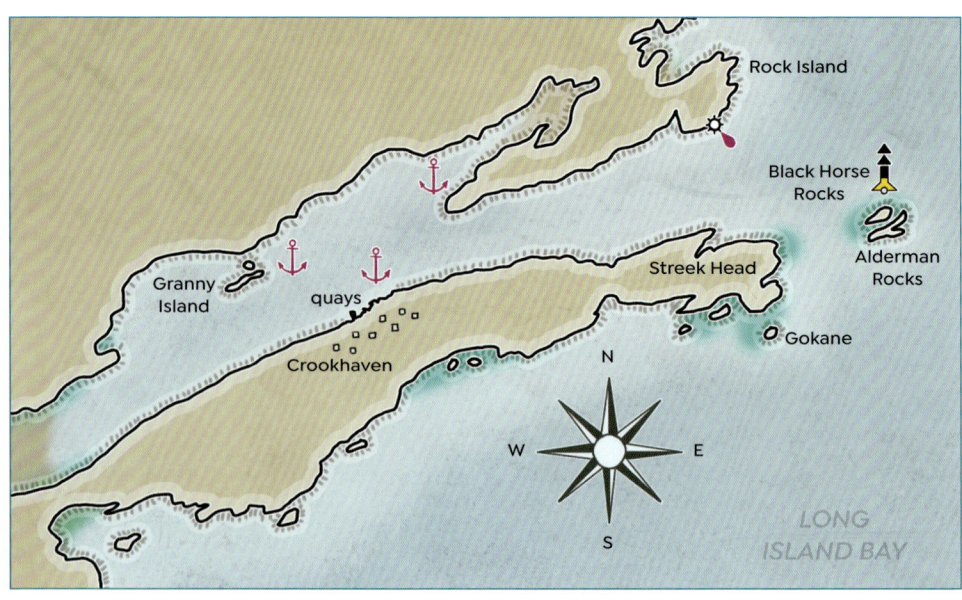

was where the Fastnet keepers' families lived. In 1902 an early Marconi radio station was built to communicate with the lighthouse (and so pass messages to and from shipping) and further to Cornwall. Arthur Nottage, a native of Cambridgeshire, came here as one of the first radio operators, married the pub landlady, and lived in Crookhaven for the rest of his long life. Arthur's party tricks were legendary. He would stick a table knife in the wooden ceiling above the bar, hand a customer a bottle and a glass of water, and invite him to put the bottle on the bar and get the knife to fall into the bottle without touching it. When the customer admitted defeat, Arthur would raise the glass to wet the knife handle, place the bottle where the drip landed, and give the ceiling a sharp (and well-rehearsed) thump beside the knife. He died at the age of 90 in 1974, but the name of Nottage is still above the pub door.

The harbour approach is very straightforward, between the conspicuous Rock Island lighthouse and the Black Horse Rocks north cardinal beacon opposite. The shores are steep-to, and the only danger is a rock, with 0.1m, a cable (185m, 600ft) or so off the point at the west end of Rock Island. This may not be shown on older charts since – surprisingly – it was first reported only in 2014. There are visitors' moorings, and anchorage is available almost anywhere with generally good holding. Shelter from easterlies is available behind Rock Island.

▲ Crookhaven village

There's a small shop, and restaurants and pubs offer excellent hospitality. The finest beach in West Cork is about 1.5km away at Barley Cove, where sand dunes form the isthmus sheltering Crookhaven Harbour from the west. Local folklore has it that these dunes were thrown up by the tsunami from the great Lisbon earthquake of 1755, but scepticism is allowed. The lighthouse museum at Mizen Head is a longish 4-mile (6.4km) walk, but a casual lift is a near-certainty given the popularity of the facility. And for those bound further by sea, the Mizen itself, by Atlantic headland standards, is not unduly challenging. – NK

▼ Crookhaven from the east

# KITCHEN COVE

DUNMANUS BAY, CO. CORK

**DUNMANUS BAY, THE** first of the great rias north of Mizen Head, is one of the least-travelled stretches of water in Ireland. Yachts tend to pass it by in their hurry to get to the more popular gluepots of Bantry Bay, which is a pity; Dunmanus Bay has several lovely anchorages, and the best of these is Kitchen Cove, beside the tiny village of Ahakista.

Kitchen Cove lies on the north shore of the bay, 8 miles (14.4km) from the entrance between Three Castle Head and Sheep's Head, and 3 miles (5.4km) from the head of the bay at Durrus. Largely surrounded by woodland, the anchorage is also protected by the low, rocky Illaunowen to the south and by reefs extending from it to the shore.

Entry to Kitchen Cove from the southwest is straightforward; the ocean swell has normally completely dissipated this far in, and while the shores on each side of the entrance to the Cove have extensive drying rocks, the clear channel is more than a cable (185m, 600ft) wide. A small red and white banded pole marks the inner end of the reefs on the port hand.

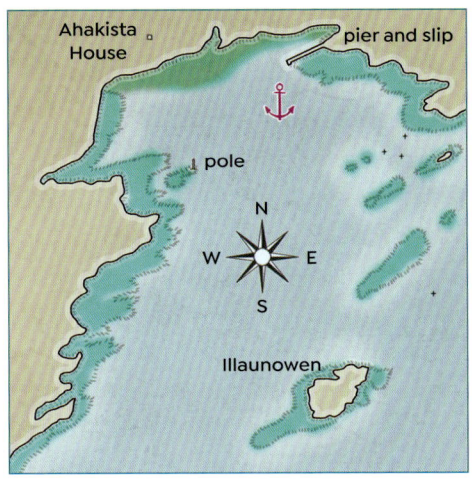

Good anchorage is available north or north-west of Illaunowen. The shallow (and very sheltered) north-west corner is taken up by local moorings, and the north-east corner, south of the pier, has poor holding on a rocky bottom. Approaching from the east, the narrow channel between Illaunowen and the reefs, used by local inshore fishermen, is not recommended. The concrete pier has 1.5m of water at LAT at its outer end, and a water tap, but for overnight berthing the local fishing boats take priority. There's a strong tradition of hospitality and good seamanship, as

▲ A shellfish boat makes her way into Kitchen Cove

we found on one occasion when we dragged an anchor and fouled the propeller on the tripping line.

There are two pubs with lovely beer gardens – the long-established Arundel's, and the Ahakista Bar, known as the Tin Pub named after its corrugated roof. Ahakista House, on the shore of Kitchen Cove, is the summer home of the popular TV presenter Graham Norton, who is a native of Bandon, also in County Cork. This is a remote part of Ireland – the bus goes to Bantry just three times a week – and running through Ahakista is the Sheep's Head Way, a 56-mile (90km) walkway extending in a loop around the peninsula and offering spectacular views of the cliff-bound coast.

A few hundred metres east along the Durrus road from Ahakista Pier is a beautiful memorial garden to the Air India disaster. In June 1985 a Boeing 747 eastbound from Montreal to London and Delhi was blown up in mid-air 180 miles (290km) off the Irish coast. The death toll of 329 was the worst in a single terrorist incident until the attack on the Twin Towers in New York City in 2001. The centrepiece of the garden at Ahakista is a sundial whose shadow is said to fall in the direction of the crash at the time of the anniversary each year. That is approximately true, but more accurate is the shadow, 13 miles (21km) to the south, of the Fastnet lighthouse. – **NK**

▼ Kitchen Cove and the tiny village of Ahakista

# GLENGARRIFF HARBOUR

BANTRY BAY, CO. CORK

**GLENGARRIFF HAS ATTRACTED** visitors for two centuries, and is often described as Ireland's prettiest anchorage. The natural harbour, studded with wooded islands, nestles in the innermost part of Bantry Bay, and it has long been renowned for its scenic beauty and its mild and largely frost-free microclimate. About 120 years ago, the visionary landowner Annan Bryce capitalised on this, and planted out a remarkable Italianate botanical garden on Garinish, the largest of the islands. The eminent Scottish gardener Murdo MacKenzie managed the gardens for 43 years. This paradise of subtropical plants is now owned by the state and open to the public.

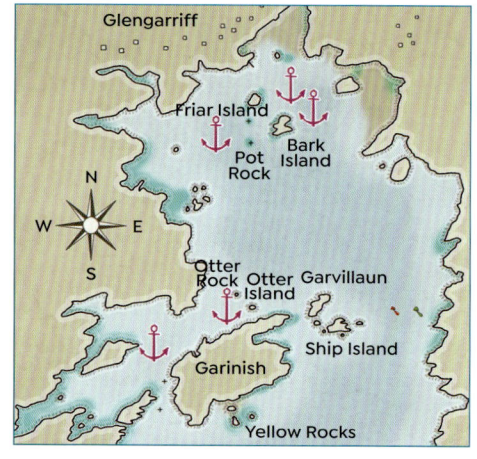

Uphill from the village is the Ewe Experience, a zany outdoor sculpture garden. Winding paths lead up among thick forest; 'a phantasmagorical landscape of weirdness and brilliance' according to the McKenna Guide, and in the words of the *Irish Times*, 'Ireland's number one garden'. Here you'll see a sheep in cardigan and slippers, relaxing in a chair; a 1930s car, half buried, nose down; a pair of trousered legs sticking out of the ground as if their owner had dived out of an aircraft; and much, much more. No more spoilers. Every corner of the path surprises and delights.

The approach to the bay is straightforward, and the entrance is marked by a pair of lateral buoys, provided principally for small cruise ships; there aren't many small enough to get in here. There's a wide choice of places to drop the anchor, and a visitor's mooring – a yellow buoy, with a tag – may be available. The most sheltered spot is north-east of the little Bark Island, but there is a charming anchorage off the north shore of Garinish. Older charts show a low overhead cable crossing to the island, but it was re-routed underwater many years ago. There's a large colony of very tame harbour seals.

The village is something of a tourist trap and so – quite apart from a breathtaking choice of Aran sweaters and general souvenirs – it therefore has excellent restaurants and pubs. Back in the day when Bantry Bay was one of the four Treaty Ports, retained by the Royal Navy after Irish independence, the well-known yachtsman Eric Hiscock wrote in 1937, 'This is, of course, what everyone comes to south-west Ireland to see, although a little spoilt by motor launches and charabancs. Large [sic] cruising liners sometimes anchor south of the island while their passengers go ashore to see the 'sights' and are usually rushed off to Killarney... A visit to Glengarriff would be wasted without paying a visit to Mrs Flynn of *Roche's Hotel* – better known to the navy and yachtsmen as "Auntie May".'

The navy left the following year when the Treaty Ports were handed over. Bantry Bay has now only one symbol of big government – it is the location of Ireland's strategic oil reserves, in a tank farm on Whiddy Island, between Glengarriff and Bantry. In 1979 the tanker *Betelgeuse* caught fire and exploded there, killing 51 people. The jetty has been derelict since, and tankers now unload at a mooring buoy north of the island. Despite its tragic recent history and the huge tank farm, Whiddy is a delightful island to visit. **– NK**

▽ Ferries bring visitors to Garinish Island from the pier at Glengarriff

# DUNBOY BAY

## CO. CORK

**DUNBOY BAY LIES** on the west side of Pipers Sound, the channel west of Bere Island to the fishing port of Castletownbere.

Castletownbere (Castletown Bearhaven on the charts) is the most important whitefish landing port in Ireland, and its quays are busy with vessels from Ireland, the UK, France and Spain. It's a characterful and bustling town, and one of its principal attractions is MacCarthy's Bar, immortalised by Pete McCarthy in his book of that name in 2000. Castletownbere is an excellent watering hole, but it may be challenging to find an alongside berth.

However, Dunboy offers a beautiful nearby alternative, and it is steeped in history. In 1607, after the defeat of the Irish chieftains at the Battle of Kinsale, the O'Sullivan fortress at Dunboy was besieged, and the surviving defenders were all

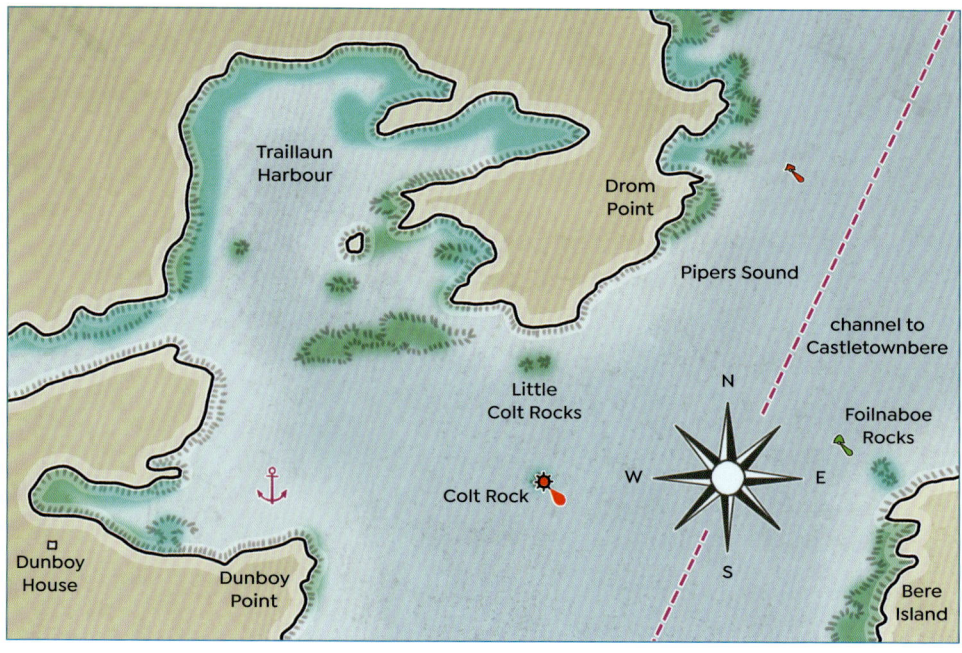

▲ Dunboy anchorage; the old house, and new apartments behind

hanged. The ruins of the old castle, on the southern point sheltering the anchorage, are no longer visible from seaward but still, grass-grown, obvious on land.

More than two centuries later, Henry Puxley built a magnificent house overlooking the bay. Puxley's family had owned the copper mines at Allihies, over the hill, and employed up to 900 miners. But the business was volatile, and whenever the price of copper fell, the miners were laid off. In 40 years, two-thirds of the local people emigrated to the mines of Butte, Montana, where the West Cork names of Healy and O'Sullivan are still common. Dunboy House was completed in 1883, but Puxley never lived in it, and for decades the house was full of furniture under dust covers, looked after by a skeleton staff. It was burned down by the IRA during the War of Independence in 1920 and restored as a hotel in the early 2000s with ugly new apartment buildings built behind. It closed again soon after.

Puxley's grandfather was a smuggler turned Revenue man, and in 1745 he was shot dead by a former partner in crime. In 1937 the famous sailor Eric Hiscock wrote of the place, 'When, in the stilly watches of the night, you hear a strange bubbling noise along the shore, remember that it is only the ghost of Puxley who was murdered nearby. Although he is quite harmless, there are but few people at Castletown who would care to venture there at night'.

The novelist Daphne du Maurier was a friend of the Puxley family and her novel *Hungry Hill* is a thinly disguised history of the family through five generations. The real Hungry Hill is several kilometres to the north-east and overlooks Adrigole.

The bay is sheltered from all directions except east. (Traillaun Harbour, to the north, is very shallow). A drying rock in the entrance to Dunboy may be avoided by a simple transit involving the conspicuous tree in front of the old house, and the rock is often unofficially marked. Colt Rock, further out, has a lighted port-hand beacon. Anchorage in 3–4m, good holding. There are no facilities – except of course for the entertainment provided by the ghost of John Puxley. **– NK**

# ARDGROOM HARBOUR

KENMARE BAY, CO. CORK/CO. KERRY

**THE KENMARE RIVER** (or Kenmare Bay), on the Cork–Kerry border, gives the enduring impression of being a great and well-kept secret. One of the four great rias of south-west Ireland, it is less well known than its neighbours Bantry Bay and Dingle Bay, yet it boasts more anchorages than either of them, and it has the famous scenic routes of the Ring of Kerry and the Ring of Beara to north and south. Tens of thousands of visitors each year enjoy the views from these roads, but both Rings are much better seen from seaward.

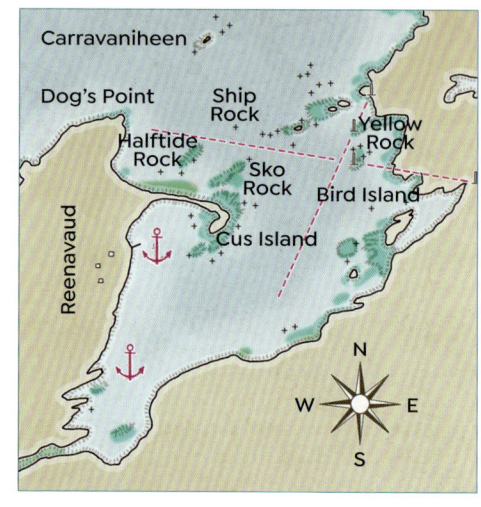

▼ Ardgroom Harbour

Ardgroom Harbour lies on the south side of Kenmare Bay about 17 miles (30.6km) from Dursey Sound. The entrance channel of the harbour passes between Halftide Rock (with its unlit beacon) and the drying Ship Rock, and continues between more rocks and shallows before opening out. The channel is marked by two pairs of (unlit) white stone leading beacons. The first pair leads from close north of Halftide Rock through the next gap in the rocks to the east. The back mark of this pair, on sloping wooded ground, tends to get obscured by rampant greenery, and care must be taken not to confuse it with the chimney of a house to the east or the tip of the gable of another to the west, also peeping above the trees. (The chart plotter is a very present help in time of need.) The second pair of beacons leads clear east of the shoals.

Much of the area of the harbour is used for rope culture of mussels. The ropes hang from parallel lines of barrels – it's safe to thread the lines but not to cross them, and safest just to skirt the outside of the farms. There's ample room around them, and plenty of space to anchor. A visiting yacht will most likely be the only one. The recommended anchorage is in the north-west corner, off the pier at Reenavaud, sheltered from the north by the long, low curving spit of Cus Island. But practically anywhere clear of the mussel farms, suitable depth is available – the main body of the harbour has 6–9m. The head of the inlet in the south-west corner offers a good anchorage

▲ The elusive back leading mark at Ardgroom, in line with the front mark

and access to the colourful village of Ardgroom, which has a shop, café, filling station and *The Village Inn*. Make your way up the little river in the dinghy, tie it up to a fence post on the left-hand side at the bridge, and walk 500m (1,640ft) to the village. Glenbeg Lough, 1.2 miles (2km) from the village, is a spectacularly scenic glacial lake between the mountains, and Ardgroom Stone Circle, a 1.8-mile (3km) walk, dates from 1000 BC.

Immediately east of Ardgroom is Kilmakilloge Harbour, similar in size and shelter, while 3 miles (5.4km) away on the north side of the bay lies Sneem Harbour, surrounded by wooded islands. Kenmare Bay stretches for a further 11 miles (19.8km) east to the bustling town of Kenmare among the mountains at its head. **– NK**

# DERRYNANE HARBOUR

## CO. KERRY

**FOR A YACHT** cruising this coast, this beautiful natural harbour is not to be missed. Protected from the south-west by the tidal Lamb's Island and surrounded by rugged rocky hills, it has fine sandy beaches on either side of the sandspit, which closes it to the south-east. The views out to the islands of Scariff and Deenish and beyond to the Skelligs are stunning, and in good weather a sunset will never be forgotten. This place, seen from the road high above, is the highlight of the renowned circular tour of the peninsula, the Ring of Kerry.

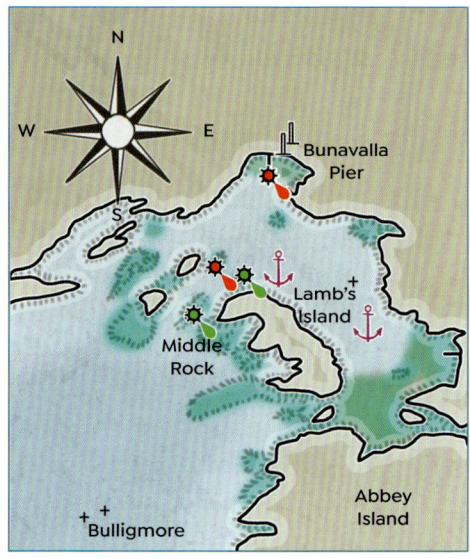

▽ Derrynane Harbour, with Derrynane Bay beyond

▲ The entrance to Derrynane; this picture predates the beacon on Middle Rock

Half an hour's walk along verdant lanes is Derrynane House, the family home of the 19th-century nationalist and reformer Daniel O'Connell. Now a National Monument, the beautiful old Georgian house, its estate and its gardens are open to the public. O'Connell was a giant of Irish history. He was a passionate believer in the political process, and he argued successfully for Catholic emancipation. A powerful orator, he is famous for the quote 'the altar of liberty totters when it is cemented only by blood', and when his Irish-born political opponent Wellington claimed to be Irish, he responded with 'Being born in a stable does not make a man a horse' – a remark often attributed to the Iron Duke himself. O'Connell's campaign for home rule was overwhelmed by the famine of the 1840s, but he is today regarded as one of the fathers of his country, and Dublin's main thoroughfare O'Connell Street is only one of many named in his honour.

Along the way to the house are the ruins of the 6th-century Derrynane Abbey, with an ogham stone beside the road. Ogham was a Celtic alphabet of the 5th and 6th centuries, and it is found on about 400 surviving monuments, mostly in Pembrokeshire and south-west Ireland; two-thirds of them are in Kerry.

The narrow entrance to Derrynane harbour faces south-west, and can become a little too exciting in strong onshore weather, but the harbour is very well sheltered, with good anchorage on sand. In the approach, the drying rock Bulligmore is easily avoided by following a well-marked leading line. Middle Rock, in the centre of the entrance, now has a starboard-hand beacon, which is useful for avoidance of the last-minute confusion, which used to afflict the visitor on the way out. (There is, however, also ample water on the south-east side of Middle Rock). Going in, care must be taken to depart from the leading line once through the entrance because a port-hand beacon, marking a rock, lies to the right of the line. A classic yacht once accidentally left that to starboard, and got away with it, but it is not to be recommended.

There are several visitors' moorings and many others mostly belonging to weekenders, but there's plenty of space to anchor in 2–4m, avoiding a drying rock on the north side. The pub is a short walk from the jetty at the head of the bay, and the village of Caherdaniel is 1.8 miles (3km) away. – **NK**

# PORTMAGEE

CO. KERRY

**THE NAME OF** Valentia Island is well known to any sailor in Irish waters as the home of one of Ireland's four Marine Rescue Coordination Centres and constantly featuring in weather forecasts. On its south side the island is bridged to the mainland at the village of Portmagee.

Portmagee Sound offers a handy stop without a lengthy detour off the rhumb line course. Valentia and the entrance to the Sound are exposed to the full Atlantic swell, and the combination of that with a high cliff coastline and the tide around the headlands can raise steep seas here. But Portmagee is accessible in almost any weather, and the zigzag shape of the Sound acts as an effective barrier to the swell. In settled conditions there's a pretty anchorage among the islets at the entrance.

The village is a minor fishing port, and its infrastructure has recently been improved by the addition of a pontoon facility with two berths on the T-head, available for visiting yachts – or, of course,

▼ The monastic remains on Loughan Island

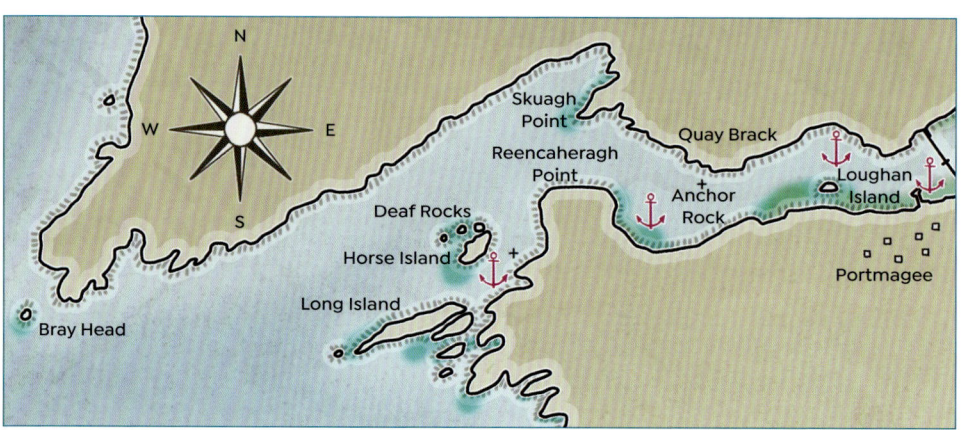

▲ Portmagee and the bridge to Valentia Island

more rafted up – while anchorage in 4m is available off the pier. This is a popular tourist spot on the designated Wild Atlantic Way road route, and has good pubs and restaurants including the award-winning Moorings. Easy walks offer commanding views from some of Ireland's most spectacular cliffs. Valentia Island has the 385-million-year-old fossilised footprints of a tetrapod, the earliest amphibian with anything that could be considered legs. It also has a slate quarry from where came the roofing for the Houses of Parliament in Westminster and the shelving for London's Public Records Office, and it was the European end of the first transatlantic telegraph cables in the mid-1800s.

Portmagee is the main base for tourist boats ferrying passengers out to the World Heritage Site of Skellig Michael, 9 miles (16.2km) offshore. The craggy 214m (702ft) high pinnacle, with its 1,400-year-old monastic beehive huts and oratories, is one of the world's most magical places, and its fame has been boosted recently by its use as a location in two Star Wars films. Sadly, that, and an increasing awareness of safety and liability issues, have led to tight restrictions on landing. A daily footfall quota of 180 is taken up by 15 small ferryboats, and no allowance is made for yachts – of which there are few in any case. One option for a yacht's crew might be simply to take the ferryboat, but they tend to be booked up well in advance and the fares for the 7-mile (11.3km) crossing are eye-watering. However, merely sailing round the island, close to its cliffs, is an unforgettable experience. The Little Skellig, nearby, has a colony of 35,000 gannets, the largest gannetry in Ireland.

Loughan Island, in the channel to Portmagee, also has some ancient monastic remains, and The Skellig Experience Visitor Centre is at the island end of the bridge at Portmagee. The bridge used to open, but not for many years past, and access to Valentia Harbour for a masted yacht is via the northern entrance at Cromwell Point. – **NK**

# PARADISE

RIVER FERGUS, CO. CLARE

---

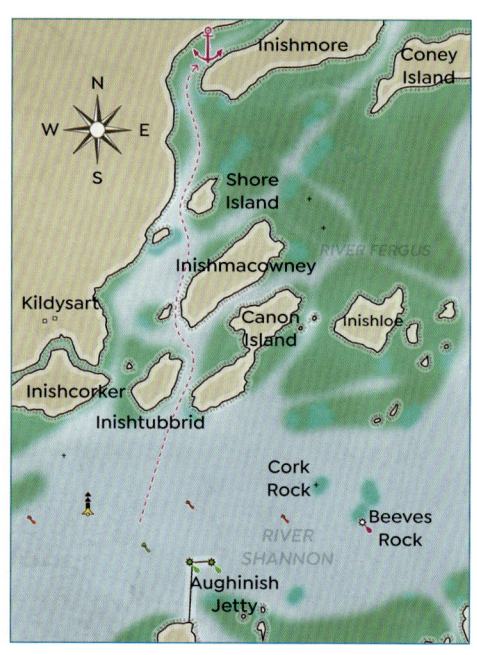

**ON A TREE-CLAD** slope not far from the village of Kildysart, the ruins of Paradise House look out over the islands that dot the tidal River Fergus at its confluence with the Shannon. Between Inishmore and the western shore, and just below the old house, is one of Ireland's most beautiful and peaceful anchorages.

Paradise, built in 1685 and rebuilt in 1863, was the home of Lieutenant William Henn, who challenged for the America's Cup in 1886 with the 102ft steel cutter *Galatea*. William and his wife Susan, together with a large crew, sailed the yacht across the Atlantic for the race series. In New York, William was taken ill and Mrs Henn assumed command of the yacht, but *Galatea* was beaten in two races by General Charles Payne's *Mayflower*. The Henns continued to live aboard their yacht until his death in 1894 and hers in 1911, and on at least one occasion they brought *Galatea* up to Paradise, a considerable achievement given her draught of 13ft 6in and the fact that she had, of course, no engine. A proper tribute to Susan Henn had to wait 139 years – in 2025 she was finally inducted to the America's Cup Hall of Fame.

▼ The ruins of Paradise House

Appropriately enough, the way to Paradise is neither wide nor straight. From the Shannon estuary north-east of Foynes, the channel leads between Inishtubbrid and Canon Island, then turns west, skirting Inishmacowney to avoid a drying rock off the north shore of Inishtubbrid and passing between Inishmacowney and the tiny Doon Island. Although the survey in the Fergus dates from 1841, the charts are still pretty accurate in respect of the bathymetry and the trend of the channels. But this is a place to practise traditional navigation skills, and watch the echo sounder. The tricky part is between Illaunbeg and Shore Island, where rocks encroach from both sides and the least depth of 0.6m at LAT is to be found. (At this point *Galatea*, 158 tons, had 1.3m (4ft 6in) between her keel and the rocks, at high water springs.)

The anchorage is in 2–3m, with excellent holding in thick mud, in mid-channel just north-east of the ruins of the old house. The tide runs at less than a knot through the anchorage; the range is 4.9m at springs, large by Irish standards. The village of Ballynacally, 1 mile (1.6km) to the north of the landing, has a shop and a pub, but nightlife in Paradise has more to do with owls, bats and foxes than loud music.

Paradise House remained in the Henn family until 1960, and was destroyed in an accidental fire ten years later. Nature has reclaimed the house and grounds to an extraordinary extent, and they are now quite hard to find from the Kildysart road. – **NK**

▼ Paradise

# ROUNDSTONE

CO. GALWAY

---

**THE PRETTY VILLAGE** of Roundstone was a planned settlement, built in the 1820s by the remarkable Scottish engineer Alexander Nimmo. Nimmo came to Ireland in 1811 at the age of 29, and spent the remaining 20 years of his short life there, leaving a legacy of 40 piers and harbours, and many of the roads, in Mayo and Galway. Roundstone today is a thriving holiday village, frequented by artists, writers and traditional musicians.

Nimmo's old harbour at Roundstone remains essentially unaltered. It faces east across a 2 miles (3.6km) by 0.5

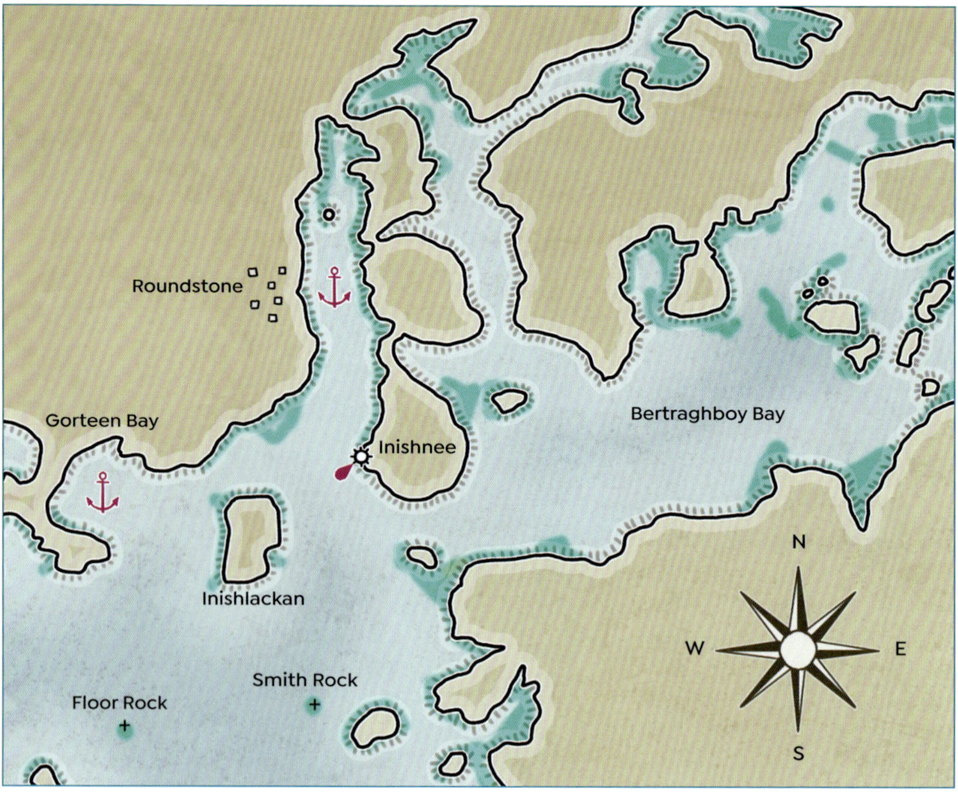

miles (0.9km) inlet, overlooked by Mount Errisbeg and with the lovely backdrop of the Twelve Bens of Connemara. The harbour itself mostly dries, but offers a good partially drying berth inside its south wall. It is home to sea-angling boats and small inshore fishing craft.

The cruising sailor on the coast of Connemara must be more than usually self-sufficient, for facilities are sparse, and so Roundstone, with its useful shops and its excellent pubs and restaurants, is a bit of an oasis. Not many yachts pass it by, and a fair number keep moorings there and use it as a summer base.

The coast around is dotted with islands, and offers wonderful daysailing and dozens of beautiful and snug anchorages. From the south, most visiting yachts will approach from the Aran Islands. South of Roundstone Bay a number of rocks must be avoided, and the little light tower on Inishnee marks the entrance. The bay is shallow – with 1–2m of charted depth – but there is deeper water off the village, and the charted drying rock in the fairway does not exist. Tidal range is 3.8m at springs, 1.8m at neaps, HW simultaneous with Galway, and tidal streams are slight.

Roundstone Harbour is sheltered in all winds although the bay can be a bit windswept in southerlies. Anchor off the harbour, to the south of the moorings. The holding is good, in mud. There are visitors' moorings on the far side of the bay, but they are a long dinghy ride from the village. Ashore are excellent pubs and restaurants including O'Dowd's,

▲ Roundstone Harbour

which has been in the same family for generations. The post office, around 90m (295ft) from the harbour, is also a convenience store and has petrol and diesel pumps. There's a good butcher and a fishmonger, as well as art galleries and antique and craft shops, including one specialising in musical instruments.

Roundstone is a centre for traditional boats like Galway hookers and their smaller cousins, and both canvas and wooden currachs. The annual regatta takes place in July. Nearby are many ancient ecclesiastical sites, and the easy walk to the summit of Errisbeg (298m, 978ft) provides beautiful views of the coast and islands.

Many of the original residents of Roundstone, nearly 200 years ago, were Scottish fishermen and their families, and so the village has an old and now disused Presbyterian church, in whose overgrown graveyard Alexander Nimmo is believed to be buried. But if his grave was ever marked, no trace of it can be identified now. – **NK**

# TOBERDENNY HARBOUR

CO. GALWAY

**THIS BEAUTIFUL, PEACEFUL** and unspoiled place, 4 miles (7.2km) west of Clifden in Connemara, is a perfect natural harbour, and reportedly – at least in recent years – has seen only one visiting yacht. That yacht was ours, and shortly after we anchored in the pool, a local boat came out to greet us. 'What brought you in here?' was the friendly and curious question, 'We never had a yacht come in before. Do you know you can't get out before the morning?'

Of course we knew, and that – to a large extent – was the reason we were there. I had spotted it on the chart, and it looked irresistible. The entrance to Toberdenny Harbour dries right across, making it landlocked at low tide. Sheltered from the south by the Ardmore peninsula and from the west by Turbot Island and Inishturk, the bay is skirted by a quiet road with a scatter of houses. A dozen shellfish currachs occupy the south-east corner, and a little local sailing boat has a mooring in the pool. The entrance is 0.25 miles (0.45km) wide, and dries up to 1.2m for a distance of 0.3 miles (0.5km). The bottom in mid-channel is sand, but Carricknahollana reef extends

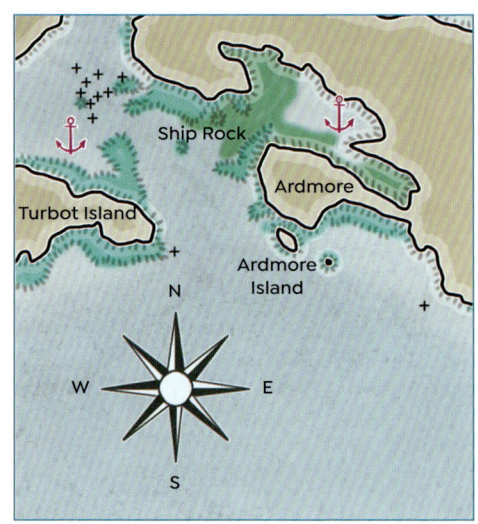

▽ Toberdenny Harbour at summer sunrise

west and north from Ardmore, and there is a drying rock off the north shore opposite. At high water neaps there's at least 2.2m of water over the bar, and the deep pool, 370m (1,200ft) by 278m (900ft), has almost 8m at LAT. Landing is easy on any one of half a dozen little beaches around the shores, and there's a small jetty in the south-east corner. It's the kind of place where you might expect to find a fish farm or mussel rafts, but there are none. It is pristine, unspoiled and achingly beautiful in the sunset.

The bar doesn't quite dry at neaps, and low water springs occurs around midday and midnight, so capturing a photograph while landlocked means spending at least a day there, which is scarcely a hardship. In the approach from the south, beware of Ship Rock, which dries 1.3m. Near HW it is possible, with great care, to rock-hop inside Turbot and Inishturk to the anchorages between these two and to the east of Omey to the north. All three islands are seasonally inhabited, but the last permanent inhabitant of Omey, the film stuntman Pascal Whelan, who was a native of the island, died in 2017. Inishturk and Turbot ceased to be inhabited year-round from the 1970s. The whole area was quite densely populated in the 19th century, but the landscape of thin soil and rock offered a very meagre living, and the potato famine of the 1840s ravaged Connemara. Ardmore is grazed now, but old 'lazybeds' – parallel ridges painstakingly built up from sand and seaweed to grow potatoes – cover the whole peninsula.

There are of course no facilities, but that only adds to the remote charm of Toberdenny. – **NK**

▽ The seascape to the north of Toberdenny; Inishturk, left, and Omey, with its lake

# INISHBOFIN

CO. GALWAY

------------

**INISHBOFIN HAS THE** best natural harbour of all the islands of Ireland, so it's a popular spot for yachts cruising the west coast. It's literally hard to avoid; it sits squarely across the course northwards from Slyne Head. The island, 3.4 miles (5.5km) long and 1.9 miles (3km) wide, has a population of 180, and a ferry connects it with Cleggan on the mainland. It's home to many seals, and the rare corncrake.

The approach to the harbour from the south-west is relatively straightforward, with good leading marks and a sectored light. Anchorage is on hard, shaly sand, and it is essential to ensure the anchor is well dug in. The main pier is in constant use by the ferries; a dredged channel leads to the old pier, used by the cargo ferry, but an alongside berth may be available.

Inishbofin is a Mecca for traditional musicians, and spontaneous sessions in the pubs are frequent. Somebody in a corner of the bar will start playing a guitar, somebody else joins in on a flute or a tin whistle, and then a bodhrán (a handheld goatskin drum of ancient design, often struck with a bone) joins in.

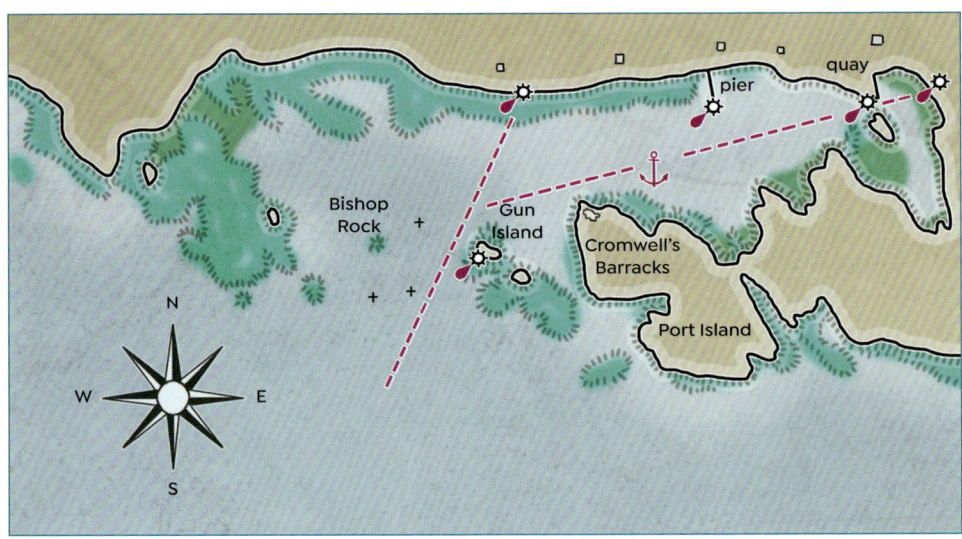

▲ Bofin Harbour

A fiddle makes up the quartet. Nothing is apparently planned or rehearsed. On one visit, we came upon such a session at seven in the evening. We staggered out at one in the morning, and it went on until four. It happens a lot. The standard of talent, and the variety of instruments, are impressive, and the craic, as they say, is mighty. The pace of life is relaxed, yet there is a lively buzz about the place.

The island has been inhabited for over 2,000 years. A monastery was founded in AD 670 and there are remains of ancient forts. It was a strategic location in the sectarian wars of the 1640s, and in 1649 it was surrendered to the forces of Oliver Cromwell, a man revered in England as a hero but reviled in Ireland for his brutality. Around 1655 a star fort was built, commanding the entrance, and until 1660 it was used, among other things, as a prison for priests arrested for continuing to minister to the Catholic population of Ireland. The imposing ruins of the fort still stand. The famine of the 1840s reduced a population of 1,400 by a third, and it steadily fell until the 1980s before recovering to its present level.

▲ Tra Geal, at the west end of Inishbofin

There are pleasant walks to glorious sandy beaches at both ends of the island, and bikes can be hired. The island is fairly low-lying, its highest point just 70m (230ft). Despite that, the north coast has some spectacular cliff scenery, and the views towards the mountains of Connemara and the adjacent islands are stunning. For such a small and remote community, facilities are good, and include several excellent restaurants specialising in seafood. There's an annual island food festival in September, and arts and music festivals in spring and summer. – **NK**

# BURTONPORT

## CO. DONEGAL

**THE HARBOUR OF** Burtonport nestles among the islands and reefs of Aran Sound, the shallow and rock-strewn channel separating Arranmore Island from the mainland. The village owes its name to William Burton Conyngham, an extraordinarily accomplished 18th-century landowner and Irish MP who inherited estates in Donegal and Meath. About 1784 he decided to build

▼ Now all but two houses restored, the extraordinary 240-year-old terrace on Rutland Island, with the Arranmore ferry, behind

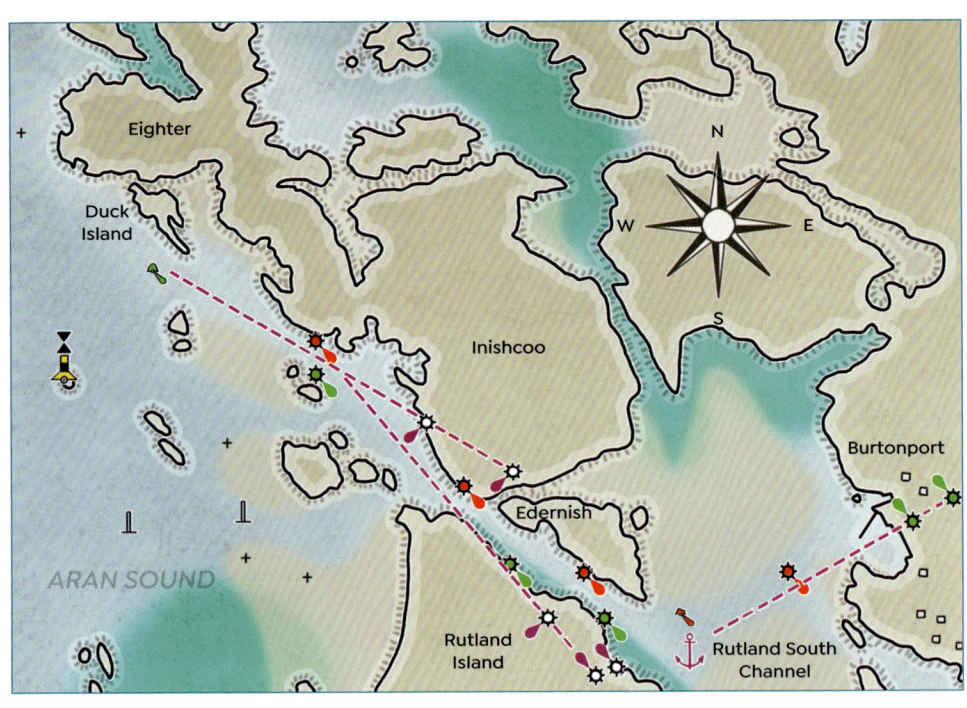

158 | ANCHORAGES OF THE BRITISH ISLES

a herring fishing station on the largest of the islands in Aran Sound, renaming it Rutland Island in honour of the Duke of Rutland, Lord Lieutenant of Ireland at the time. Conyngham built quays and warehouses, a salt store, streets of houses and even a pub.

It didn't prosper, and was abandoned after 14 years. Many of the buildings on Rutland fell into disrepair and were inundated with wind-blown sand, but some have been restored and there's an extraordinary little urban-style street of terraced houses, and several new-builds, all second homes. The owners of these have to provide their own transport across from Burtonport.

The village remained a minor fishing port, but today this is all but confined to inshore potting for shellfish. The main channel into the pier comes from the north, behind the islands, but this was blasted clear only within the last century and a half or so; in Conyngham's time shipping used the south sound, strongly tidal and tricky in pilotage. In 2009, local divers came upon a wreck near the channel, which dates from the late 16th or early 17th century, and may be linked to the fate of the Spanish Armada.

The pier at Burtonport, reached via a dredged channel, can offer an alongside berth, and anchorage is available close to Rutland Island south of the seaward end of the pier channel. Facilities in the village are few, but include access to mechanical and electrical repairs, and there's a good pub and restaurant. Arranmore, connected with Burtonport

▲ Burtonport Harbour (top left), Rutland Island (right)

by the car ferry, has Ireland's second-largest island community, numbering 478, and several good anchorages around its shores. Its lighthouse, dating from 1798, was the first to be built in Donegal, and is one of the oldest working lighthouses in Ireland. The lifeboat station on Arranmore dates from 1883, and for many years was the only one between the Aran Islands (County Galway) and Portrush (County Antrim), a coastline of over 200 miles (320km). Five more stations established since 1980 now fill the gaps.

Burton Conyngham never married, and died in 1796. His library, auctioned in 1810, was the biggest collection of books and papers ever sold in Ireland. His estates, also including Slane Castle in County Meath, passed to his nephew, who later took the title Earl of Mountcharles from an estate near Donegal Town. He was a direct ancestor of the present owner of Slane, now a noted venue for rock concerts. Conyngham is still the family name. – **NK**

# GOLA

GOLA SOUND, CO. DONEGAL

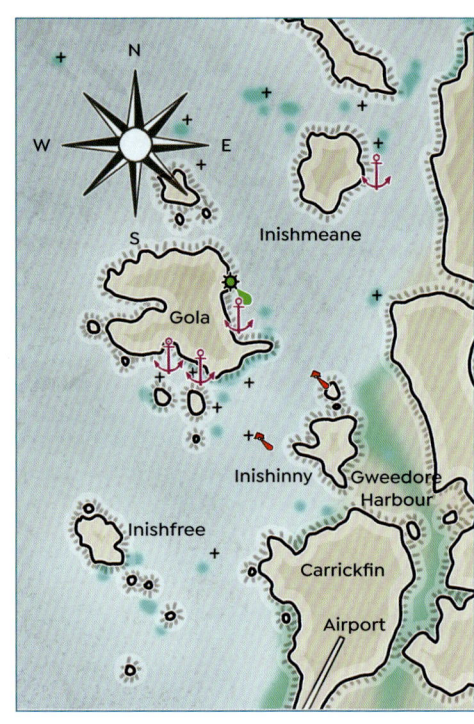

**FOR 15 MILES** (24km) south of Ireland's north-western extremity, the west-facing coast of Donegal is known as The Rosses. The coast, exposed to heavy seas in winter, is broken and studded with islands and rocks, and the local granite makes for sudden changes in depth, while its pink colour, particularly in the setting sun, is the derivation of the headland's name – Bloody Foreland. This is a stunning coast of cliff scenery and intricate channels, making for fascinating exploration. The largest island, Arranmore, has a population of 478, while the smaller ones to the north were all abandoned during the mid-20th century. But two of them, Owey and Gola, have seen surviving natives and their descendants return for at least part of the year, and Gola in particular is a heart-warming example of what can be done with resource and determination.

Gola had 160 people in the 1920s, but was evacuated in 1967. It remained grazed by sheep in summer, but since 2000 it has seen a remarkable transformation. On the initiative of its own people, the old houses have been reclaimed and tastefully renovated, and power and water have been connected from the mainland. There are no poles and overhead lines – the cables were run underground. The island is now inhabited almost year-round and a ferry service operates to the mainland in summer. We called there in 2011 and 2019, and on each visit the same man was on duty in the little wooden tearoom building,

160 | ANCHORAGES OF THE BRITISH ISLES

entertaining his guests. He was a leader of the restoration and repopulation project. A native of Gola, his accent of English was unlike the typical West Donegal lilt – in some ways more like the Southern Hebrides. I asked him if he could understand the Scots Gaelic of Islay. 'Yes, of course, I was at the fishing. I know Port Ellen, but the old people are the easiest. I have trouble catching what the younger ones are saying'. I suspect that schools in both countries are teaching standardised pronunciations, which don't really fit the nature of the old tongue. The Gaelic language – Irish and Scottish – is a continuum from Kerry to Lewis. Donegal can understand Islay, but Lewis can barely understand Barra, let alone Kerry.

The most secure anchorage at Gola, sheltered by the islets of Allagh and Go, is on the south side of the island off the jetty at Portacrin. But the bay off the main pier on the east side of the island offers good shelter. The west coast of the island has some classified cliff climbs, and near the west end is a memorial to two of the victims of the 2001 Twin Towers attack, descendants of Gola natives. It has become something of a place of pilgrimage. **– NK**

▲ Portacrin, the best anchorage at Gola

▼ Gola pier, with Umfin and Torrorragaun, beyond

GOLA SOUND, CO. DONEGAL | **IRELAND** | 161

# LOUGH SWILLY

## CO. DONEGAL

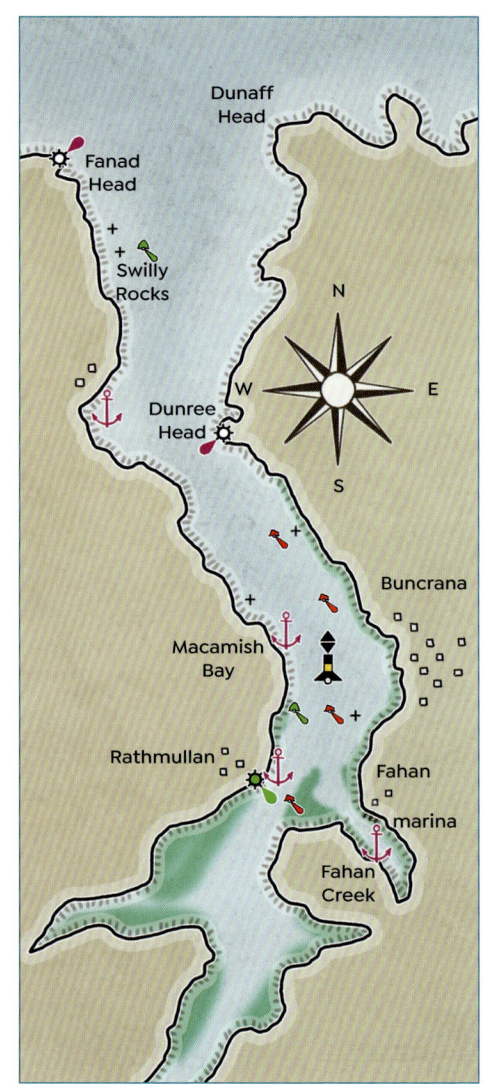

**THE DEEP AND** sheltered inlet of Lough Swilly is the principal sailing centre on the north coast. Geologically a fjord, the Lough is surrounded by beautiful scenery and has several fine anchorages. It is also rich in history. In 1607, in an act confirming their defeat in the great Anglo-Irish wars of Tudor times, the Ulster leaders Tyrone and Tyrconnell left for exile in France, an event commemorated as the Flight of the Earls. For centuries the Lough was an important naval base, and was heavily fortified: three pairs of Martello towers were built in Napoleonic times, and forts with naval guns guarded it during the First World War. It was one of four Treaty Ports retained by the British until ceded to what was then the Irish Free State in 1938. Overlooking all from a strategic hilltop to the south is the ancient Celtic ring fort of the Grianan of Aileach, almost 2,000 years old.

Lough Swilly is entered between Fanad Head and Dunaff Head, and a starboard-hand buoy marks the drying Swilly Rocks 2 miles (3.6km) to the south. The lighthouse on Fanad Head, often dubbed the most attractive in Ireland, was built following the wreck in 1812 of the frigate

▲ Macamish, the prettiest anchorage in the Lough

▲ Portsalon and the golden sands of Ballymastocker Bay

HMS *Saldanha*, with heavy loss of life. She got her name from a British naval victory in the bay of that name in South Africa, and she gave it to Saldanha Head, where she came to grief.

The holiday village of Portsalon, 4 miles (7.2km) within the entrance, offers a handy passage anchorage in its bay, and there are visitors' moorings and an old stone pier. The village has a friendly pub, and the bay has a glorious 2-mile (3.2km) stretch of sandy beach. Further up the lough and also on the west shore is Macamish, undoubtedly the lough's prettiest anchorage. Three sandy bays divided by rocky outcrops are overlooked by one of the Martello towers – now a private house – and backed by a little nine-hole golf course. A reef in the southern half seldom covers but a rock with 0.5m in the northern half must be guarded against. Anchorage is in 2–4m on sand, sheltered from south-east through south to north-west.

About 11 miles (19.8km) within the Lough is the village of Rathmullan, with a long pontoon attached to its deep-water pier, and on the east shore opposite are the town of Buncrana and the village of Fahan. Fahan Creek is the base of Lough Swilly YC, and has a marina. The border with Northern Ireland, and the city of Derry, are only 5 miles (8km) from here, and most of the yacht club members cross the border to go sailing on Lough Swilly. Two round-the-world racing skippers, Sean McCarter and Richie Fearon, and the designer of the Shannon class lifeboat, Peter Eyre, learned to sail at LSYC. In 2016 Lough Swilly RNLI station at Buncrana received the first Shannon lifeboat in Ireland. – **NK**

# PORTMORE

INISHTRAHULL, CO. DONEGAL

------------

**SOME ISLANDS HAVE** an almost magical air of remoteness. Tucked in at anchor on a dark night, you have the feeling of being hundreds of kilometres from the next living soul, no matter that the mainland may be only a few kilometres away.

Such a place is Inishtrahull. Six miles (10.8km) north-east of Malin Head across a tide-swept sound, it is Ireland's northernmost land. The 34ha (83 acre) island was inhabited until 1928, and a map dating from 1900 shows 14 houses,

▲ Ruined cottages dot the rocky slopes of Inishtrahull

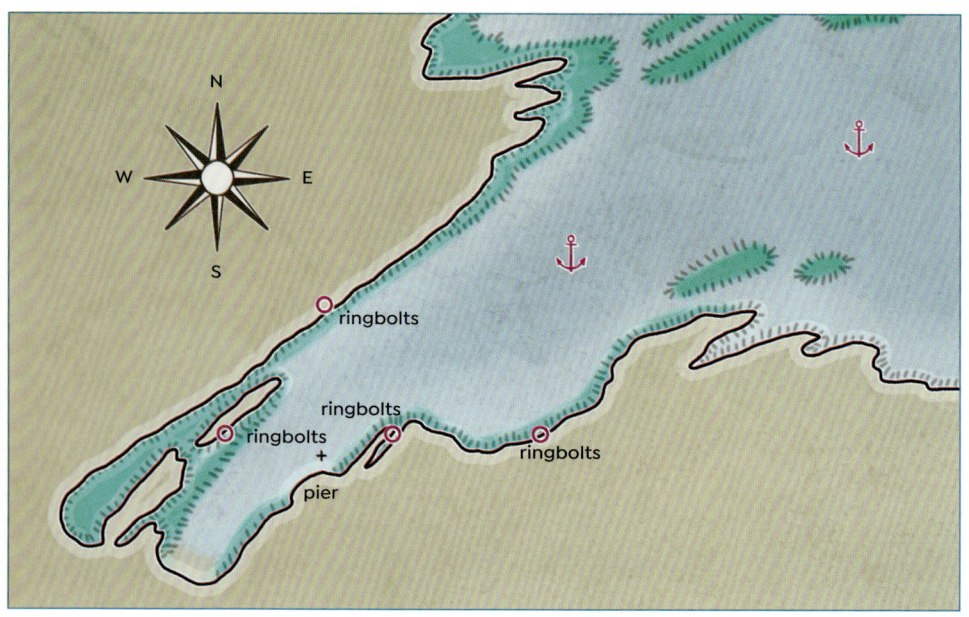

▲ The anchorage at Portmore

occupied by McLaughlins, McGonagles, Dohertys and Houtons. But those names were seldom used; they were Teeker, Wee Davey, Nellie Rua, Big Barney, Catherine Ned. It was a tough and dangerous existence. A lighthouse keeper wrote in the 1870s, 'It is a melancholy fact that most of the men meet their end by drowning.'

The remains of the old houses can still be seen, along with the roofless school, with its misspelt nameplate 'Inishtrhull National School'. The lighthouse, on the western summit, dates from 1957, and replaced an older tower on the eastern hill; the last lighthouse keepers left in 1987. The island is a Special Protection Area and a breeding ground for the grey seal, and for many seabirds. There is also a small herd of red deer, which has to be kept in check because the deer eat seabirds' eggs. This unusual diet is apparently occasioned by the fact that on an island of unyielding metamorphic rock (Inishtrahull shares its 1.7 billion-year-old Lewisian gneiss with the Outer Hebrides and Greenland) there are no other sources of dietary calcium. But how do the deer know that?

The waters around the island are a hot spot for whales, dolphins and basking sharks. The tide runs at up to 4 knots at springs in Inishtrahull Sound, running west for only three hours out of 12. This is the windiest corner of Ireland, and with strong winds against the tide, the sea state in the Sound can be steep and confused. For those passing by, Garvan Sound, close to the mainland side, is often the most convenient route, but Inishtrahull makes a fascinating stopover. The anchorage is at Portmore, a north-east-facing gut with a stone pier used to service the lighthouse. The entrance is flanked by two rocks, both of which almost always show above water. The gut has 10m decreasing to 4m abreast the pier, and offers shelter in winds from south-east through south to north-west. It is completely out of the tidal stream. Weed may choke the anchor, so be careful to ensure it is well bedded in. The pier has 3m alongside, but there is a rock with 1.1m, just 8m (26ft) away from it, which can be a hazard at very low tides. The spring range is 2.9m. The largest-scale chart depicts the whole island just under 2.5cm (1in) long, but the ICC Sailing Directions have it well described.

There are – not surprisingly – no facilities ashore. **– NK**

# STRANGFORD LOUGH

CO. DOWN

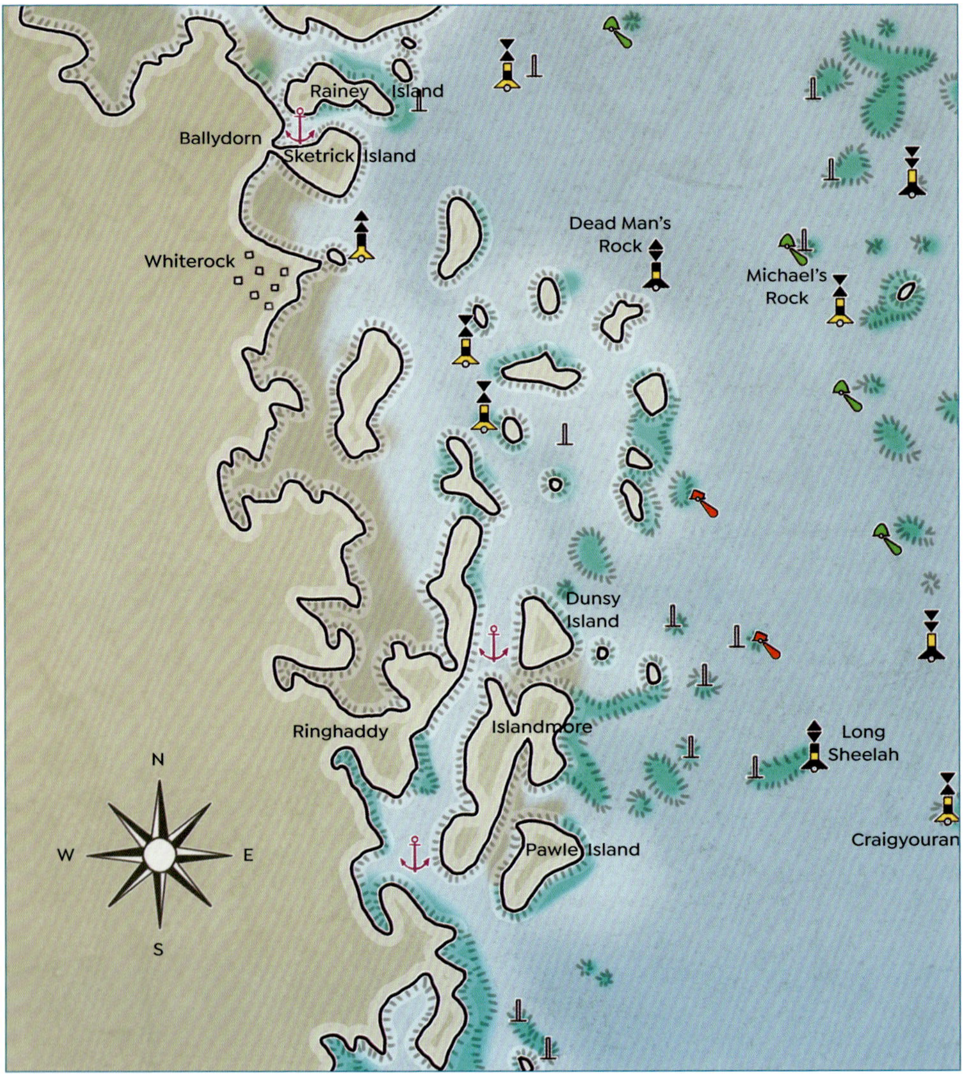

**STRANGFORD LOUGH IS** an extraordinary inland sea of 58sq miles (150sq km), connected to the Irish Sea by the Narrows, a deep channel 4 miles (7.2km) long, through which the tide runs at up to 8 knots. Much of eastern County Down is 'drumlin country', a landscape of small rolling hills, boulder clay deposited by retreating ice more than 10,000 years ago. Where rising sea levels flooded some of this terrain, the drumlins became low islands, or boulder shoals underwater. The islands are often bafflingly similar; many of the shoals, or 'pladdies' are now marked by IALA beacons and buoys, replacing unofficial perches. Only a few kilometres from the city of Belfast, this beautiful and peaceful place is the finest sheltered sailing area in Ireland. There are no large towns on its shores, and no marinas north of the small one at Portaferry in the entrance channel. Despite the constriction formed by the Narrows, the tidal range inside the Lough is 2.4–3.6m.

Eleven sailing clubs are based around the lough, each one different in its character and ambience, and there are many places where an anchor can be dropped in solitude. To nominate the best anchorages is not an easy task, but Ringhaddy Sound vies for the title. Splendidly sheltered by Pawle, Islandmore and Dunsy Islands, it is the home of Ringhaddy Cruising Club. There are almost 100 moorings in the Sound, but ample room to anchor on a secure mud bottom at either end in 3–5m. The approach from the south-west leads between the above-water Black Rock, with two drying shoals outside it, and the drying Verde Rocks, the underwater hazards being marked by perches. The northern entrance to the 1.5 miles (2.7km) long Sound is through the maze of small islands. Ringhaddy is relatively remote by road and there are no facilities ashore.

Around 2 miles (3.6km) to the north is another gem. Sketrick Island is connected to the shore by a causeway, and between it and Rainey Island lies Ballydorn. This is the home of Down Cruising Club, whose clubhouse is the former lightship *Petrel*, built in 1917 and sold to the club by the Irish Lights in 1968. The ship is moored to a pontoon beside the coast road. It didn't escape the notice of the shrewd purchasers that lightships tended to have very thick plating and lasted a long time.

At the end of the causeway on Sketrick Island is a renowned and long-established pub and restaurant, Daft Eddy's; the eponymous Eddy was an 18th-century smuggler who met his end in a shoot-out with the Revenue men. The inner anchorage at Ballydorn is pretty well taken up by local boats on moorings, but between Sketrick and Rainey Island to the north, anchorage is freely available. The entrance is marked by lateral buoys. **– NK**

*See page 5 for a photograph of Strangford Lough.*

# WALES

BRISTOL CHANNEL TO THE MERSEY

------------------------------------

Cruising the Welsh coast can be challenging, with its strong tides, few marinas, the intimidating Bristol Channel and Mersey Estuary and the predominant south-westerly winds generally making Cardigan Bay a lee shore. Having said all that, it really rewards the more adventurous sailors with some amazing peaceful anchorages, stunning wildlife and fascinating history to explore.

Along the south coast the tidal streams and range will test your maths when calculating how much chain to let out. Around Pembrokeshire's beautiful coast you'll be able to edge into bays and harbours before braving a crossing of Cardigan Bay. The Llŷn Peninsula can provide a few interesting locations, with atmospheric Bardsey at its tip. To reach the north coast of Wales you can either run the gauntlet of the Menai Strait or circumnavigate Anglesey, trying anchorages en route.

The anchorages that are described here are just a taster of what you can find around the Welsh coast, and hopefully will set many off on new experiences.

*Aurial* waiting for the tide ▶

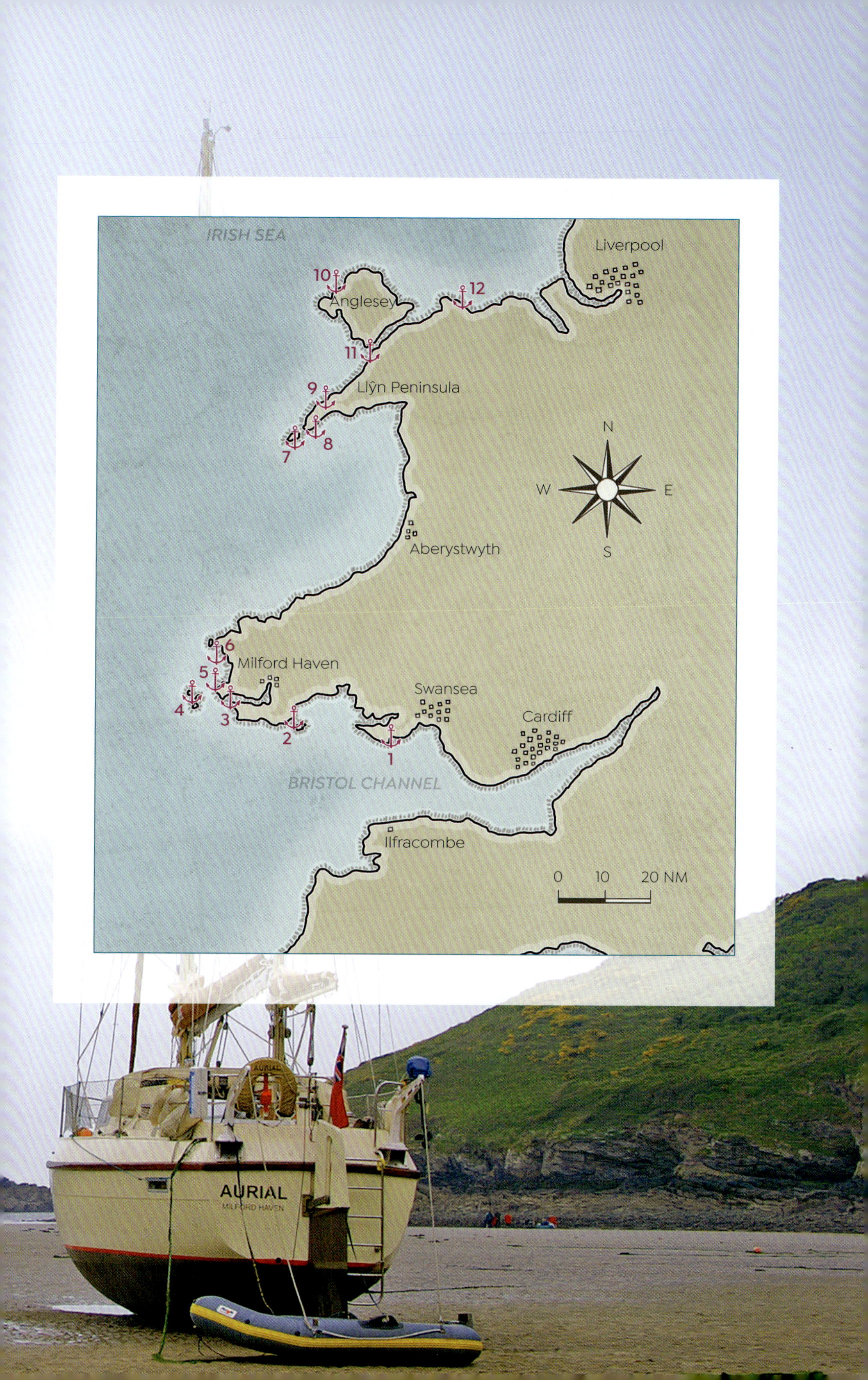

# PORT EYNON

GOWER, SWANSEA

-------------

**THE NAME SUGGESTS** you might find a harbour here, but all you have at Port Eynon is a long, curved stretch of beach with headlands at either end that can offer you a degree of shelter for a night at anchor. The bay is located on the south coast of the Gower Peninsula, which is one of the most beautiful coastlines in South Wales, and marks a departure from the industrialised

▲ Port Eynon

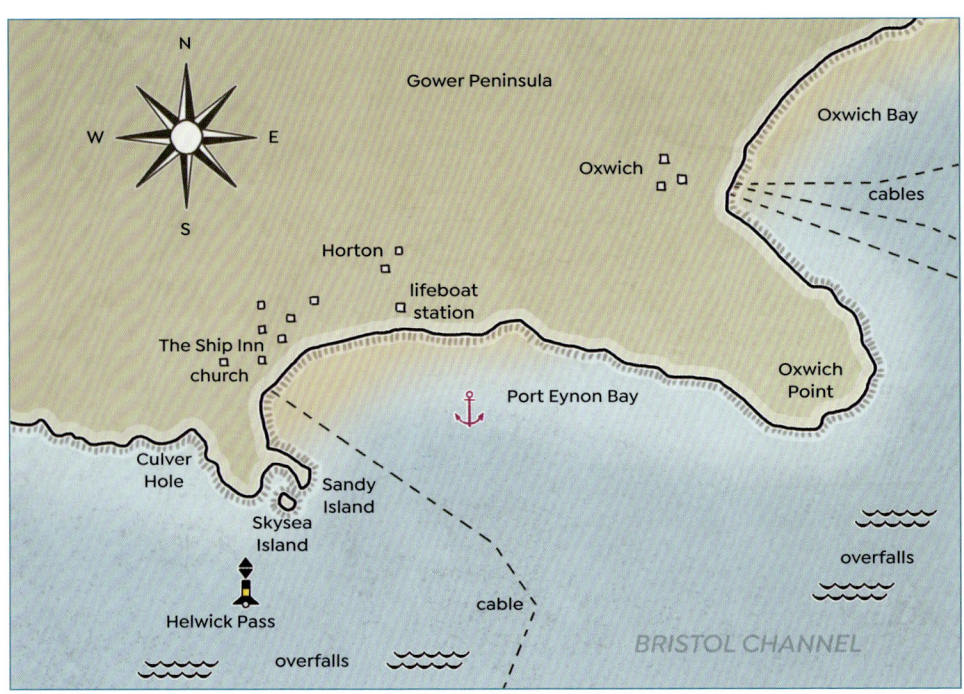

170 | ANCHORAGES OF THE BRITISH ISLES

sections of Wales further east. Port Eynon and the neighbouring Oxwich Bay are two useful anchorages for sailors seeking respite from an adverse tide or somewhere to drop the hook. Although larger, Oxwich Bay to the east loses some of its attraction because of the seabed cables that restrict the available space for anchoring.

Port Eynon also has a cable on its seabed but this is located at the western end close by the rocky patches, so there is considerable space left for the anchorage. Here, there is not quite the same level of protection from the westerlies that can plague this area, but there's good protection when the wind swings round to anywhere in the northern sector.

The name Port Eynon reflects the history of this bay; in the distant past it served as a port where ships would beach at HW and load cargo during the falling tide. There was also a flourishing smuggling trade here.

For yachts, there is space for anchoring in the centre of the bay, and the best plan is to feel your way in with the sounder running until you find a safe depth. The new inshore lifeboat house is a useful marker but it does not stand out too well, so the GPS is probably your most reliable guide.

If you fancy a run ashore you'll almost certainly head for *The Ship Inn*, a traditional pub that serves steaks and burger and chips, but there is also a dedicated fish and chip shop in the village. In the height of summer, you

▲ A campsite next to the beach

may find these places fairly crowded, as Port Eynon has been rather overrun by caravan sites. The bay itself can also get busy on a fine day during the summer months, as day trippers come out from Swansea to enjoy time in the sun. The other problem going ashore is that the beach dries out for quite a distance. Landing by tender, you might have a long way to carry the dinghy up or down the beach.

Access to Port Eynon is straightforward, with no off-lying dangers. However, there are strong tides running outside the bay, and you can find some tide rips off both of the headlands enclosing the bay in what is known as the Helwick Pass. Once out of the main channel, these should disappear as you enter the peace and quiet of the bay. While it looks like you can enjoy a reasonably quiet night within the shelter of Port Eynon, you can find yourself exposed to swell entering from the west as it is refracted around the westerly headland. Port Eynon is an interesting anchorage, but it is one you might only want to use when the weather is fine and settled. **– DP**

# PRIORY BAY

CALDEY ISLAND, PEMBROKESHIRE

----

**SEVERAL KILOMETRES SOUTH** of the popular Pembrokeshire town of Tenby lies the monastic island of Caldey, separated from the mainland by a relatively shallow sound. Its ecclesiastical history dates back to the 6th century, though Viking raids interrupted monastic devotions until the 12th century, when a cell of Benedictines based at St Dogmaels monastery near Cardigan arrived, remaining until Henry VIII's 1536 Dissolution of the Monasteries. In 1906 an Anglican Benedictine community built the present abbey and restored St

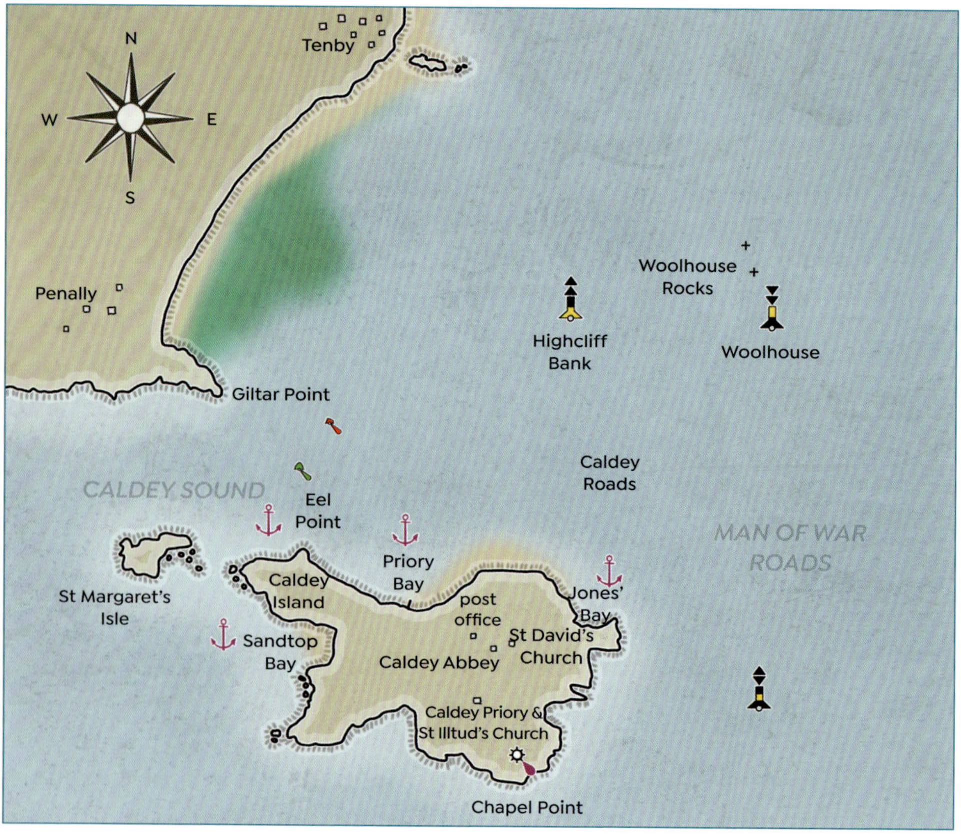

David's Church, and the Cistercian Order took up residence in 1929. This group of monks still uphold Caldey's long monastic heritage of work, study and prayer. Their avoidance of unnecessary speech has not prevented the 40 or so residents gaining financial independence by welcoming tourists (over 50,000 visit each year) and developing a perfume, cheese and chocolate industry.

The principal Caldey anchorage is in Priory Bay on the north coast off the quay and beach that is the island's main access point. It is well sheltered in westerly and south-westerly winds but less so in northerlies and easterlies. Even so, it is still considered a safe (though potentially uncomfortable) anchorage in all winds; we have not been troubled by swell on our visits. Strong currents flow through Caldey Sound, so it is advisable to tuck in as close as possible to the beach while keeping clear of the moorings. There's plenty of space and the access is straightforward; we've safely entered and anchored in the dark. The bottom offers good holding in sand but bear in mind the impressive 9m equinoctial spring tidal range here; take care to calculate the depth and put out adequate anchor rode.

The approach from the west through Caldey Sound between St Margaret's Isle and Giltar Point is easy if conditions are reasonable and the tidal stream taken into account; spring flows of 3 knots can not only cause slow progress but also create nasty wind over tide situations – choose a favourable current. Keep midway between the red and green lit channel buoys, and only make a starboard turn towards the beach 280m (910ft) beyond the starboard Eel Point marker in order to clear Eel Spit. From the east, give a good offing to Woolhouse Rocks before leaving the Highcliff Bank north cardinal to port, then head for the same approach point in Caldey Roads.

The island is closed on Sundays but open on weekdays and Saturdays between 10am and 6pm. As the island and foreshore are in private ownership, landing can only be with permission; landing from yacht dinghies is frowned upon, although offering to pay the entrance fee might avert offence. The preferred option is to go to Tenby and arrive by ferry when the entrance fee is included in the ticket. Caldey Island requests that no landings take place on its other beaches.

Once ashore, attractions include the historic Old Priory, the medieval churches of St David and St Illtud, a walk up to the lighthouse, and village shops selling the perfumes, chocolate and shortbread made on the island. The village post office hosts an interesting museum of Caldey historic life, and a cup of tea and a cake from the café will refresh visitors after their exploration.

Whether going ashore or simply enjoying life afloat, wildlife sightings of seals, guillemots, razorbills, cormorants, gannets and puffins are frequent, and the views beautiful. This anchorage is well worth a visit on passage or as a destination in its own right. **– JP**

# 3

# WATWICK BAY

MILFORD HAVEN, PEMBROKESHIRE

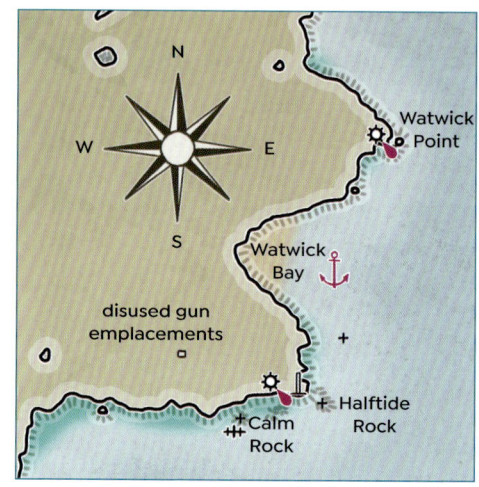

**IF YOU'RE SEEKING** an easily accessed, quiet and secluded beach anchorage near Milford Haven then Watwick Bay surely fits the bill. It's often described as one of Pembrokeshire's best-kept secrets as it's only accessible from the Coast Path; the nearest car park is over 2 miles (3.2km) walk in either direction, which tends to discourage land-based families. In settled, sunny weather the bay can become busy with passing yachts and motorboats during lunchtime, but there's ample room for all.

▼ Watwick Bay is just inside the entrance to Milford Haven, on your port hand

The beach is sited on the eastern side of the narrow Dale Peninsula on whose southern tip stands St Ann's Head Lighthouse. Watwick faces south-east and is warmed quickly by the morning sun, with good shelter to winds from any westerly quadrant; at low tide there's a sizeable area of golden sand with nearby rock pools and caves to explore. Pembrokeshire can experience spring tidal ranges of over 8m, but even at high tide a postage stamp of sand remains to satisfy sunbathers. This huge rise and fall of spring tides means that Watwick Bay might be better visited during neaps to provide enough anchor depth without being excessively far from the sand.

The approach is straightforward, and hazard-free. The area outside the Heads where the ebb tide makes a 90° encounter with the main tide flowing up and down the coast can cause confused seas. The two main big-ship channels are well buoyed and it is best to stay outside them; tankers constrained by their draught regularly use these busy channels.

Watwick Bay is easily found between the tall beacons that form a leading line into the West Channel. From seaward leave an offing of around 370m (1,215ft) round West Blockhouse Point and its commanding fort to avoid rocks and reefs off Watwick's southern boundary. Having carefully calculated the height of water, drop the hook anywhere in the bay clear of the margin; the holding is good in sand and mud. If swell develops there's always the option of relocating to

▲ Overlooking Watwick Bay to the entrance to Milford Haven

Dale round the corner. There's no shelter from easterly winds, and Watwick Bay has no facilities; the nearest village is Dale, 2 miles (3.2km) along the Coast Path, where you'll find a restaurant, pub and a shop in the water sports centre.

The remains of the British First World War submarine HMS *E39* lie off the southern margin of Watwick Bay. Having outlived her usefulness, she was being taken to be scrapped in Pembroke Dock but broke her tow and foundered on the rocks of Watwick Bay in December 1922. Substantial portions of the vessel were salvaged but 65ft of her original 180ft length still lies at a depth of 10–14m under the south side of the bay, below the steps as marked on the charts.

This beautiful suntrap bay, with its red cliffs surrounding a stunning crescent of light sand, comes into its own when the day visitors depart and peace descends. Sit back and admire the views as the light fades. **– JP**

# SOUTH HAVEN

SKOMER, PEMBROKESHIRE

------------

**NESTLED INTO THE** south-east corner of the nature reserve of Skomer Island, South Haven is a true classic anchorage. Conveniently placed between Milford Haven and St Brides Bay, it is not only a destination in its own right but also a handy passage anchorage while waiting for favourable tidal streams in nearby Jack Sound.

The inlet is surrounded by high cliffs that teem with avian wildlife, especially from April to mid-July; puffins, Manx shearwaters, kittiwakes, razorbills, guillemots, choughs and buzzards as well as the occasional peregrine falcon busily criss-cross the bay as they hunt or bring home food from the local maritime larder. The moaning of seals echo in the

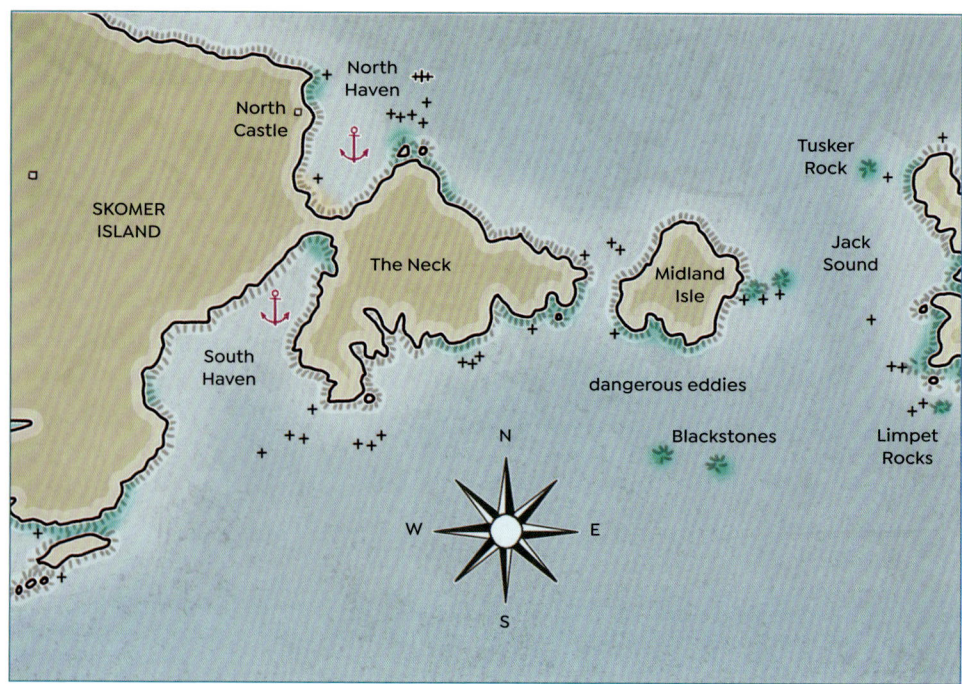

cliff caves and their music can often be heard through the evening, while during the day their inquisitive heads pop up between the boats.

South Haven experiences the 8m spring tides of Pembrokeshire, but with a gently sloping bottom there is ample depth and space for 20 yachts. However, it is rare for us to have seen half that number, and even at the weekend there's usually only a handful of boats. We've spent many delightful nights alone here – Pembrokeshire is not exactly crowded! The holding is excellent and, ringed by enfolding cliffs, the shelter superb. It is true that in any strong wind, cliff-edged havens like this suffer downdraughts and gusts, but as long as the wind is not from the open south-east, protection is complete. At times swell can be its downfall; even though the prevailing Atlantic waves come from the south-west, they sometimes sweep round the island to make the anchorage uncomfortable. Indeed, in heavy conditions both South Haven and its companion North Haven, situated on the north-east of Skomer and only separated by a narrow cliff isthmus, can suffer swell. Occasionally I have chosen to pass through Jack Sound to escape an untenable South Haven, only to find that North Haven is no better. But such occasions are rare and are easily predictable; when it's going to be that bumpy I head for the complete shelter of Milford Haven.

Entry is straightforward, though beware a charted rocky patch that lies

▲ The anchorage in South Haven on Skomer is surrounded by steep cliffs and landing is prohibited

to the south of the eastern entrance promontory. It's best to approach from due south and leave the Mew Stone to port before heading north, keeping 185m (600ft) from the west steep-to cliffs before entering the haven itself, which is clear of hazards.

There are no facilities. Landing is not only forbidden by the Wildlife Trust of South and West Wales but virtually impossible due to the steep-to cliffs lacking any path. For shore access head to North Haven, where the *Dale Princess* docks with day trippers carried across from Martin's Haven on the mainland. Visitors are welcome during opening hours, subject to a fee and the requirement to report to the warden for an island briefing. However, there's no restriction on the joys of pottering round South Haven in the tender, enjoying the wildlife and fauna at close quarters. **– JP**

# MARTIN'S HAVEN

HAVERFORDWEST, PEMBROKESHIRE

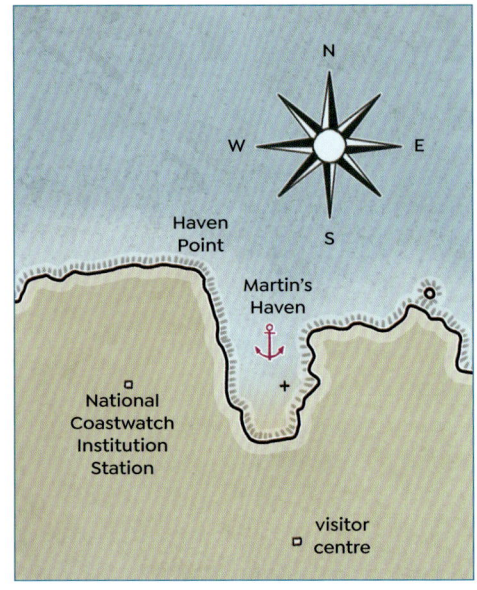

**THE WEST COAST** of Wales has some of the most stunning coastal scenery in the country, and the area around St Brides Bay comes somewhere near the top of the tree. Much of the coast here is still wild and remote, and access can be quite challenging.

Martin's Haven at the southern end of the bay is a great anchorage, but to get to it you have to either navigate through the tide races of Jack Sound, if sailing from the south, or those of Ramsey Sound, if approaching from the north. Transiting these tidal races requires precise timings to make sure

▽ Martin's Haven

you sail through both of them at slack water. There is the option of taking the long way round and coming in from the west, but even then you'll have to cope with the strong tides that stretch quite a way out to sea. If you're approaching the area from Jack Sound then do not sail too close to the eastern headland, which is Wooltack Point, as there's a drying rock about 200m (655ft) to the west of the point. Otherwise there are no off-lying dangers.

Martin's Haven is worth the challenge if you're seeking an anchorage away from the hustle and bustle of the modern world. Tucked into the shore where it turns back to the east just north of Jack Sound, this cove is home to the boats that take people out to the nature reserve of Skomer Island, on the west side of Jack Sound. These boats operate from spring through to autumn, making several trips a day, so the cove can get a bit busy. Ashore, the National Trust car park attracts its share of visitors, but once evening approaches all goes quiet, so you may have the place to yourself overnight.

The ferry to Skomer has its own mooring buoy in the middle of the cove where it moors up overnight. Dive boats also moor here on their own buoys, but there's still room to anchor towards the mouth of the cove in about 6m of water. If it feels too cramped for you, there are more coves further to the east along the coast that tend to remain empty. There's also another anchorage just inside Wooltack Point which offers shelter from the west, but you might get refracted waves coming round the headland in a fresh westerly.

All of these coves offer shelter from southerly and westerly winds but if there are any northerlies, these bays become exposed and are not viable. Make sure you check the weather forecast before anchoring here. St Brides Bay is wide open to the west, so there's always the risk of a swell running in to disturb your night at anchor, but the rewards of these anchorages are considerable in terms of wildlife and scenery. There are no facilities at Martin's Haven, but it's a beautiful location and, if the weather allows, is peaceful and quiet. A cottage on the shore has been converted into a visitor centre for the Wildlife Trust, but if you want a pub then there's an anchorage in the small bay close by Marloes village, where you'll find *The Lobster Pot Inn*. **– DP**

▼ The end of the Welsh coastline

# 6

# SOLVA

PEMBROKESHIRE

---

**SOLVA IS ONE** of Pembrokeshire's picturesque gems, with a wonderfully sheltered tidal inlet leading to a bustling village finding space for a selection of cafés, restaurants, pubs, art galleries and gift shops. While there are some food shops, it's best to get the bus to St David's if resupplying the galley, and this can be combined with a visit to the famous cathedral.

▼ The pool at Solva

The inlet is boomerang-shaped with a south-facing entrance guarded by high headlands, making Solva one of the safest and most sheltered harbours on the Pembrokeshire coast. At high tide, the beach is just a narrow strip at the head of the creek, but at low tide the sands stretch to within 100m (330ft) of the entrance rock, leaving a huge expanse of sand beloved of walkers, swimmers and small children. A stream permanently runs down the middle of the harbour between the dried-out local boats, providing hours of entertainment for youngsters to catch fish, shrimp and crabs. Towards the mouth of the inlet are rock pools and caves, ready to explore. When high tide covers these delights, jumping off the harbour wall provides hours of fun – truly a holiday paradise!

Solva was once one of the busiest trading ports in Pembrokeshire, though as the thrust duly changed towards leisure boating its boat community developed, becoming the Solva Harbour Society Limited in 2020. This Community Benefit Society (CBS) purchased Trinity Quay and the Sand Quay and leases and manages Solva Harbour. Information on facilities is available from the helpful harbourmaster; there are showers and toilets, and a café overlooking the boats. Water is obtainable from a tap, but the nearest fuel and gas is at St David's 3 miles (4.8km) away.

Careful calculations must be made when making for Solva from either Milford Haven or Cardigan Bay in order to pass Jack Sound and Ramsey Sound respectively; the local pilot books are

▲ Overlooking Solva harbour

invaluable to aid balancing slack water with an adequate depth for Solva. The harbour is hidden behind Green Scar and the entrance only becomes evident 1 mile (1.8km) or so off. Having rounded Green Scar and its companions, I usually choose the eastern entrance between Black Rock and St Elvis Rock; Black Rock is marked by an iron post behind which lies 'The Pool', where there is space for up to three yachts to anchor; the alternative for deep-keeled craft is to continue up to Trinity Quay and dry out against the wall (though book ahead to avoid disappointment). Boats able to dry out usually choose one of the eight yellow mooring buoys to the east of the main channel leading to the quays; each marker buoy hosts two bow lines and a single stern line with a carabiner to split the span line if necessary. The moorings dry at half-tide, so careful calculations are required.

Once safely settled, the fleshpots of Solva beckon, although the walks along the ridges alongside the inlet are perfect for working up a thirst. Just remember to return aboard before the tide comes in!

– JP

# 7

# BARDSEY ISLAND

GWYNEDD

**IN MEDIEVAL TIMES** it was considered that three pilgrimages to Bardsey Island gave the equivalent benefit to the soul as one to Rome. Its Welsh name, Ynys Enlli, translates to 'The Island in the Currents', and indeed Bardsey Sound carries a formidable reputation, with 6 knot tides and vicious overfalls. Despite being only 0.6 miles (1km) wide and 1 mile (1.6km) long, Bardsey occupies a prominent place in history; St Cadfan built a monastery here in AD 516, which survived until Henry VIII's Dissolution of the Monasteries in 1537. Today all that remains is the 13th-century bell tower and a Celtic Cross to commemorate the 20,000 saints said to be buried on the island.

Owned by the Bardsey Island Trust, the island remains a place of pilgrimage – not purely religious, but also for visiting ornithologists and naturalists. Bardsey is not only a Site of Special Scientific Interest (SSSI) and National Nature Reserve (NNR), but is also sited on the migration routes of thousands of birds in addition to the 30 or so species who regularly nest on the island including choughs, oystercatchers and little owls. By far the noisiest visitors are the 10,000 pairs of Manx shearwaters, whose nocturnal return to their mates in burrows near the lighthouse is trumpeted by the cacophony of their eerie cry. Their

▼ The anchorage at Bardsey with the lighthouse in the background

'song', together with the barking of the hundreds of grey seals that bask on the shores of the anchorage, make visits a unique auditory experience.

The anchorage at Henllwyn Cove does not enjoy good holding – weed and rock can make dragging a regular feature unless a fisherman's anchor is deployed. While there is one mooring buoy, this belongs to Colin Evans, the boatman who transports visitors across Bardsey Sound, and should not be used without his permission. His usual landing is in Y Cafn; a narrow inlet terminating in a slipway used to draw his ferry safely out of the water, as both the anchorage and Y Cafn are exposed to the south-east and cannot be considered tenable in any wind with an easterly component.

The approach and entry in settled weather is fairly straightforward, although care must be taken with the tidal flows that swirl through Bardsey Sound and spread out over both Bastram Shoal, rising to a depth of 6m, and The Devil's Ridge, which can produce dangerous breaking seas in wind over tide conditions. Henllwyn Cove anchorage, easily marked by the dominating lighthouse, should be approached on a bearing of 270°T. Avoid the hazards of the visible rocks to the south of the entrance, and beware the rock at a depth of 1m in the south-western third of the bay. A shingle drying beach to the north allows landing. There are no shops or facilities apart from a small souvenir stall in the Bird Observatory.

Visiting Bardsey requires a determined effort that can only be achieved in settled weather, though the rewards of success make it all worthwhile. Bardsey's peace, isolation and wildlife really feels a world apart – those 20,000 saints knew a good thing when they saw it. **– JP**

# 8

# ABERDARON

LLŶN PENINSULA, GWYNEDD

**LOCATED AT THE** top end of Cardigan Bay, Bardsey Island creates quite a barrier to the tidal current flowing round the bay and in turn this can generate some nasty seas, overfalls and riptides around the island. With tides running at up to 6 knots and the area wide open to the west, Bardsey Sound, between the island and the mainland, has quite an evil reputation and is not a place to take lightly. The place names – Hell's Mouth and The Devil's Ridge – say it all. However, the wide bay at Aberdaron just to the north of the sound can be a good place to find an anchorage if you're waiting for slack water or conditions to improve before turning the corner at Braich-y-Pwll and heading north.

There's good shelter in the bay from any wind from the west right round to the north-east, but it is wide open to the south. Even with a westerly wind, you can get the swell running into the bay unless you tuck in close under the cliffs on the west side. A good spot is off the little cove of Porth Meudwy, where there is adequate water quite close in, but if you want to go ashore for a drink or a meal then choose a spot off the village of Aberdaron itself.

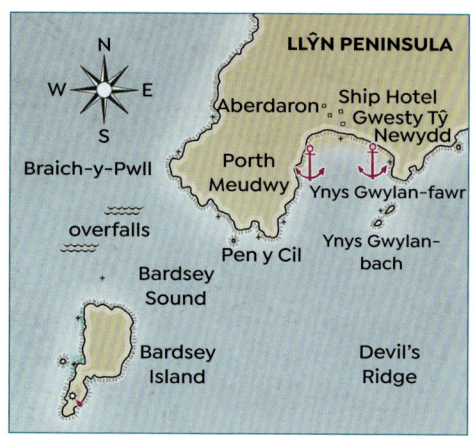

Keep to the eastern side; there are boulders on the western side, brought down by the river that exits on the beach. Landing here involves using the beach, which could leave you with a long carry if the tide is ebbing. Ashore, you have the *Ship Hotel* and the *Gwesty Tŷ Nwydd* for food and drink; the latter is a large white building which is a good guide into the anchorage.

The approaches to Aberdaron Bay are clear of danger apart from two islands – Ynys Gwylan-bach and Ynys Gwylan-fawr – that mark the eastern edge of the bay. You can pass inside the inner island with a clear passage if you're coming from the east. From the west there are no off-lying dangers and you can head close round the Pen y Cil headland.

Porth Meudwy is a lovely little cove that is a National Trust property. The ferry that links Bardsey Island with the mainland operates from here, and it's also home to fishing boats that launch off the beach with tractor assistance. There are no facilities here. At Porth Meudwy you can anchor under the cliffs that run sheer into the water, but it's probably best to anchor a bit to the south of the cove to avoid traffic. Look out for lobster pots.

In summer months Aberdaron Bay can get busy, with many boats coming out from Abersoch and Pwllheli to spend the day at this delightful anchorage. Most of this activity will die down as evening approaches, so you should get a quiet night at anchor, but you might want to choose a spot a bit further south towards Pen y Cil because the dayboats tend to head for the beach areas. **– DP**

▽ Aberdaron

▽ Bardsey Island from the hills above Aberdaron

# PORTH DINLLAEN

GWYNEDD

---

**TUCKED IN BEHIND** a sheltering bluff on the north-west shore of the Llŷn Peninsula, Porth Dinllaen is a perfect passage halt for coastal travellers as well as being a haven in its own right. Sailors from Cardigan Bay, fatigued by Bardsey Island's tides and chop, will delight in rounding Trwyn Porth Dinllaen, passing by the lifeboat house, and dropping the anchor at the periphery of the moorings. Not then to land on the sandy beach fronting the welcoming *Tŷ Coch Inn* and enjoy its good beer and fine food would seem a missed opportunity. Those travelling from the north across Caernarfon Bar or past Holyhead will likewise delight in this perfect rest stop before proceeding southwards into Cardigan Bay. Porth Dinllaen is the nearest refuge for those waiting for the right conditions to cross Caernarfon Bar, an attribute made all the more

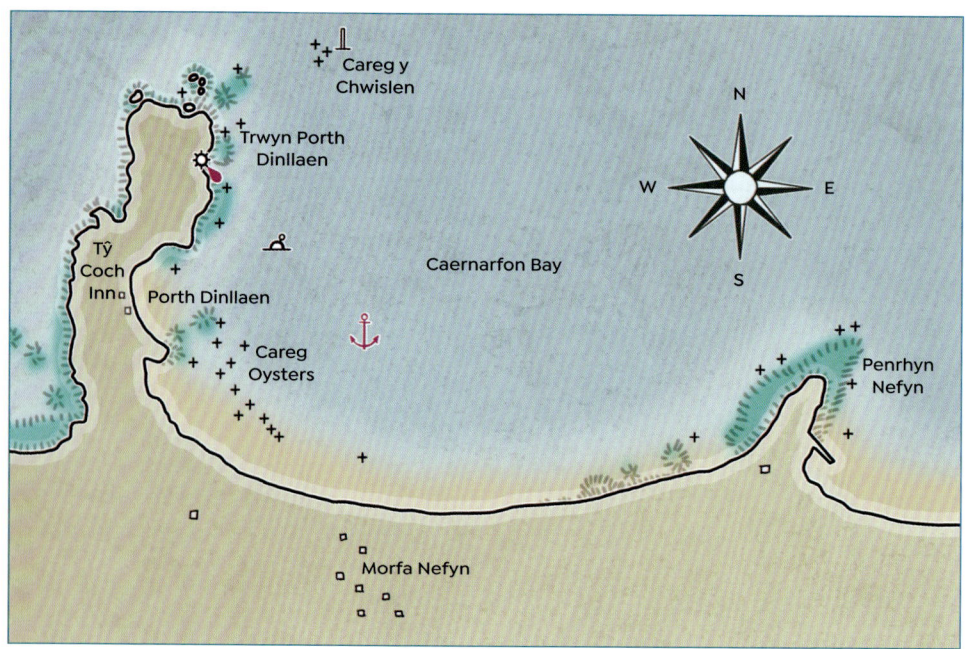

▲ The popular *Tŷ Coch Inn* at Porth Dinllaen

pleasurable by its hostelry.

The main approach hazard is the rock of Careg y Chwislen north-east of the headland, marked by an isolated danger pole beacon. Approaching from the north or west it is wise to give this danger a couple of cables (370m 1,200ft) offing, as the tidal stream can set onto it from inshore, though in calm conditions it is possible to use the 1 cable (185m, 600ft) wide channel to the west of the beacon. Coming from the north-east you are safe if you keep the beacon open of the extremity of the headland.

The anchorage offers excellent holding in sand and mud with a depth of 3m, and is sheltered from the south round to the north-west. A swell can set in if the wind veers further north, and the anchorage is exposed to the north-east. The bay off the *Tŷ Coch Inn* is full of moorings, and rocks crowd the shallows inshore and south of the ruined jetty, and more lurk to prevent anchoring down the southern part of the beach as far as Morfa Nefyn. Beware the rocks of Careg Oysters south-east of the pub, but otherwise there is ample room to anchor outside the moorings. The chartlet clearly shows the hazards, and they are easily avoided. The moorings may not have been checked, so I prefer to anchor.

Other than the Tŷ Coch, facilities are sparse. The village of Morfa Nefyn offers small shops and a bus service but lies nearly 1 mile (1.6km) away. This is a place to gently stroll ashore before a pleasant beer on the beach. One of my fondest memories is dining on a beach table in the sun with the incoming sea lapping at my bare toes while watching the boaty comings and goings.

Porth Dinllaen's attraction is shared by many, and is better suited to people-watching than idyllic isolation. It's a popular beach tourist destination, so be warned – when the sun shines in the summer months you'll have plenty of company in both the anchorage and the pub. This is definitely a place to sit back and watch the world go by – I could linger for days. **– JP**

# CEMLYN BAY

ANGLESEY

------------

**ANCHORAGES ALONG THE** northern coast of Anglesey are not exactly two a penny, and sailors traversing the top of the island tend to experience a sense of foreboding as they sweep past the hazards, marks, rocks and currents that aid or abet their passage. With challenging pilotage and navigation, the prevailing weather conditions can make all the difference between what might look on paper to be an easy trip and the harsh reality of an adverse rodeo-riding slog at the helm of a wave-tossed

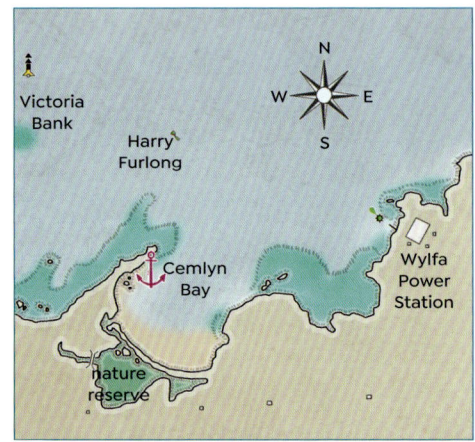

▼ Sunset at Cemlyn Bay

188 | ANCHORAGES OF THE BRITISH ISLES

boat. It's at times like this that a period of quiet for a peaceful cuppa becomes irresistible, and Cemlyn Bay is one of the places to achieve it. This north-east-facing anchorage provides good shelter from the prevailing south-westerlies, and the long low point of Trwyn Cemlyn creates a natural breakwater on the western side of the bay that abates swell. Indeed, in the right conditions the bay makes an excellent overnight destination rather than just being used as a lunch stop.

Situated on the north-west coast of Anglesey, Cemlyn Bay consists of a steep 600m (1,970ft) long shingle beach with rocky outcrops to the east. While offering a little bit for everyone – sea fishing, kayaking, walking or just taking in the beautiful scenery – it is especially beloved of birdwatchers. Cemlyn Bay is home to hundreds of seabirds and has the only breeding Sandwich Terns in Wales. The Cemlyn estate is owned by the National Trust and holds AONB and SSSI status as well as being a North Wales Wildlife Trust reserve. Behind the beach is a partly man-made brackish lagoon where, aside from assorted terns, can be found wildfowl, oystercatchers, ringed plover, stonechat, whitethroat and sedge warbler, as well as seabirds such as skuas and gannets. During the winter, divers and grebes visit the bay.

Around 2.5 miles (4.5km) east of Carmel Head, Cemlyn offers shelter in winds from the south-east through the south to the west; it is exposed to the north-east. There are no facilities at

▲ The long beach at Cemlyn Bay on the north coast of Anglesey

all. The approach from the east is fairly straightforward after passing Middle Mouse. The former Wylfa nuclear power station makes a prominent landmark; once past Wylfa Head, turn into Cemlyn Bay well before the green Furlong buoy to avoid Harry Furlong's Rocks. From the west, pass Carmel Head and keep close inshore until West Mouse is to port, before aiming directly for the green Harry Furlong buoy; you'll leave Victoria Bank and its north cardinal to port. Leave the Furlong buoy to starboard before entering the centre of the bay. Anchor as close off the beach as depth allows, or, for more shelter, east of Trwyn Cemlyn on the western side of the bay, though ensure you are clear of the rocky shore.

While Wylfa nuclear power station dominates the skyline to the east, it soon fades from your awareness. On gentle summer evenings Cemlyn Bay is a lovely place to rest and watch seals, porpoises and the occasional dolphin pod enter and cavort under the wheeling seabirds.
– JP

# 11

# FORT BELAN

MENAI STRAIT, GWYNEDD

---

**FORT BELAN PROVIDES** a good anchorage at the south-west entrance to the Menai Strait. It is a useful stopping-off point for those waiting for the right tides before making the passage through the strait. It also offers a quiet place for the night for sailors who would rather avoid the bustle of Caernarfon a bit further up the channel. On the chart it looks like it could be a useful anchorage spot before navigating the busy waters around the top of Anglesey, but to get to Fort Belan you have to tackle the entrance over the Caernarfon Bar.

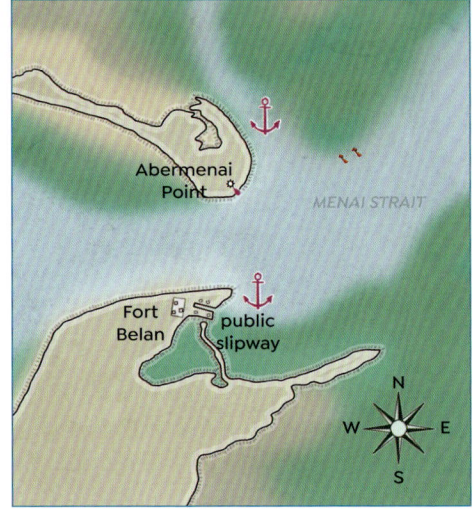

▽ Fort Belan harbour

190 | ANCHORAGES OF THE BRITISH ISLES

▲ Fort Belan is on the southern side of the Menai Strait

The sands of this bar are constantly changing, particularly after a westerly gale. Although well marked, the positions of the buoys often alter and frequently don't correspond to what the chart might indicate. It's best to talk to the harbourmaster at Caernarfon, who is responsible for the buoys, before attempting an entrance. Details are also available at www.caernarfonharbour.org.uk. With the tides running at up to 5 knots through the channel where Fort Belan lies, you'll probably want to make this entrance on the flood.

If this has not put you off even attempting to get to Fort Belan, then follow the buoyed channel over the bar to the point where it narrows, with Abermenai Point to the north and the low greyish buildings of Fort Belan to the south. Here, there is adequate water quite close up to the land, as the channel is scoured out by the strong tides. After rounding the tip of Fort Belan, you'll find the anchorage, which has depths of two or more metres at LW. Head into the shallower water with the echo sounder going. A couple of mooring buoys mark the best location in the anchorage.

The fort here was built as protection from privateers during the American Civil War, but is now privately owned, with the buildings converted into holiday lets. It looks so inviting and there is even a dock that was constructed originally for a private steam yacht, which today provides protected drying berths for local yachts. There are no facilities ashore and you need the owner's permission to land. The waters off Fort Belan offer a quiet anchorage for an overnight stop and it is well sheltered, provided you can tuck yourself into the small bay.

A tidal inlet runs south, a few kilometres from the anchorage, which might be interesting to explore on a rising tide, but there's little else on offer apart from peace and quiet.

There is another well protected anchorage on the opposite side of the main channel created in the form of the narrow channel running north on the east side of Abermenai Point. The channel is only a little over 100m (330ft) across, but it offers shelter from the west. In both anchorages, the sandy bottom offers good holding ground. **– DP**

# RHOS ON SEA

CONWY

---

**LOCATED BETWEEN THE** major holiday resorts of Llandudno and Colwyn Bay in North Wales, Rhos on Sea is a quiet anchorage for the night when the wind is in the west. The town has a small harbour, but while most harbours have long historical origins based on commercial activity or fishing, the harbour at Rhos on Sea was only developed in the 1980s as part of a flood protection scheme. Evidence of the fish weirs that were used to funnel fish into nets in the 13th century are still visible, with a P-shaped fish trap still partly shown on the Ordnance Survey map of the harbour.

The sea wall along the coast here is quite low and, in storms, there used to be a serious risk of the waves overtopping the wall and flooding the properties along the sea road. To address this, a breakwater was built some 300m (985ft) offshore, with the surplus stone from the construction used to extend the groyne that runs out from the nearby point. The result is a harbour with a half-tide opening at its northern end, with the breakwater running parallel to the shore, extending south. The harbour almost dries out at LW, with the majority

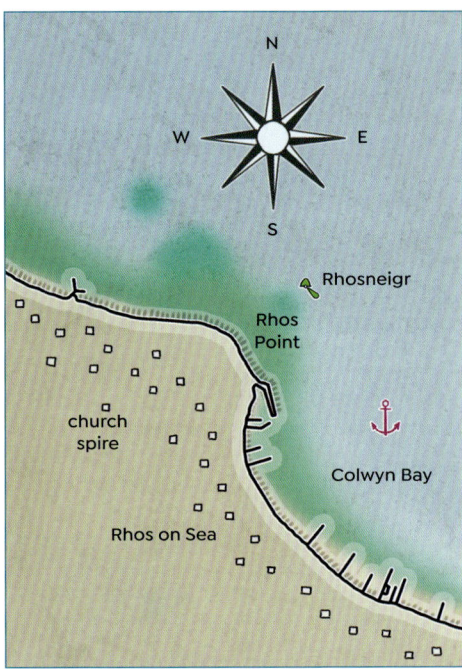

▼ The tiny chapel of St Trillo

192 | ANCHORAGES OF THE BRITISH ISLES

▲ The drying harbour at Rhos on Sea

of mooring buoys allocated to the local angling fleet, so you're unlikely to find space here even if you can dry out.

Instead, take a wide sweep around Rhos Point where the Rhosneigr buoy marks the wreck of a paddle steamer, and you can find an anchorage for the night off the southern end of the harbour breakwater. Give the end a wide berth because shoals extend out, and there is a partially submerged jetty running out from the shore. Beacons mark both. Keep well south to avoid the submarine cable marked on the charts.

Your guide as you run in with the echo sounder is the remains of an old pier on the beach at the southern end of the harbour. Here you can anchor in about 2.5m, roughly 0.5 miles (0.9km) offshore. This should be well sheltered in south-westerly winds but you can get some swell sweeping round the headland if the wind swings to the west. There's a slipway on the shore adjacent to the remains of the old pier for landing by tender.

Ashore you'll find all the facilities of a small, friendly town, with pubs and eateries along the promenade. It's busy in the height of the summer, but if you want to escape the crowds, it's well worth exploring the Rhos on Sea Heritage Trail, which takes in 25 historic sites in just three hours, including St Trillo's Chapel, reputed to be the smallest church in Britain at Rhos Point, a short walk from the anchorage. The chapel can seat just six people and is named after the 6th-century St Trillo. Further inland, there are the remains of Bryn Euryn, a 5th-century hill fort that promises stunning views across the bay.
– DP

# NORTH WEST

THE MERSEY TO THE SOLWAY FIRTH

---

The northern part of the Irish Sea, between North Wales and Scotland, tends to be unfairly overlooked as cruising boats head north or south to the better publicised lure of the Scottish west coast. It's true that potential destinations are fewer and further apart, but an exploration of the North West coast and the Isle of Man will reward the more adventurous cruising sailor. Anchorages are slightly more elusive, and timing your arrival and departure anywhere in the vicinity of Morecambe Bay is critical, so getting to know this coast will test your seamanship.

For many people, any reference to the North West only evokes the Lake District, but the coast of Cumbria is dramatic and beautiful and rewards exploration.

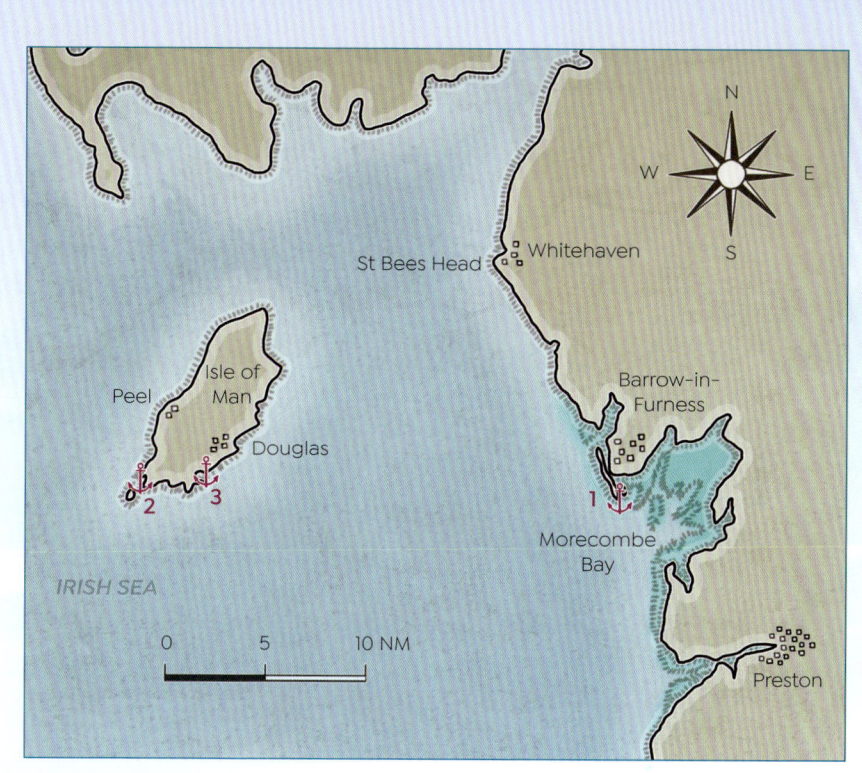

▼ The unspoilt coast of Cumbria

# PIEL ISLAND

MORECAMBE BAY, LANCASHIRE

------------

**IN THE OFFING** as you approach Morecambe Bay there are now several wind farms covering a significant area west of the low-lying shingle bank of Walney Island, which may make it easier to spot your destination. The island is linked by a bridge to Barrow-in-Furness, with its port which serves the offshore energy industry and is well known for BAE Systems and submarine-building.

The north edge of Walney Island is bounded by the Duddon Estuary and in its SSSI there are natterjack toads and a rare dune hellebore. It is also the only place in the world where a particular species of geranium grows. The southern part of Walney Island is a nature reserve and home to a grey seal colony as well as being a breeding location for several species of seabird and on the autumn migration route for others.

Between the south-east of Walney Island and the mainland is Piel Island, just 20ha (50 acres), which feels barely above tide height. There's an interesting anchorage in behind the island on the edge of Walney Channel, which leads up to Barrow-in-Furness.

The channel fairway buoy is about 1 mile (1.8km) south of Hilpsford Point and you follow the buoys in on a leading line of 041°T until you pass the Bar buoy just off Haws Point. As you come abeam

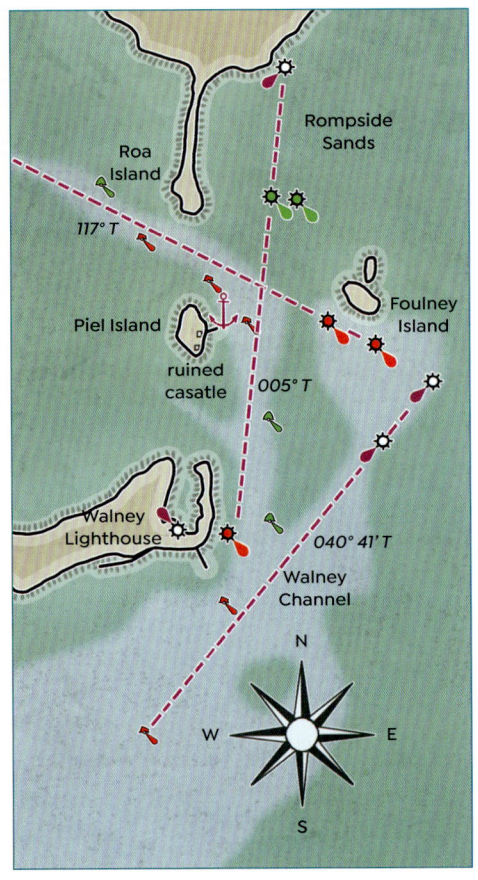

▼ The old castle on Piel Island

Walney red buoy, head on to the next leading line at 005°T until you reach Castle red buoy with Piel Island on your port hand. The ruins of the castle on the south of the island are conspicuous as you approach and there's a landing pier on the south-east, opposite Roa Island, which is no longer an island as there's now a road on to the mainland. A ferry runs regularly between Roa and Piel islands from Easter to October.

Unless you can take the ground, nudge in towards the pier and anchor in mud away from the moorings just off the channel. There's an alternative anchorage to the east of Roa Island for bilge keelers or a lifting keel.

Piel Island has a fascinating history. The ruins of the 14th-century castle are now owned by English Heritage, but entrance is free. The castle was owned in the 14th century by Furness Abbey, and was probably fortified to protect the abbey against raids from Scots and pirates, as well as to protect trading routes into the harbour. Furness Abbey was said to be involved in smuggling; merchants from Calais accused the abbot of not paying dues on wool from Piel Island. After the Dissolution of the Monasteries during Henry VIII's reign the castle was allowed to fall into ruins.

On the island is the Ship Inn, a convivial and friendly pub. Tradition has it that the landlord is King of Piel and the ceremony, which involves quite a lot of beer being poured over the king's head, may date back to the 15th century. As part of the tenancy agreement the landlord has to preserve the helmet and chair used during this event.

At the turn of the 20th century Piel Island was owned by the Duke of Buccleuch. When he wanted to sell it in 1919, the Mayor of Barrow-in-Furness intervened and the island was given to the town as a memorial to those who had died in the First World War. **– JC**

# PORT ERIN

ISLE OF MAN

---

▼ The Milner Tower on Bradda Head is a good marker for Port Erin

**THE HEADLAND TO** the north of Port Erin Bay, Bradda Head, has a conspicuous tower on the top, Milner's Tower, making identifying the bay straightforward. The tower is supposed to be key-shaped and is a memorial to William Milner, a safe maker who was born in Sheffield. He visited the island often and finally retired to Port Erin in 1860. He was also a philanthropist, building a row of cottages, St Catherine's Terrace, for poor fishermen and the first hotel in the village, the *Falcon's Nest*. He helped to

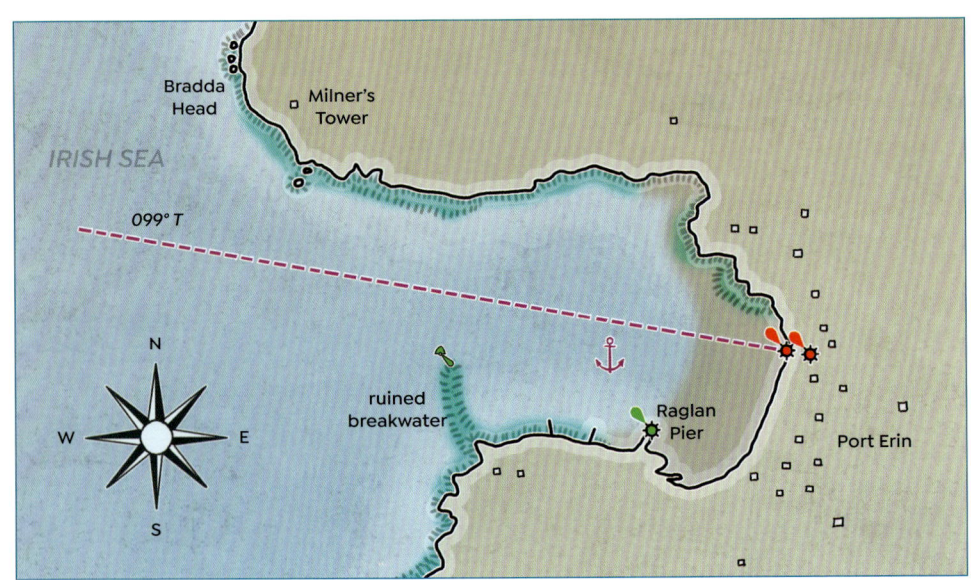

▲ Raglan Pier in Port Erin

have a breakwater built, although this was destroyed in a storm 20 years later. After his death his estate funded the construction of St Catherine's Church.

The leading line into Port Erin is a white tower with a red band on the beach and a white pole with a red band above it on the shore. The bearing is 099°T – this will keep you clear of the old ruined breakwater, which also has a green buoy off its north end. The leading line is lit so it is possible to enter at night, though probably not recommended for a first visit.

The bay is sheltered from all easterly weather but is exposed to wind from south-west to north-west. If you can take the ground it is possible to tuck in behind Raglan Pier in the south-west corner of the bay, but you are likely to find several local boats here. There's also a large yellow visitors' buoy in this area and three others are laid during the season. There are now two underground cables across the southern part of the bay with a beacon on the shore. They run about half a cable (90m 300ft) north of Raglan pier and off the green buoy marking the end of the ruined breakwater, so avoid these when anchoring. The holding is generally good.

Port Erin is a popular beach and the town offers good restaurants and cafés, shops and attractions. It is one end of the Isle of Man Steam Railway and the railway museum will keep enthusiasts happy for hours. You can take a trip on the railway

▼ The lower leading mark on the beach at Port Erin

to Douglas, the island capital, which takes about an hour, but there are stops on the way so you can visit places inland. The Kerroo Brewing Company has premises a short walk in from the beach. The taproom is only open at certain times, so you'll need to check their social media pages before you go.

You can land by dinghy at Raglan Pier or at the jetty a bit further west, though this partially covers at HW. From the village there are coastal footpaths north to Bradda Glen and out to the headland, or south back to view Calf Sound and the Calf of Man if you came through here on your way.

To learn more about the south of the Isle of Man call in at the Rushen Heritage Centre in Bridson Street. As well as holding special exhibitions, it's also a visitor information point working with Visit Isle of Man. **– JC**

▽ Looking out to Bradda Head

# 3

# DERBYHAVEN

ISLE OF MAN

**ON THE SOUTH-EAST** corner of the Isle of Man you can find good shelter tucked into the bay at Derbyhaven with winds from south, through west to north, but north-easterlies and anything from the east sends in a heavy swell, making the anchorage untenable. At times this may not be the quietest anchorage as it's just to the east of Ronaldsway airport, though this is no Heathrow.

Derbyhaven is on the north side of the isthmus joining the long Langness peninsula to the mainland. The very northern end is St Michael's Isle, joined to

▼ The anchorage at Derbyhaven is sheltered by St Michael's Isle

▼ Peaceful evening light in Derbyhaven

Langness by a causeway. With the ruins of St Michael's chapel and the circular Derby Fort, it is often referred to as Fort Island. Named after the Earls of Derby, the fort you see today was built on the site of earlier fortifications, some of which can be traced on the island. You can't go into the structure but can look inside through an iron gate.

The approach from the north is fairly straightforward but be sure to give the north end of St Michael's Isle a wide berth, as rocks extend north of the island and the tide will tend to push you towards them. In Derbyhaven there's a detached breakwater, but only yachts that can take the ground should consider anchoring inside. Access should be made at the south end of the breakwater where there is a white light, and just to the south is a red beacon on rocks, which must be left to port. Anchoring outside the breakwater, it's best to go towards the south end where there's reasonable holding in about 3m on a sand and mud bottom. A large yellow visitor buoy is laid here during the season, about 100m (330ft) south-east of the south end of the breakwater.

The southern part of the Langness peninsula protects the drying harbour of Castletown, which was the capital of the Isle of Man until 1869. If you land on the beach at Derbyhaven it's just over 1 mile (1.6km) walk to Castletown, where you can visit Castle Rushen. Built over 800 years ago and used by the rulers of Man for centuries, it is one of the best-preserved medieval castles in the British Isles. You can climb up to the roof, from where there are amazing views across the south of the island. The castle is on the side of the harbour where the Silver Burn joins the sea.

Don't leave Castletown without a visit to the Nautical Museum on the opposite side of the harbour. Here, you can learn about *Peggy*, the oldest-surviving schooner in the world, built in 1789 for the politician George Quayle as an armed yacht. At the time of writing she is undergoing conservation work elsewhere, and there are plans to create a new museum with an atrium so she can be exhibited fully rigged – watch this space! In the museum there are exhibits about the Georgian era of the late 18th and early 19th century, the Napoleonic wars and the life of George Quayle. There's also a sail loft with tools of the period.

If you fancy eating ashore you have a good choice of restaurants and pubs in Castletown. **– JC**

▼ Low water in Castletown harbour

▼ Derbyhaven is on the north side of the isthmus, with St Michael's Island to the east

# SCOTLAND

## OUTER HEBRIDES TO THE SOLWAY FIRTH

-------------------------------------

The west coast of Scotland has enough islands and anchorages to keep most sailors busy for a lifetime, and whole books have been written about them. This selection is an attempt to cover the coast from Lewis and Skye to the Solway Firth, with a few tried and tested favourites and some more challenging possibilities. As you peruse them, either in the cockpit or from an armchair, you'll sample the stunning grandeur of nature and some of the (possibly disturbing) history of the people and events that have shaped them. A few have become very popular, so you may have to pick your time, but others are remote and you are likely to be the only boat in the anchorage. Most of them have few facilities so your boat needs to be well prepared before setting out. You'll have ample opportunities to see wildlife that is never spotted further south, so it's important to give due consideration to the environment and leave nothing that might harm it. And don't forget to pack insect repellent, or better still, hatch screens!

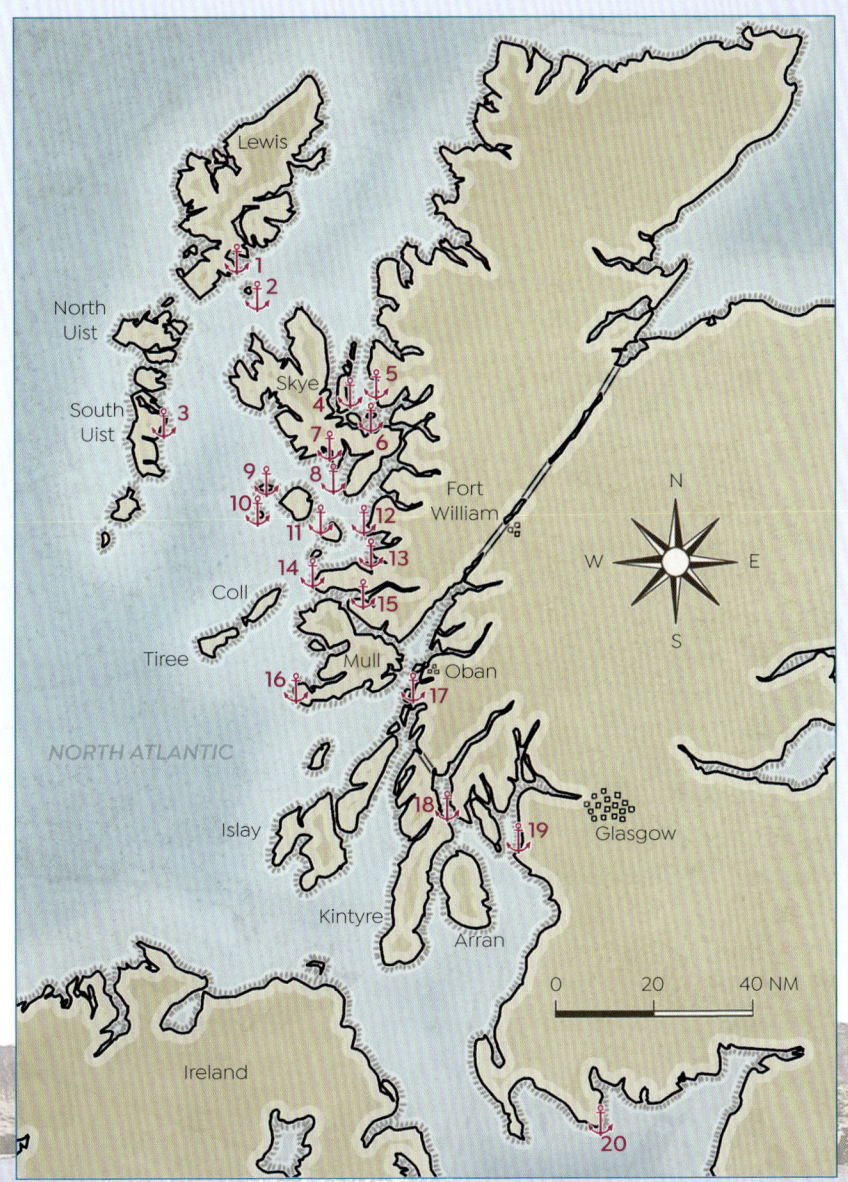

▼ Soay Harbour in near perfect conditions

# LOCH SCADABAY

HARRIS, OUTER HEBRIDES

- - - - - - - - - - - - -

**A FAVOURITE ANCHORAGE** in the Outer Hebrides is Loch Scadabay. Hidden away off the west shore of The Little Minch between the Isle of Skye and The Hebrides, this secluded Harris gem is worthy of inclusion in any *Swallows and Amazons* adventure. Accessed through a narrow 30m (100ft) wide cleft in an apparently unbroken line of cliffs, intrepid yachts will suddenly find themselves in a sheltered circular hurricane hole, protected from all sides by gently rolling Hebridean countryside dotted by crofts and grazing sheep.

There are no facilities, but those who ask politely might find water available at the houses; a Harris Tweed weaver and a small shop do not seem to have stood the test of time and neither were in evidence on my last visit.

To the east side of the entrance channel is a small quay used by local fishermen, but for water and general supplies the nearest port of call is North Harbour on Scalpay, some 6 miles (10.8km) to the north-east. The nearest 'town' is Tarbert, some 5 miles (8km) north by road, though Scadabay is an anchorage to be visited for its peace

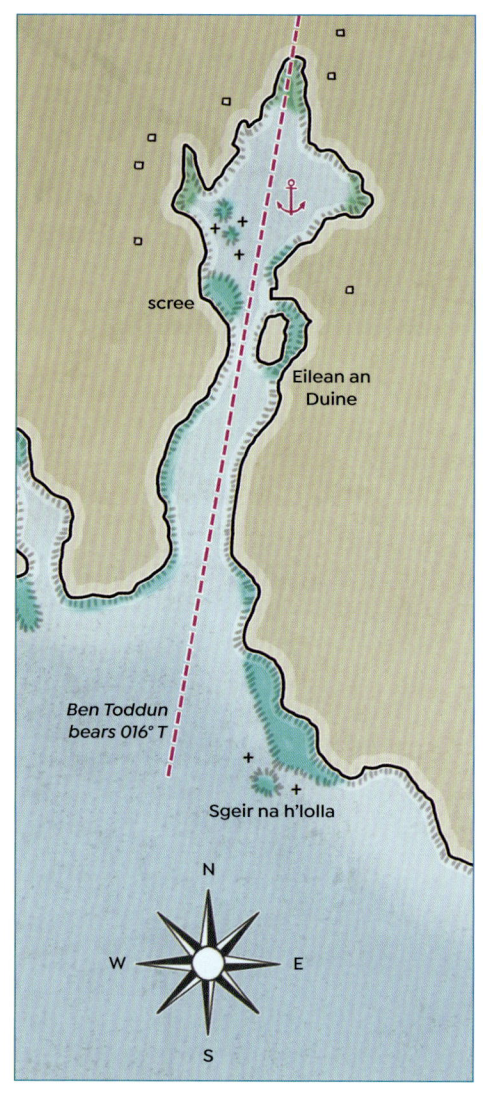

rather than the local high life. Those with bicycles can enjoy the narrow roads and gentle hills, secure in the knowledge that their yacht can be left safely.

In days gone by the redoubtable Mr and Mrs MacLeod used to weave Harris Tweed in a tin shed by the cottages on the shore – indeed, one of my treasured possessions is an indestructible pair of tweed stockings now used as bedsocks on chilly nights afloat. Mrs MacLeod's hospitality was renowned, and she provided visitors with a proper 'High Tea' complete with home-made cakes and scones – her nautical guests even included royalty.

Pilotage is simple – from the north and east stay 5 cables (925m, 3,035ft) off Rubha Brocaig's shore, ignoring the first wide entry to Loch na h'Uamha before seeing Loch Scadabay's entrance open up when the 526m (1,726ft) hill of Toddun (north of East Loch Tarbert) bears 016°T. From the south, keep 3 cables (550m, 1,800ft) off Rubha Chluar and Eilean Dubh and head for the entrance, keeping mid-channel before leaving Eilean an Duine to starboard as you pass over the 1.7m least depth of the narrow entrance cleft. Veer to starboard past the jetty to keep clear of drying rocks to port before following the rocky point round to starboard as the pool opens up.

The bottom is soft mud with excellent holding – anchor in any area clear of the few local fishermen's mooring buoys, and don't be concerned about the depth – fin keelers can sink safely into the deep mud without heeling. Keep clear of the

▲ The anchorage at Scadabay

rocks as marked on the west side, but the centre of the pool is safe and has a least depth of 1.8m.

With such a narrow entrance even a rough swell is denied entry, and the wind can whistle all it likes from any direction without finding any chinks in the total shelter. This is truly a treasured haven of seclusion that calls its devotees back time after time. **– JP**

▼ Getting underway to leave Scadabay

# SHIANT ISLANDS

OUTER HEBRIDES

----

**MENTION THE SHIANT** Islands to any sailor and their ears will prick up, especially if wildlife is one of their interests. The Shiants are a small group of islands in the Outer Hebrides, 4 miles (7.2km) off the coast of Lewis and 12 miles (21.6km) north of Skye. The main islands are Garbh Eilean (rough island) and Eilean an Taighe (house island), which are joined by a narrow isthmus, and Eilean Mhuire (Mary island) to the east. The sea cliffs on the north side of Garbh Eilean are similar to those of St Kilda, with volcanic columnar basalt rock protruding out of the sea to form jagged cliffs over 120m (390ft) high, while the waters surrounding the Shiants are among the most productive for cetaceans anywhere in Britain with minke whales, harbour porpoises, Risso's dolphins and super pods of common dolphins all a regular sight.

But it is the bird population that makes the Shiants stand out as one of the marvels of the Hebrides. Time your visit to coincide with the breeding season (late April to mid-July) and you will never forget the extraordinary experience of a plethora of seabirds flying in all directions, zipping overhead

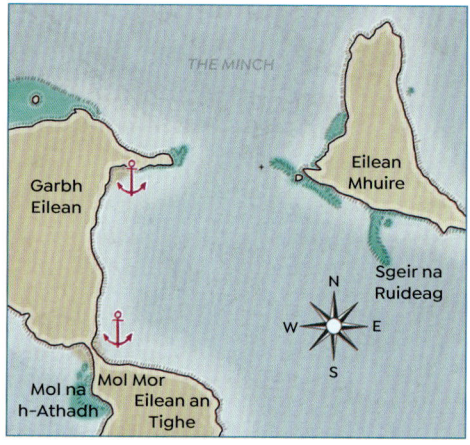

▼ Landing on the Shiant Islands at the shingle beach

▲ A sheltered quiet day off the Shiant Islands

as they return to their young with beaks full of fish. Perhaps most treasured, the Shiant's puffin population – 'the clowns of the sea' – is one of the largest in the UK with around 240,000 puffins nesting on the grassy banks of the islands each year. The colony accounts for about an eighth of the British total and 2 per cent of all the puffins in the world. Aside from the puffins there are thousands upon thousands of other birds including kittiwakes, Manxies, guillemots, razorbills, fulmars and, if you're lucky, even sea eagles. The sheltered bay teems with rafts of razorbills, the rocks of Garbh Eilean are home to a myriad guillemots, while puffins shoot round the bay like avian bullets before returning to their burrows above the natural arch in the north-western corner of the bay.

As an anchorage it has to be said that the Shiant Islands fall short. Unless the conditions are settled, the Shiants are best considered a lunchtime stop, although I have frequently stayed overnight safely. Good shelter and reasonable holding can be found to the east of the shingle landing beach between Eilean an Tighe and Garbh Eilean, but I have struggled to set the anchor on the east side of Garbh Eilean and off the arch in the north-west corner. Fortunately, the pilotage is simple and, rarely for the Hebrides, the bay is clear of hazards, though be aware of the eddies and heavy overfalls that can occur around the islands.

The Shiant Islands have been privately owned for centuries and in 1937 they were bought by Nigel Nicolson, of the Nicolson publishing house, from Compton Mackenzie. Nigel gave them to his son, Adam, as a 21st birthday present who subsequently handed them on to his son, Tom. There are, of course, no facilities. The bothy on Eilean an Tighe is only occasionally used as a shelter by ornithologists, and the 'landing' is a rough shingle beach. Rather than struggling ashore, my preference is to relax aboard, soak up the great sense of wilderness and watch the birds flying in on late summer evenings. Unforgettable. – JP

# WIZARD POOL, LOCH SKIPPORT

SOUTH UIST, OUTER HEBRIDES

**SLICING INTO THE** island of South Uist in the Outer Hebrides chain, Loch Skipport is a haven of peacefulness offering several classic anchorages within its varied branches and pools. Once one of the main seaports of South Uist, its now ruined pier near the top of the loch accommodated steamers from Glasgow and Oban. While no longer a centre for coastal trade, Loch Skipport is still a popular leisure destination for crews sailing in the Hebrides.

The Penguin Cruising Club's long-favoured retreat within the area is the aptly named Wizard Pool, the first inlet on the south side after Loch Skipport's easy entry. The large pool is clear apart from Wizard Island and its attendant drying reef in the south-west corner, and a drying rock off the channel between

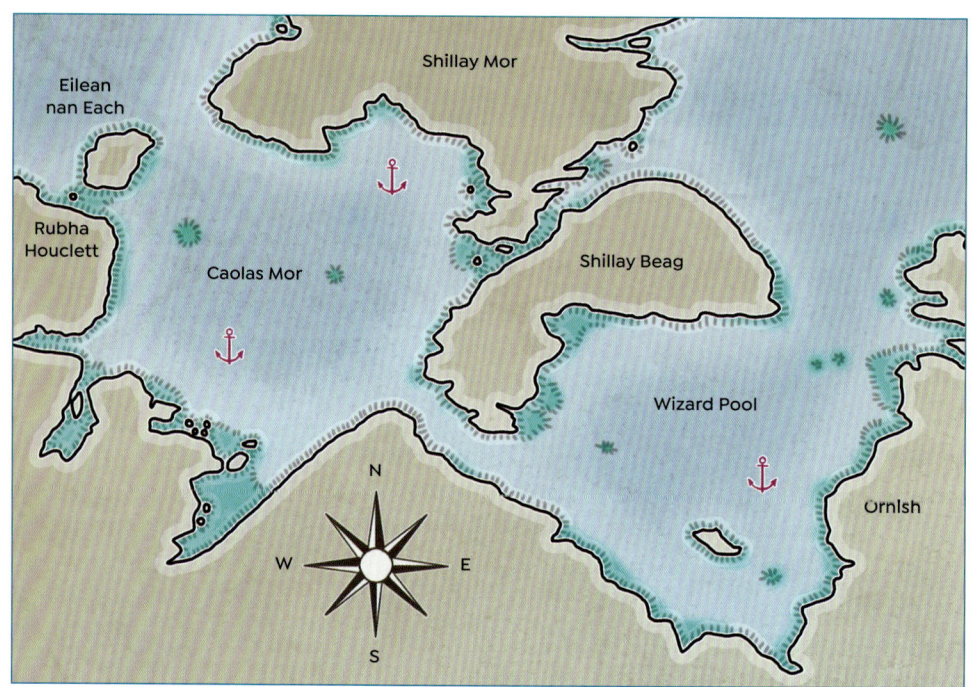

210 | ANCHORAGES OF THE BRITISH ISLES

Wizard Pool and the adjacent Caolas Mor pool. The holding is soft south of Wizard Island – mooring rings are reported on both the island and the adjacent land but their current provenance is untested. Anchor anywhere round the sides of the pool but be aware that while Hecla, the 606m (1,988ft) high hill to the south, looks picturesque, it can be the source of strong gusts in southerly gales. I would tend to anchor close to the south shore west of Wizard Island in southerly sector winds, and nestle in the north-west corner of the pool south of Shillay Beag in north-westerlies. If there is a north-easterly swell, this latter location also gives the smoothest water, but in truth, once within the pool the shelter is excellent in all but the most unreasonable weather and the holding is good. There's ample space to absorb high-season popularity, though I'd be surprised to share its peace with other boats in low season.

When approaching Loch Skipport from the south give Ushenish lighthouse a good offing before passing to the north of Ornish Island. Once within Loch Skipport, passage to the anchorages is free of hazards except for Float Rock to the north of Wizard Pool. From the north, establish your position before turning into Loch Skipport. Once inside steer towards the island of Shillay Mor until a cable (185m, 600ft) off to avoid Float Rock; fish farms lie to your east. Pass Shillay Beag to the west of mid-channel to avoid drying rocks off Ornish and enter the pool. Beware the drying rock east of the south end of Shillay Beag.

▲ An aerial view of Wizard Pool

Wizard Pool and its adjacent Caolas Mor (Kettle Pool) are wild anchorages and offer no facilities. While water can be collected from a burn to the south of Wizard Island, the closest marina-type services are at Lochmaddy to the north and Lochboisdale to the south. Ensure your stocks of fuel, food and gas are adequate as there are no small shops round the corner! Indeed, this isolation and shelter are the main reasons to stay here; the opportunities for swimming, hiking and dinghy exploration abound while afterwards the spectacular situation forms the perfect backdrop to refreshments. **– JP**

▼ The anchorage of Wizard Pool

# ACAIRSEID MHOR

RONA, HIGHLAND

---

**THE PENGUIN CRUISING** Club describes this hidden haven on the west coast of the island of Rona, north-west of Skye's Portree, as 'the dream harbour of the north-west'. Its beauty and remoteness are matched by its total shelter from all directions. Add good holding, and what more could you wish for? Well, OK, the entrance could be easier, though it is not as difficult as the Clyde Cruising Club Sailing Directions suggest. It does, however, still involve some rock dodging, which all adds to the thrill, once safely inside.

The population of Rona peaked at 181 in 1891, but there are now only two

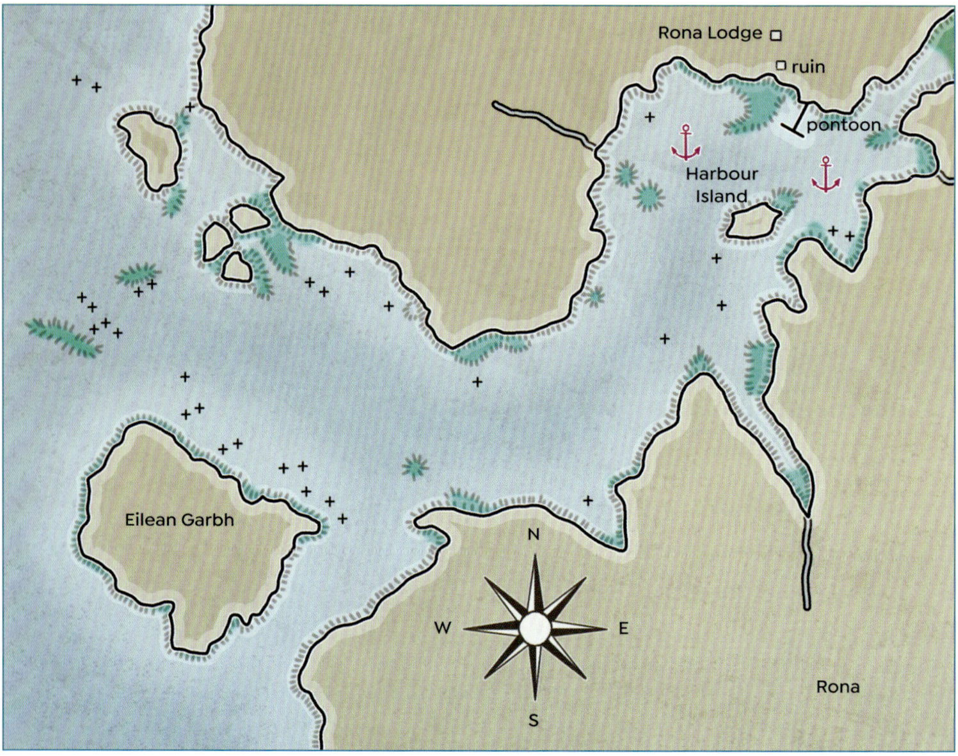

▲ The anchorage offers good shelter but few facilities

full-time inhabitants living up the track from the pontoon at Rona Lodge, a newly completed house. Local produce and Rona stamps are available, though sadly the hot shower facility has closed. For those keen to stretch their legs, the choice includes a track to the north that leads towards the old village of Acairseid Thioram, or south to the village remains of Doire na Guaile and the ruin of An Teampull, a chapel on the southern tip of Rona. A popular shorter walk is to Church Cave on the east coast across the island from the anchorage. Here, behind a high Gothic type of arch, is a cavern where the islanders used to worship using a natural rock depression as a font.

Small patches of mixed woodland and Scots pines around the anchorage provide good bird habitat, and seabirds, seals, otters and even sea eagles are a regular sight. The absence of rabbits and sheep helps the variety of local flora, and cattle and red deer thrive after their reintroduction.

Access is by a channel south of Eilean Garbh at the entrance to Acairseid Mhor, clearly marked with a white arrow painted on the rock face. Leave this starting point to port and aim to leave a rocky point on the south shore directly east of Eilean Garbh close to starboard in order to pass between the point and the rock that dries at 3.7m to the north of it: when covered this rock can be seen as a pale area below the water. Once clear, steer directly for the north-west edge of Harbour Island, taking care not to deviate over the rocks lying to the north and south of the track between Eilean Garbh and Harbour Island. Once the latter is 95m (300ft) to starboard, the anchorage opens up, with options to anchor either to the north-west or to the north-east of Harbour Island keeping clear of the five moorings (£15 per night). Those opting to anchor may choose to pay a fee of £1 for use of the pontoon. The holding is in good black mud in 4–6m.

In the summer it is rare to be on your own, but I have enjoyed many stays with only fellow club boats and the local wildlife for company. This is an entrancing anchorage that draws its admirers back many times. – JP

# POLL CREADHA

APPLECROSS PENINSULA, HIGHLAND

- - - - - - - - - - - - -

**POLL CREADHA IS** an easily overlooked and underused anchorage on the east side of the Inner Sound which separates the remote Applecross peninsula from the islands of Raasay and Rona, with Skye itself further to the west. Historically, the isolated village of Applecross was accessible only by boat until the early 19th century, when a road was created over the notoriously treacherous Bealach na Ba (Pass of the Cattle) which crosses the peninsula via the 792m (2,598ft) Sgùrr a'Chaorachain. In 1975 the settlement was connected via a winding coastal road to

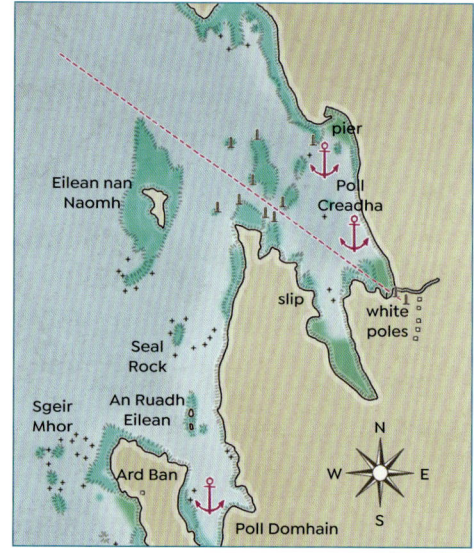

▽ The anchorage at Poll Creadha

Shieldaig and Torridon. Poll Creadha lies several kilometres south of Applecross village and still serves as the best haven for any nautical visit.

At first glance the approach and available shelter might seem inauspicious; the approach is through a series of drying reefs and the anchorage seems perched on the edge of the land. But fear not: the pool is surprisingly inset into the coastline, offering good shelter in all but north-westerlies, while the safe track through the reefs is marked with perches and a leading line. That said, entry should not be attempted at night, in adverse conditions, or when any swell is running.

Once through the challenge of the reefs, a couple of sunken rocks separate two refuges; my preference is to turn to port for the northern anchorage area, though the one more to the south might give slightly more shelter from westerly winds. The inlet to the far south is crowded with moorings. The drying reefs do give protection from swell until they are covered; once in, this is a very snug anchorage. Access to the slip is possible from half-tide, and water and diesel are available there. For other supplies the village of Applecross is 3 miles (4.8km) from the north of the anchorage. For groceries the Applecross Shop and Post Office is halfway to the village itself; the Applecross Inn and other outlets are on the main 'street'.

First-time visitors may be edgy about the entry, though it is straightforward in good conditions. Start your approach from the north of Eilean nan Naomh, leaving a good two cables (370m, 1,200ft) clearance. Head south-east towards the outer perches to pick up the leading line marked by two white poles at the head of the bay on a bearing of 126°T. The rear pole is hard to see from far out; the right-hand edge of the extension of the second cottage from the north can be used instead providing it is not obscured by a tree. Follow the track through the perches, leaving a good offing to each before either heading straight ahead for the southern anchorage or turning tightly to port to avoid the rocks as per the chart to reach the northern anchorage.

This is a peaceful haven in one of Scotland's most remote communities and makes a wonderful base for hiking, kayaking, fishing or cycling. Relax and enjoy the breathtaking sunsets across the reefs before heading below for an untroubled sleep. – **JP**

▼ Sunset at Poll Creadha

# CROWLIN ISLANDS

INNER SOUND, HIGHLAND

------------

**TUCKED INTO THE** sheltered space between the Isle of Skye and the Scottish mainland lies the stretch of sea known as the Inner Sound, whose 324m maximum depth earns it the title of being the deepest territorial water in the UK. Bounded to the west by the islands of Rona and Raasay and to the east by the Applecross peninsula, the Inner Sound's south-eastern margin is formed by the Crowlin Islands. This uninhabited tight-knit group of three isles is home to one of my favourite anchorages.

The Crowlins' two main islands are split by a narrow channel, creating a fairly shallow landlocked pool enjoying impressive shelter. This creek is entered from the north end by passing over a bar whose least charted depth is 0m; while I've never seen it actually dry, careful tidal calculations for arrival and departure are imperative. A 2m draught usually limits access to approximately HW +/-2hrs depending on the spring/neap range. The impassable southern end dries at 3.1m, resulting in a perfectly sheltered pond bordered to the east and west by land, and to the north and south by a narrow shallow or drying barrier; swell

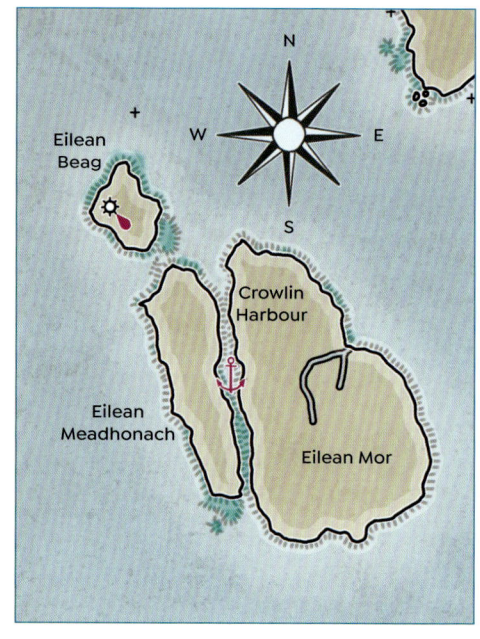

is not a problem here, though the tide does run through when the south end is covered. The bottom is clean sand with good holding.

The approach must be made from the north, having passed the Crowlin Islands if coming from Plockton or the Skye Bridge to the south, or directly towards the island group when heading southward through the Inner Sound past Rona, Raasay and Applecross. It's worth

▲ A quiet day in the Crowlin Islands

noting that the Inner Sound is used for submarine exercises and weapons testing; daily information broadcasts are made on Ch 8 at 0800 and 1800, and when the area is operational safety vessels will request yachts to stay clear, though passage is usually allowed within about 0.5 miles (0.9km) of either shore.

When closing the northernmost, Eilean Beag give, a good offing to the drying rocks off its north end as well as to the reef extending eastwards halfway down; similarly, when rounding Eilean Mor from the east keep well clear of its northern point. The area north of the bar is otherwise clear, and the anchor can be dropped once between the arms of the main islands. Tidal height permitting, I prefer to continue south over the bar into the main pool, noting a reef that extends from Eilean Mor's west shore at the pool's entrance. Bob Bradfield's Antares Charts usefully cover the anchorage and indicate 4.9m depth in the centre of the pool. There is ample room; on several of our cruises, three yachts have not proved a crowd.

The very absence of any facilities is one of this anchorage's charms – the only company (assuming the probable absence of other visitors) will be the wildlife. Once the tender is launched, Eilean Mor can be explored; bare of trees and providing sustenance for only grazing sheep, its peak of 114m (374ft) and the small Loch nan Leac (translating as tombstone loch) prove the main features, though a walk to the north-east leads to a ruined village once occupied by crofters opting for a remote, hard life rather than emigration following the Highland Clearances.

This is a peaceful spot devoid of the bustle and noise of humanity; the evenings are frequently enhanced by clear skies and, if it is warm enough to sit in the cockpit, it's a delight to nurse a postprandial whisky while watching the bright stars until the light and warmth of the cabin beckon. **– JP**

# LOCH NA CUILCE

SKYE, INNER HEBRIDES

----

**THE DRAMATIC LOCH** na Cuilce, tucked under the Cuillins on the south coast of Skye at the head of Loch Scavaig, can rightly claim to be one of the most awe-inspiring anchorages in Britain. Dominated by the stark, jagged peaks of Skye's Black Cuillin, walls of rock surround its northern aspects while the bulk of Eilean Glas stands guard to the south to bar entry to swell.

Although the shelter looks near complete, Loch na Cuilce nevertheless

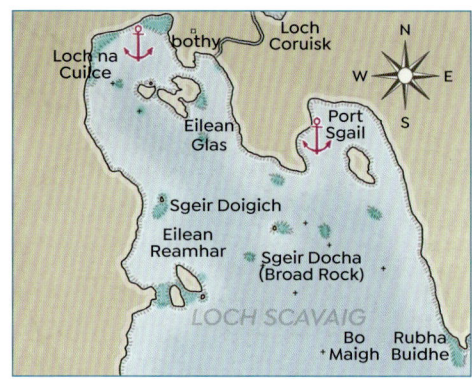

▼ Although it looks sheltered, beware strong winds which cause downdraughts

cannot be recommended in strong winds. Those towering 'protective' mountains are also the anchorage's Achilles heel, as they generate katabatic downdraughts with the power to literally blow your anchor out. Even in settled weather the gusts can bluster boats about – in heavy winds it can be truly terrifying. At night blasts of cool wind funnel down the steep slopes above the pool, causing squalls capable of dragging anchors across the loch. Indeed, I 'enjoyed' one such experience the night before I proposed to my wife on the shore of Loch Coruisk; one of our companion boats was driven ashore during a gusty night. While it managed to pull itself into deep water again, it was at the cost of wrapping its kedge anchor cable round the propeller. In the dark, we secured it to our safely anchored yacht by knotting all our mooring warps together, and managed to clear the problem next day. Our conclusion was to avoid Scavaig in high winds – it is not, despite its looks, a hurricane hole, although in established settled weather there can be few more spectacular places to drop the hook.

There are no facilities; only a climber's bothy nestles on its shoreside, though Scavaig's beauty draws day-trip launches from Elgol to tie up at an iron jetty so that visitors can enjoy the gentle freshwater outflow of neighbouring Loch Coruisk as it slithers over smooth rock slabs to the sea. Depth is no problem apart from at low spring tides near the jetty, which in any case should be kept clear for the tourist boats.

▲ Delicate pilotage is needed to find Loch na Cuilce anchorage

While the anchorage rewards the arrival, the approach does deter some, though the use of Bob Bradfield's Antares Charts is a godsend. Passing east of Eilean Reamhar and Sgurr Doigich with sensible clearance carries no hazard; it is the wriggle past Eilean Glas that requires care. A sunken rock lying 50m south of the north-western tip of Eilean Glas must be left to starboard – a bow spotter and low speed is reassuring here – and, once passed, a starboard turn leaving the north-west corner of Eilean Glas 20m off avoids the drying rock 50m to the west that is the final sentinel of the entrance. The holding is in sand. Tellingly, mooring rings are fixed to Eilean Glas and the Skye shore, though their condition cannot be relied upon.

Once inside relax, and enjoy the panorama before walking up beside the gentle waterfall to Loch Coruisk to marvel at the sublime view of the Cuillin ridge.
– JP

# SOAY HARBOUR

SOAY, INNER HEBRIDES

**SOAY IS A** sandstone island south of the contrasting towers of Skye's Cuillin range. Low-lying, with a height of only 141m (463ft) at Beinn Bhreac, the dumbbell-shaped island is virtually cut in half by inlets that form Soay Harbour to the north and the main bay, Camus nan Gall, to the south. The main 'settlement', Mol-chlach, is on the shore of Camus nan Gall, but though the population peaked at 158 in 1851, the Highland Clearances followed by the requested evacuation of most of the inhabitants in 1953 has left a mere single household as permanent residents. The island's name derives from Old Norse *Sauða-ey* meaning Sheep Island, though the Soay sheep breed actually comes from the Soay Island in the St Kilda archipelago. This Soay is better known for once being owned by the author Gavin Maxwell, who established a basking shark oil factory there in 1945. Never successful and operational for only three years, the experience provided Maxwell with material for his first book, 1952's *Harpoon at a Venture*. Perhaps disturbed by his wartime experiences, it seems incongruous that the naturalist Maxwell opted to attack basking sharks with

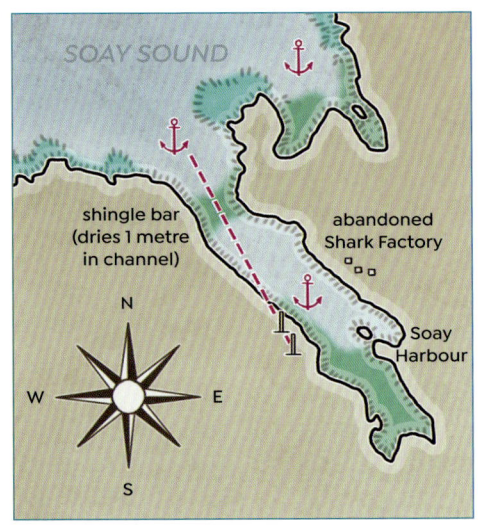

machine guns, shotguns and harpoons; the book describes how difficult these placid plankton-feeding giants are to kill. This violence was perhaps an antidote to the 'ennui of peacetime'. Far from today's ethical nature writing, *Harpoon* was followed in 1960 by the conservation-inspiring *Ring of Bright Water*, written at nearby Sandaig.

The ruins of the factory still stand on the shoreline by Soay's excellent harbour anchorage. The island is separated from Skye by the Sound of Soay; this channel is free of dangers, though a permanent

▲ Soay Harbour in near perfect conditions

westerly set of the tide can create confused seas in strong south-westerly winds. Keep at least 400m (1,300ft) offing from the Soay shore whether approaching from the north-east or the south-west before turning into the harbour entrance.

The landlocked inlet that forms Soay Harbour is entered through a channel less than a cable (185m, 600ft) wide over a bar that dries to 1m, so careful tidal height calculations must be made before entering. In the approach to this channel note that reefs extend half a cable (95m, 300ft) from the south shore and over one cable (185m, 600ft) north-west from the north-east point of the entrance; keep in the centre. A heading south-south-east on approach avoids these hazards. When crossing the bar keep slightly east of mid-channel before steering 20° to starboard in order to line up two barely visible white posts on the south-west shore. The anchor can be dropped just inside the bar or about half a cable (95m, 300ft) north-west of the pier; the holding is good in thick mud and the shelter excellent.

There are no facilities, though on the short walk across to Camus nan Gall you'll find a solar-powered telephone among the abandoned houses. Apart from its walks, wildlife, industrial archaeology and fantastic scenery Soay's greatest attributes are its quietness and peace. Rest assured that you are anchored in total shelter and let Soay's tranquillity enfold you. **– JP**

▲ The quay and old shark factory in Soay Harbour

# CANNA

SMALL ISLES, INNER HEBRIDES

----

**THE WESTERNMOST OF** the Small Isles, Canna is also my favourite. Only 4.3 miles (6.9km) long and 1 mile (1.6km) wide, it is linked to its sister island Sanday by a road and sandbanks. Canna was left to the National Trust for Scotland by the Gaelic scholar Sir John Lorne Campbell and his wife Margaret Fay Shaw, who were fascinated by Gaelic folklore, ancient culture and language. During their lifetime they amassed an enormous collection, leaving a Literary Archive consisting of thousands of individual items, photographs, transcribed music, original letters and manuscripts. The sound archive alone comprises over 1,500 field recordings of Gaelic song and story from the 1930s and 1940s, which are all stored in Canna House and the St Edwards Centre – well worth a visit. There are only about 20 buildings on Canna and Sanday, three of which are churches; the population of around 20 are well served religiously. The tiny active community hosts a café, satellite public telephone, self-catering cottages, a campsite, a post office and a community shop.

This small island south of Skye is kept lush and fertile by the Gulf Stream, with green shores ringing a natural

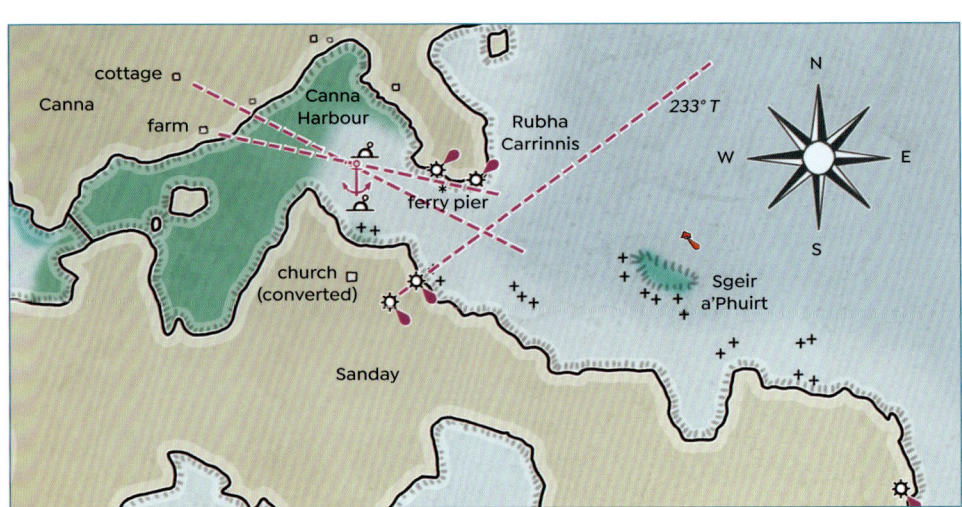

▼ The anchorage on Canna

anchorage. The bay is well sheltered from almost all directions and offers plenty of space for anchoring around and among the moorings. The holding is in mud and sand but with some kelp, so it is best to dig the anchor well in; the cleanest area is between the two chapels. Avoid anchoring within 100m (328ft) of the pier. The ten serviced yellow visitor moorings are available on a first come, first served basis at £20 per night. All have pickup lines and are suitable for vessels up to 35ft. A slipway at the pier has space for tenders at the top, but keep the pier and slip clear for the island services. Toilets are located at the pier and the community shop, while showers are usually available at the campsite. Water can be accessed from a tap at the shop, a short walk from the pier. There's no gas or fuel.

The approach is easy from the northeast – aim for the white beacon transit due south of Rubha Carinnis on a bearing of 233°T, keeping well clear of the port-hand can guarding Sgeir a'Phuirt. Turn to keep the leading line of the hill cottage over the double cottage on the shore open to the left until you've left the rock by the pier to starboard. There's plenty of space around the moorings to anchor but do watch out for the kelp.

Stretch your legs round the tranquil bay or go for a hike over Compass Hill, named for the magnetic deviation its iron-rich basaltic rock causes to passing ships; we climbed it to check but were unconvinced – maybe the deviation is muted on its pole. Our trek was nevertheless rewarded by magnificent views of the jagged ridges of Skye's iconic Black Cuillin to the north, seeming part of a mystical world out of our reach across the sea. **– JP**

▼ Canna

# HYSKEIR LIGHTHOUSE

HYSKEIR, INNER HEBRIDES

------------

**OIGH-SGEIR, NOW GENERALLY** known by its Norse name of Hyskeir, is about as far from being a hurricane hole as is possible – it can only really be considered a fair-weather anchorage as the shelter is minimal and the pool and quay are prone to swell. Oigh-Sgeir is a low-lying isolated group of skerries 5 miles (9km) south-west of Canna in the Sea of the Hebrides. Its rocky ledges claimed enough shipwrecks to justify the construction of Hyskeir lighthouse, completed in 1904. Initially it was manned by three lighthouse keepers whose shore base was in Oban; on Hyskeir they grew vegetables in a walled garden, kept goats and even amused themselves on a three-hole golf course – an eccentricity that earned them an appearance on TV. The main island's three parts are linked by a footpath over bridges and historically supported enough pasture to have warranted the transport of sheep across from Canna for grazing in the early 20th century. After the lighthouse was automated in 1997 the keepers moved out, and only traces remain of the walled garden and golf course.

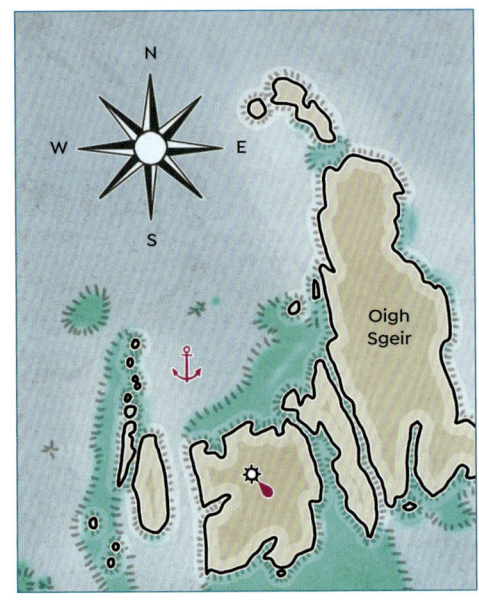

▼ Anchored at Hyskeir lighthouse

Now uninhabited, Hyskeir is deserted apart from the occasional visit by trip boats and birdwatchers. There's an anchorage to the north-west of the lighthouse itself and a quay in the main channel that bisects the island group; this was built for the monthly relief of the lighthouse keepers and the landing of stores and fuel before helicopters became the norm for service access, though heavy items such as oil and equipment still had to be landed by lighthouse vessels. The quay boasts concrete steps and it is possible to tie up alongside, although ample fendering, ideally with a fender board, is wise. The quay is often rendered untenable by swell. The best place to anchor is north-east of where the channel narrows in 4m depth on a sandy bottom.

While it is possible to enter the channel from the south it is unwise to do so without perfect calm conditions and the benefit of Bob Bradfield's Antares Charts; the accepted safe approach is from the north. The immediate sea area north of Hyskeir is clear of hazards, though Humla Rock, Jemima Rock and Emma Rock lie on a line between Hyskeir and Canna. Humla Rock is the closest to Hyskeir at about 3 miles (5.4km) offing and is protected by a starboard-hand buoy. Mill Rocks, 2.25 miles (4km) south-west of Hyskeir, should also be avoided. Approach on a bearing of 170°T, staying one cable (185m, 600ft) west of Hyskeir's northern end while keeping the narrow channel between Hyskeir and Garbh Sgeir open in order to avoid a drying rock in the bay north of the anchorage.

▲ Trip boats at the quay at Hyskeir lighthouse

Visits should only be made in good conditions during a settled weather pattern when there is no swell. The tide runs briskly through the channel and the islands are low-lying and give minimal shelter; sailors should always be prepared to move on if the conditions start to deteriorate. Dinghies can be landed on the shore or, preferably, by the steps. There are, of course, no facilities and, apart from the lighthouse, the scenery and the seabirds, the main attractions of this anchorage are its remoteness and inaccessibility. In fine weather it's a beautiful spot to stop and stretch your legs or just bob at anchor beside the towering 39m (128ft) tall lighthouse. I can no longer recommend bringing your golf clubs.
**– JP**

# EIGG

SMALL ISLES, INNER HEBRIDES

------------

**DURING A WESTERN** Isles cruise with retired vascular surgeon Martin Thomas, aboard his beautiful 40ft Fife, *Charm of Rhu*, I was keen to visit a new island, as is the box-ticking bent of sailors, so I was pleased when it was decided that Eigg should be one of our destinations.

With judicious use of the chart plotter, good visibility and a light offshore wind, we decided Poll nam Partan, on the south-eastern corner of Eigg, was a challenge worth taking. There are metal beacons in red and green marking the rocky shoals which cover at HW, and we motored slowly in at close to LW, until we found the 3m contour, happy that the tide would drop no further than that. The island appeared like a giant green submarine, it's conning tower the sugar loaf crag known as An Sgùrr, the largest volcanic column in Britain and inspiration to former resident JRR Tolkien when writing *Lord of the Rings*.

The bay was shoal and yet calm: the light north-north-westerly winds were set in under high pressure. However, anything from south round to east would make the place untenable. Ashore we found a stunning new restaurant, the

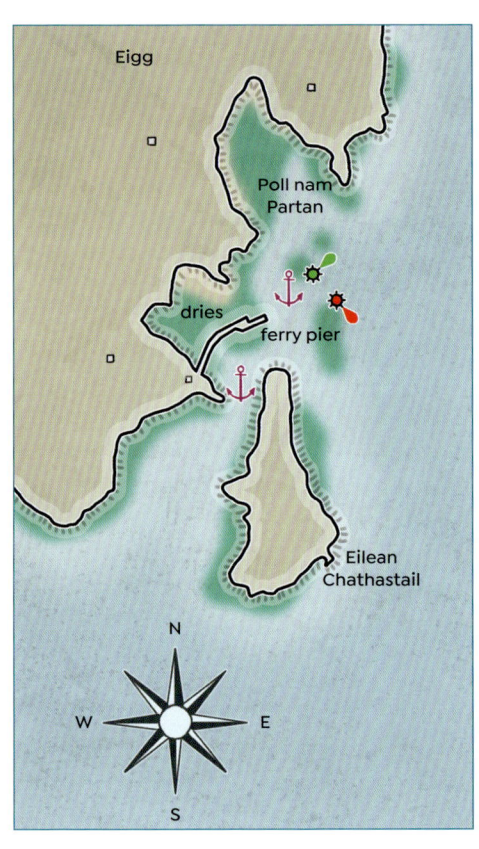

*Glamisdale Bar and Café*, right at the landing place with a plate-glass window that made you feel you were dining in a living picture of the Sea of the Hebrides. Every male on the island sported a beard, noted one of our crew, and they were all

▲ The anchorage off Eigg
*Charm of Rhu* anchored off Eigg ▶

very large: the descendants of Clansmen. It was as though Netflix were making a biopic of the Highland Clearances.

We spent the night here with one other craft: a ketch-rigged Dutch barge, *Steady*, who had made her way from the Netherlands via the Caledonian Canal.

If you have two hours to spare then you can hike up the An Sgùrr tor, which at 393m (1,289ft) is the second-highest (after Rùm) of the Small Isles. Many come across on the ferry from Mallaig to do just that. Eigg is popular with birdwatchers as an average of 130 species can be spotted during the year, and it's particularly noted as a breeding ground for raptors – peregrine falcons, golden eagles, hen harriers, kestrels and buzzards.

If you prefer caves then take a look at the Massacre Cave, so-called because it is said that 395 MacDonald islanders hid there – it was called St Francis Cave at the time – and died of smoke inhalation after the MacLeods lit brushwood fires at the entrance. The vendetta began in the winter of 1577 when some MacLeods from Skye were sent home castrated after being caught raping MacDonald girls on Eigg. Since the MacLeods and the MacDonalds, there have been other owners of the island, but in June 1997 it was bought by the islanders and is now owned and run by the Isle of Eigg Heritage Trust. **– DD**

# ARISAIG

LOCH NAN CEALL, HIGHLAND

---

**THE VILLAGE OF** Arisaig lies at the head of Loch nan Ceall, the most westerly loch in the area of Morar. Set among locations full of romance and history, Arisaig is a wonderful centre hosting sheltered moorings and good services. The Road to the Isles (A830) gives good access for cars and the West Highland Railway Line (inevitably nicknamed the 'Iron Road to the Isles') carrying the steam-powered train *The Jacobite* during summer months stops at the village; it has been voted the most scenic railway line in the world and gained further fame when its Glenfinnan Viaduct was chosen as a film location for Harry Potter's *Hogwart's Express*. Glenfinnan itself lies inland to the east, while to the south lies Loch nan Uamh, from where Bonnie Prince Charlie took wing to France, never to return to Scotland after the failure of the 1745 Jacobite rising. Further down the coast, Moidart offers spectacular anchorages before the bulwark of the Ardnamurchan peninsula (the most westerly part of mainland Great Britain) separates the

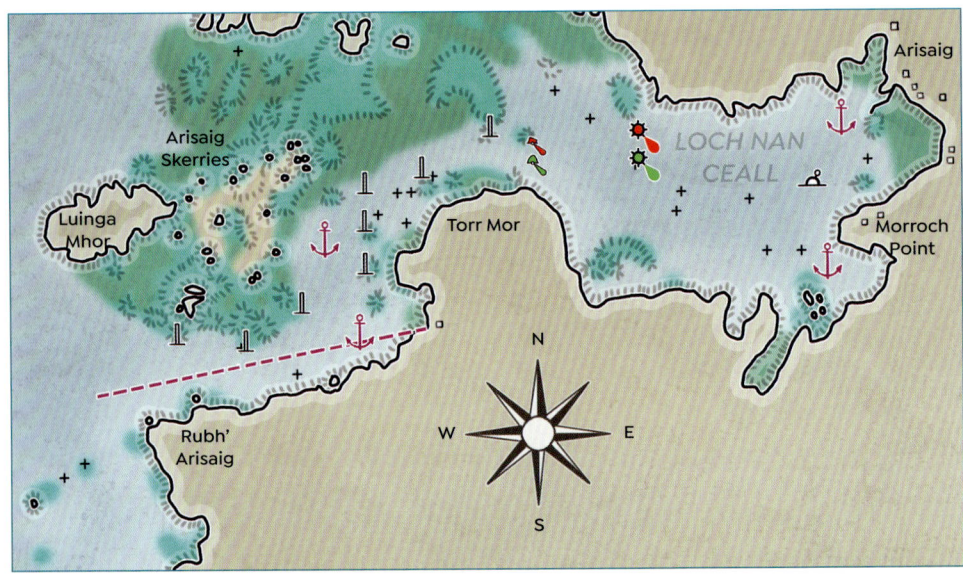

▲ There are now a lot of moorings at Arisaig

eastern part of the Sea of the Hebrides from the environs of Mull. The Small Isles (Canna, Rùm, Eigg and Muck) lie westward while to the north, Mallaig, Skye and Knoydart's Inverie beg a visit. Arisaig is truly the perfect base to explore this historic and spectacular area.

From the sea Arisaig's entrance can look daunting across its half-tide reefs but is well marked, and the pilotage in the Clyde Cruising Club book is clear. The use of Antares charts with GPS position gives further confidence. It is best to enter under engine. Correct identification of the starting point is essential; pass between the flat island of Luinga Mhor and the higher promontory of Rubh' Arisaig, usefully marked with a 40×40cm blob of white paint. Once positioned, head for the grey two-storey cottage on a bearing of 080°T. Pass the remaining two red perches (the first port perch was washed away) to port. The reefs, rocks and convolutions of the channel make the layout of the perches and the safe passage confusing so take it slowly, not moving on until the next objective is certain; the route becomes obvious. Follow the perches sequentially according to the pilot and beware being set off course by cross-tidal streams. Enter Loch nan Ceall between red and green buoys with a final pair of perches before the moorings lie in front of you; beware several drying rocks to either side of the fairway.

There's plenty of room to drop an anchor outside the 60 moorings provided by Arisaig Marine. Their pontoon provides water as well as enabling easy transfer of crew and stores while the premises include a café, chandlery, launderette and showers. Diesel in cans and Calor Gas are available, and a marine engineer can arrange repairs. In the village a café/restaurant and *The Arisaig Hotel* contribute to the choice of eateries, while a shop, post office, nine-hole golf course and visitor centre add to the local services. **– JP**

# LOCH MOIDART

HIGHLAND

---

**I HAVE ENJOYED** many land-based family visits to Loch Moidart over the years. Our favourite spot is the dramatic looming ruin of Castle Tioram, which looks imposingly down the loch towards the open sea. Perched off the beach on its own tidal islet, the causeway covers at HW, leaving it marooned. Indeed, we lingered too long on one birthday visit and were cut off, only reaching the sanctuary of the car and my birthday cake after a deep wade moments before the causeway became impassable. It was the best birthday ever, and Castle Tioram has become a place of pilgrimage for me ever since.

Imagine my delight when a club cruise from Skye down to Loch Linnhe bestowed the boon of a visit afloat. While the entrance to Loch Moidart might resemble a troll's garden, careful attention to pilotage advice, such as that offered by the Clyde Cruising Club Sailing Directions, allows a path to be picked through the scatter of guarding islets and rocks. We chose to anchor in

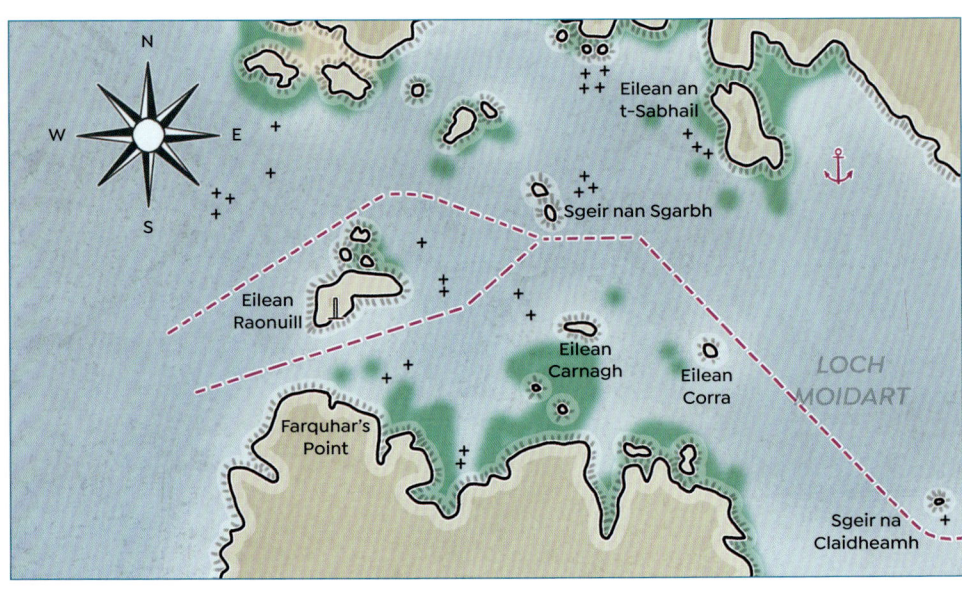

▲ Late summer sun, Loch Moidart

▲ The looming ruins of Castle Tioram

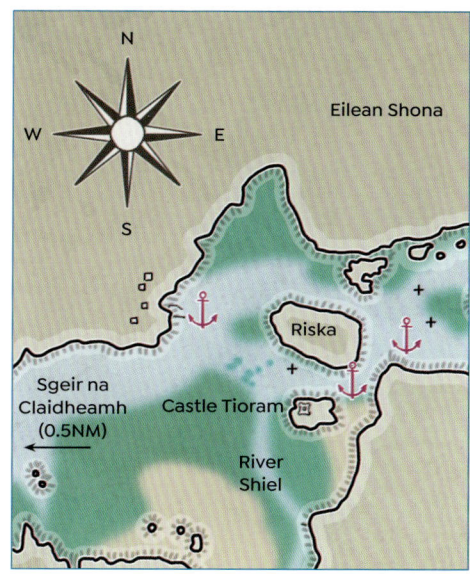

the shadow of the castle between the island of Riska and the shore, and, safely rafted, admired the setting sun dipping over the castle to glint off our incoming track between the islets from the sea.

Aside from its perfect beach, ruined castle and the 4-mile (6.4km) snaking Postman's Walk leading through to the venerable 'Seven Men of Moidart' trees at Kinlochmoidart, the area offers little other than truly breathtaking scenery. I've often spotted golden eagles soaring over the towering crags that overlook the substantial foundations of Dorlin House, which occupied a shoreside position so enviable that its still vacant site remains an enigma. Perhaps the bloody echoes of Castle Tioram's troubled history were a disturbing neighbour – the castle was finally fired by its owners in 1715 to prevent it falling into the hands of the Campbells. For us, though, the aura espoused nothing but peace and tranquillity – here

HIGHLAND | SCOTLAND | 231

the isolation is the allure, and no facilities such as shops, pubs, showers or even a water tap intrude to spoil the ambience. This is a place to unwind and relish one of Scotland's hidden treasures.

To enter the loch, first identify Eilean Raonuil, with its summit perch in the centre of the channel to the south of Eilean Shona. Make your approach to this island on a bearing of 100°T, though if Castle Tioram can be seen it can be used as a leading line over Eilean Raonuil until that island can be left 0.5 cables (95m, 300ft) to port, when a bearing of 73°T will clear the rocks to the south-east. When the grassy tops of Eilean Carnagh and Eilean Cora come into line, steer 30° to port towards Sgeir nan Sgarbh until it is 55m (185ft) to the north, before turning due east until the small cone of Eilean Cora is well open on Sgeir na Claidheamh. Pass Sgeir na Claidheamh to port, taking note of the rock to the south-west of it, and head across to leave Ru a Bhaile 1 cable (185m, 600ft) to port before circling Riska clockwise. We anchored to the south of the island, taking care to avoid the submarine cables supplying Shona.

The sandy beach is a stone's throw away, and the lure of exploration strong, but first breathe in the atmosphere of this most precious place and let your life slow down to the snail's pace the noble setting deserves. **– JP**

▼ Sunset over the anchorage at Loch Moidart

# 14

# SANNA BAY

ARDNAMURCHAN PENINSULA, HIGHLAND

------------

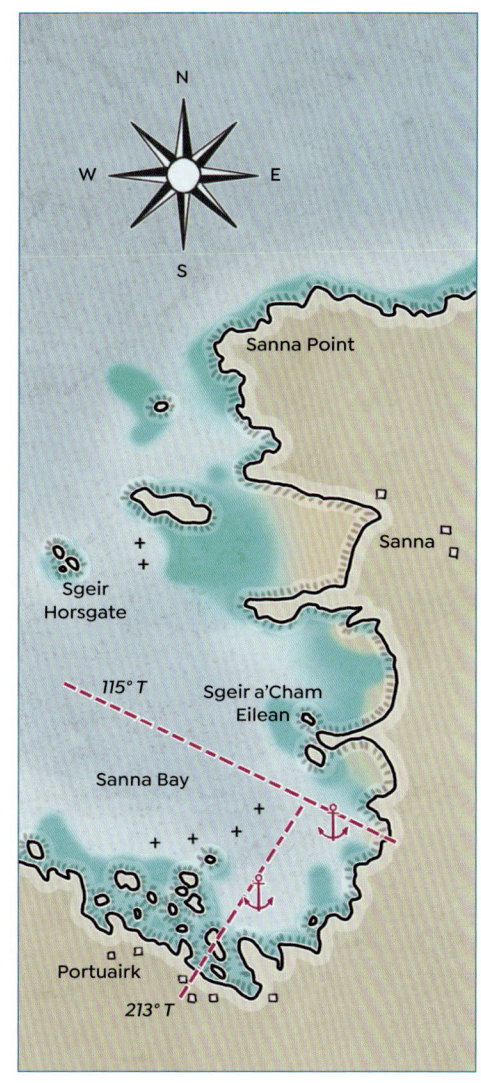

**AN IDYLL OF** turquoise sea over white sand, Sanna Bay is notable as the most westerly anchorage in mainland Britain. Situated just north of the lighthouse on Ardnamurchan Point, its only road access is by a stunning single-track road that winds a scenic 9.7km (6 miles) from the nearest shops in Kilchoan. Before the road was 'upgraded' the bay was used to service the impressive Ardnamurchan lighthouse. Well known for its magnificent beach of fine shell sand and tranquil coastal scenery, Sanna offers fabulous views of Ardnamurchan Point and the Small Isles of Rùm, Eigg, Muck and Canna.

Seaborne visitors do not come here for the facilities; there are only a few houses and the area is sparsely populated, with supplies far away. The draw is the remoteness, white sand, tropical-coloured water, wildlife and scenery. Those with an interest in geology might know that the Ardnamurchan peninsula was formed by a collapsed volcano – a caldera – which, though hard to spot from the sea, is clearly visible on the road to Kilchoan or on aerial photographs. The lighthouse

▲ Sanna Bay looks almost tropical with white sand and turquoise water

is open to visitors and is well worth a visit; a cross-country tramp of several kilometres or the easier walk along the road might generate a thirst easily slaked by its welcoming café. A steep climb to the lighthouse top platform is rewarded with panoramic vistas of Mull, the Small Isles and the Cuillins, while dolphins or whales might be spotted in the sparkling sea. The Highlands in fine weather is unrivalled, and this most westerly mainland peninsula is breathtaking on a still summer day. However, I would not sing such praises of its beauty during gales of horizontal rain or wet days of grey mist (though even these conditions have their own grandeur) – the sea state off Ardnamurchan Point in brisk wind over tide conditions can be horrendous, rendering the whole area as one to avoid. It must also be said that Sanna Bay, while providing safe shelter, can be prone to swell and is best considered a fair-weather anchorage.

The entry to the anchorage cannot be recommended in failing light or bad visibility but is better than the pilot books suggest. Avoid mistaking White Sand Bay, five cables (930m, 3,040ft) east of Sanna Point, for Sanna Bay and maintain enough offing to clear the submerged rock Bo Kora Ben just to the south. Once at a point two cables (370m, 1,200ft) south of Sgeir Horsgate aim for the more southerly of the two white sandy beaches on a bearing of 115°T. Pass half a cable (95m, 300ft) south of the rocky Sgeir a'Cham Eilean before steering to starboard when a group of three buildings bear 213°T, then steer 204°T towards the white cottage to the east of the group; anchor as close inshore as possible behind the reef, which provides some shelter from the wind and swell.

Sit back and admire the scenery and seascapes while being alert for a glimpse of some of Scotland's most elusive wildlife, including pine martens, otters and sea eagles. – JP

# 15

# LOCH NA DROMA BUIDHE

HIGHLAND

---

**WHEN DISILLUSIONED BY** the fleshpots of Tobermory, wearied by the rocking swell of Kilchoan, or exhausted by buffeting gusts and rain in the Sound of Mull, where can a simple sailor go? How about a beautiful small, sheltered loch almost completely enclosed by deserted protecting shores with an easy entrance and good holding? Loch na Droma Buidhe is your answer. This offshoot off the mouth of Loch Sunart is safely tucked between the island of Oronsay and the Morvern mainland with a narrow entrance at the western end and a drying tail at the eastern end. It provides shelter from almost all directions and, having decent holding in mud, Loch na Droma Buidhe is one of the more popular yacht anchorages on this part of the west coast.

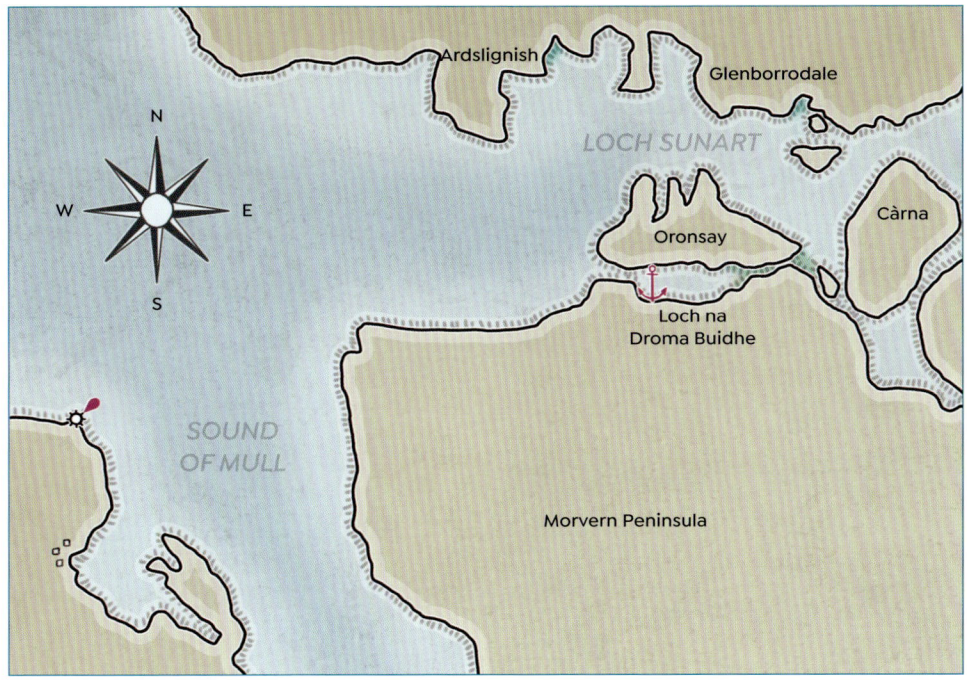

The loch is large – about 1-mile (1.8km) long and 0.5 miles (0.9km) wide – so crowding is never an issue. There are options for anchoring all around the edges, but the prime spots are marked on the chartlet. The most popular spot is probably off the burn on the south shore, where there seems to be a tradition of crews writing their boat's name in white stones or shells on the beach. In a westerly, the most sheltered spot is the south-west corner; take care here as the seabed shelves steeply and the holding isn't particularly good. There may be fish cages in the inlet off Oronsay on the north shore, though on my last visit there was no sign. I'd still use a tripping line here as the bottom may not have been left clean. While the east end of the loch has good holding and is usually quiet, Antares Charts do indicate some shallow spots in the middle of the eastern end; the safest spot is north-east off a drying bay on Oronsay's south shore.

▲ Heading out of the anchorage

It can get quite busy in high season, especially as Loch na Droma Buidhe is an ideal place for yachts to wait for a quiet weather window to round Ardnamurchan Point; it's not unheard of to be stuck here for a week, which could be trying as there's nothing here but nature. While there are no facilities, good walking is to be found on both shores. The whole area is sparsely inhabited for 5 miles (8km) in any direction; supplies are best sourced from Tobermory, about 6 miles (10.8km) westward across the Sound of Mull.

The approach and entry are straightforward provided the cluster of rocks 2 miles (3.6km) to the west in the middle of the Sound of Mull are avoided. There are also rocks close off the west coast of Oronsay, but these can be ignored if the entrance is approached from directly due west. Hug the north side of the 0.5 cable (95m, 300ft) wide channel to clear a rock and shoals at the eastern end of the entrance channel on the south side, and refrain from cutting the corner if heading for the south-west anchorage. Once safely ensconced this is a truly tranquil setting in which to chill out. **– JP**

▼ The anchorage of Loch na Droma Buidhe

# TINKER'S HOLE

MULL, INNER HEBRIDES

**ERRAID IS A** small island on the southwest tip of Mull famed for the forging of a lighthouse and being a location for the classic book *Kidnapped* by Robert Louis Stevenson. The hero of the tale, David Balfour, staggered ashore and was marooned here after his ship, the *Covenant*, had been wrecked on the nearby Torran Rocks. These two apparently disparate facts are linked, as Stevenson's father Thomas was instrumental in the construction of nearby lighthouses with the consequence that the young Robert visited the island on several occasions.

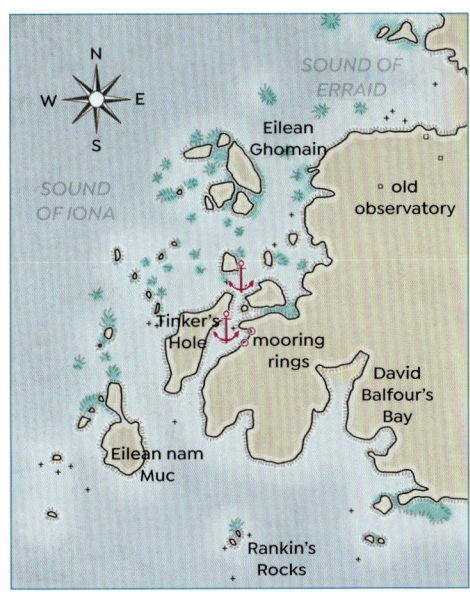

▽ Looking down into Tinker's Hole

In the 1860s the peace of the island was disrupted when it was transformed into a building site by the lighthouse engineers David and Thomas Stevenson, who chose Erraid as the shore base and quarry for Dubh Artach lighthouse 15 miles (24km) south-west of Mull. The island granite was of excellent quality, and they built a small village and port where the cut stones could be loaded; the Stevenson method involved checking the precise fit of each interlocking stone (which could weighed several tons) prior to shipping out to the rock. The disused signal station for the Dubh Artach and Skerryvore lighthouses is still visible and the well-built lighthouse keeper's cottages remain on the island, now used by a small community from the Findhorn Foundation to run courses and retreats. The 2.6sq km (1sq mile) island is rugged and tidal, and is considered to be one of the driest, sunniest spots on the west coast of Scotland.

Just over the hill from the pink granite-lined beach 'David Balfour's Bay' nestles the excellent anchorage of Tinker's Hole. This very snug and scenic anchorage is popular but offers limited space; at peak season it can be packed with yachts, though at quieter times of year its peace and beauty make a visit essential if time and weather allow. Surrounded by the pink rocks of Devonian granite on all sides, there are many small bays in between rocky islands. Indeed, two cables (370m, 1,200ft) to the north further space to anchor can be found. It is possible to put lines ashore to usefully placed (though rather rusty) rings in the north-east corner to ensure a good night's sleep, but avoid the 0.9m submerged rock at the south-west tip of the promontory where these rings lie. The holding is good on a bottom of sand and weed. The tide does flow through the anchorage; staying on the east side avoids the worst of it.

Although fishing boats sometimes use the narrow passage between En nam Muc and En Dubh (the island forming the anchorage's western side), there's no clear leading line to follow, and it's safer to approach from the south. Rankin's Rocks should be left well to starboard and a rock drying to 2.5m lying south of En Dubh should be avoided; many of our club's skippers would endorse that! Once safely settled, a nice cuppa will be in order to soak up the peace. – **JP**

◀ A quiet anchorage in Tinker's Hole

# PUILLADOBHRAIN

SEIL, ARGYLL AND BUTE

-------------

**A DEAD-RUN IN** sunshine down the Sound of Mull and round into the Firth of Lorn saw *Charm of Rhu*, a Fife 40, heading for the most perfect anchorage in the world: Puilladobhrain. This is how the inlet was once described by the late author Eric Hiscock, who, having sailed round the world at least once, was well qualified to make such a grand claim.

Whether his promotion still resounds throughout the cruising community or whether the fact that the anchorage is well placed for yachts heading north or south in the Western Isles (Oban is just 6 miles (10.8km) away), I cannot say, but as we sailed in, six other yachts were already in place, their anchor balls twirling in the breeze.

Entry is from the Firth of Lorn rounding the Eilean Duin – or Fort Island – followed by Eilean nam Beathach – isle of the brutes – and then heading west of south into the Puilladobhrain ('pool of otters') anchorage. The fact we could see the masts of yachts in the anchorage disembodied over the rocky approach was a navigational boon, as the entrance is deceptively hard to see since the pool itself is narrow. Once in, we lay in good

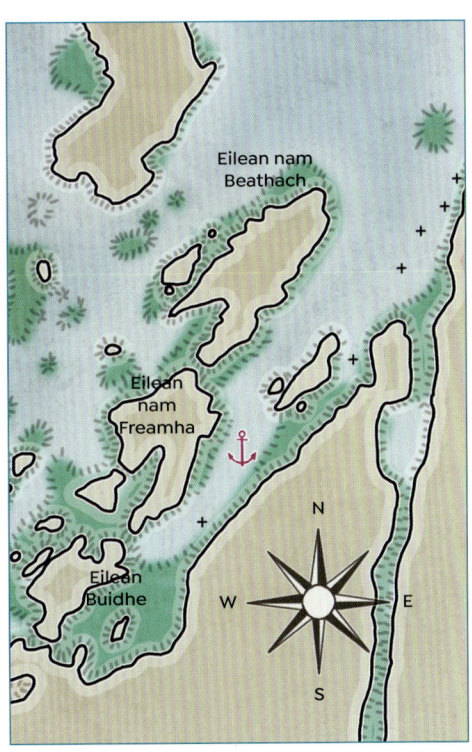

holding with 4m beneath us at LW and with shelter from all quarters.

Puilladobhrain nestles in the north of Seil island, once famous for its slate quarrying, and connected to the mainland via the Clachan Bridge built in 1793 and known as the Bridge over the Atlantic, presumably as a local joke as

▼ The anchorage at Puilladobhrain

the sound it crosses is narrow and dries out. Perhaps Hiscock kept his booze locker filled and had no need to leave his boat, because the crew of *Charm*, seeking a hostelry, stumbled over weed and rock to get a footing ashore: one thing that's not perfect about Puilladobhrain is the landing.

However the pub – *Tigh na Truish* – which I couldn't spell on the way in and couldn't pronounce on the way out, is worth finding for its real ale. The pub's English name is The House of the Trousers because when Highland dress was banned following the Jacobite Rebellion, clansmen swapped kilts for breeches here before venturing further inland.

Easdale village on the west side of Seil was featured in the 1969 film *Ring of Bright Water* based on the Gavin Maxwell book about a man with a pet otter. When I interviewed the late Hamish Haswell-Smith, whose book *The Scottish Islands* was described by the *Sunday Times* as the Rosetta Stone of island exploration, he mourned the fact that the popularity of Puilladobhrain had seen the otters depart. **– DD**

▼ Leaving Puilladobhrain

# BARMORE ISLAND

LOWER LOCH FYNE, ARGYLL AND BUTE

---

**BARMORE ISLAND IS** not really an island as it is linked to the mainland by a narrow neck of land that remains above water. Situated about 1.5 miles (2.7km) north of Tarbert on the west side of Lower Loch Fyne, there is a possible anchorage either side of this causeway. The bay to the south dries for 2 cables (370m, 1,200ft) from the head and it's best to anchor to the west of a small islet, Sgeir na Dubhaidh, which lies south-west of the tip. Continuing up the loch, you can round the island and nudge well in to the northern bay.

This is a pleasant anchorage if you have rounded Bute, either by the Kyles

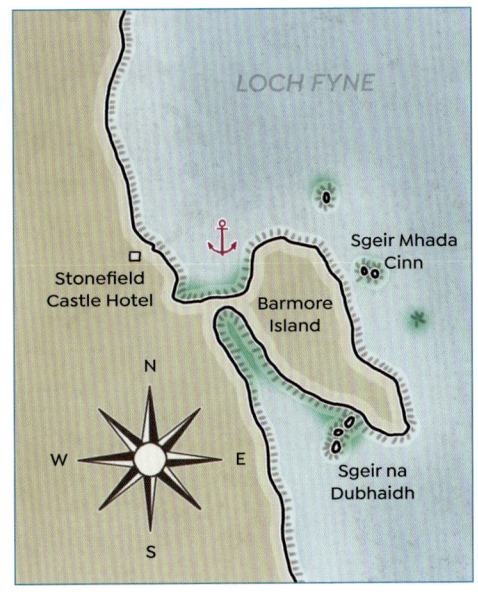

▼ The anchorage at Barmore Island in Loch Fyne

or between Bute and Arran, and you're heading towards the Crinan Canal entrance at Ardrishaig, about 7.5 miles (13.5km) to the north. You need to keep an eye out for the reef, Sgeir Mhada Cinn, just to the north-east of the island which is surrounded by rocks, but having avoided that, the anchorage is quite clean and straightforward. Clear Sgeir Mhada Cinn by about half a cable (95m, 300ft) before turning south-west into the anchorage and choosing your spot. You are well protected from westerlies in either bay but anything from the north-east will funnel down Loch Fyne, making the north bay uncomfortable.

You can land at a slip below the *Stonefield Castle Hotel* and then follow the path round to the causeway and cross to the island, which has a path right round its edge. This is not a strenuous walk but later in the season, when the bracken has grown up, you need to be careful about ticks, so probably best not to be wearing shorts. The centre of the island rises to about 60m (200ft) but is heavily wooded. In the 19th century a monkey puzzle tree was planted on the summit as an eyecatcher from the castle, but is now indistinguishable. There has been a castle on this site for centuries but the present building was designed by the architect William Playfair for John Campbell, in the 1830s. The Campbell family owned Stonefield for just over 200 years until 1948, before it became a hotel. You can take tea on the terrace overlooking your boat at anchor or sample some wonderful Scottish food either at the bar or for dinner ashore.

The grounds around the hotel are fun to explore; you may discover a bridge across Barmore Burn, a crenelated tower near the stream or a walled kitchen garden, part of which now grows vegetables for the hotel. There's a fine collection of trees and shrubs, much of which was planted in the 19th century, with rhododendrons, azaleas, pines and many unusual and rare species, including a redwood over 40m (130ft) tall. The maritime climate from the Gulf Stream, high rainfall and steep wooded slopes behind ensure the survival of this eclectic collection.

Sitting quietly at anchor the atmosphere is intoxicating, and the views up and down the loch from your cockpit are stunning. There are no facilities for yachts here but diesel is available at Tarbert fish quay, Monday to Friday, or across on the east side of the loch at Portavadie Marina, which offers all the facilities you would expect. **– JC**

▼ Landing on the slip below the *Stonefield Castle Hotel*

# MILLPORT

GREAT CUMBRAE, ARGYLL AND BUTE

------------

**THE APPROACH TO** the Clyde is dotted with islands, and on a cruise in this region you are spoilt for choice for places to anchor overnight. One of the best spots is in the bay off the town of Millport, which is located on the island of Great Cumbrae, just a short hop across from the Scottish mainland. Millport is a small harbour that has seen its share of ups and downs, and today the harbour and the bay are mainly a destination for yachts rather than commercial traffic.

In the past, Millport was home to the revenue cutter that patrolled the approaches to the Clyde and it was also a considerable fishing port. Then it was developed to export the high-quality stone from a local quarry and later, it became a destination for the excursion steamers coming out of Glasgow on day trips. This was the main reason for extending the pier, while tucked inside is the older harbour with its stone walls.

Millport Bay is littered with small islands and rocks that provide shelter in what is almost a perfect anchorage. Unfortunately, like many of the Scottish anchorages, mooring buoys have taken over the best places. There is a range

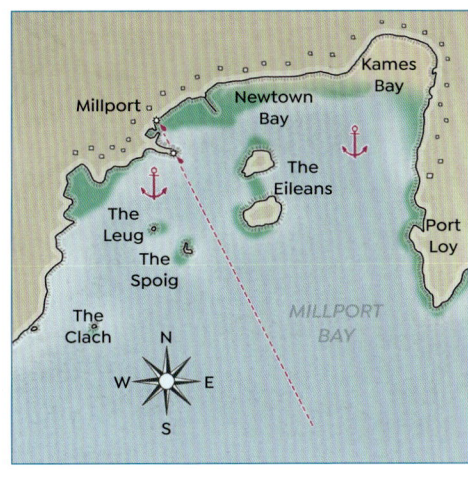

of visitor moorings laid in the summer inside the islands, but if you want to have a quiet night away from the crowds then it is possible to find anchorage space either to the east of the Eileans or to the west of the pier.

Both of these areas are a bit more exposed to any wind from the south, which is probably why they have not been used for mooring buoys, but nowhere in this bay is fully exposed to any wind because you have Little Cumbrae Island providing shelter from a southerly wind. I prefer the westerly spot, but it does mean identifying the small patches of drying

▲ The drying inner harbour at Millport

rocks that lie offshore before heading in. Space can be limited but you can find 5m of water close inshore. The masts of the yachts in the boatyard give a distant clue of the location, and coming in from seaward they will be aligned with the southernmost rocky patches, known as The Clach.

If you want to try your luck in the main anchorage area there are lights to guide you in between the rocky islands towards the main pier. Payment is by an honesty box on the quay. Watch out for the submarine cable in this area. In the summer months this is a very popular spot and perfect for day sails from mainland marinas. Ashore, the small town has plenty of facilities, including a few shops and a number of bars and restaurants, although some are only open in the summer. The stone-walled inner harbour dries out and suggests a lot of history. It is home to local fishing boats and small motor craft. Further round the bay the Cathedral of the Isles, Britain's smallest cathedral, is worth a visit. **– DP**

▼ The Cathedral of the Isles, Millport

# ISLE OF WHITHORN

SOLWAY FIRTH, DUMFRIES AND GALLOWAY

---

**THE ISLE OF** Whithorn is a bit off the beaten track for many cruisers unless you are exploring the Solway Firth. Located on the southern coast of Scotland, it may be too much of a deviation for those heading north or south through the North Channel and looking for an overnight anchorage, but do not dismiss this quiet, peaceful anchorage that gives access to a decent pub.

Tucked inside the prominent Burrow Head, the Isle of Whithorn boasts two possible anchorages, both of which offer good shelter from west and south-westerly winds. It's called the Isle of Whithorn because it was originally an island separated from the mainland by a very narrow channel, but this has now been filled in by a short causeway and it's on the west side of this that the harbour has been created. A stone pier sticks out into the harbour to offer further shelter for the local fishing fleet and a variety of small yachts that have to dry out over LW.

It may be possible to get a mooring for the night by contacting the harbourmaster (07734073420) but these are drying moorings, so if you want to stay afloat then you need to use one

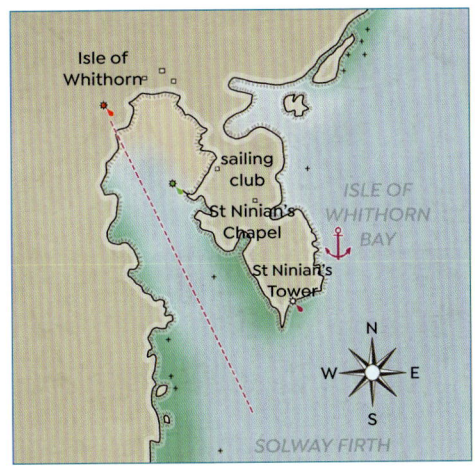

of the two anchoring possibilities. The obvious one is in the entrance channel where there is adequate water to stay afloat. There are rocks on either side of this channel but by using the echo sounder, you should be able to work your way in. The best place is on the west side of the channel, which is a bit more sheltered, but don't go in further than when the tip of the 'island' on the east side comes abeam, as by then you're entering the low water shallows.

The alternative anchorage is on the east side of the 'island' and here you can find adequate water further in, but beware a patch of rocks where you start to close the shore. There's a beach a little way inside the headland and this could be a good spot to anchor with landing by tender on the beach. Otherwise you can land by tender at most states of tide on a slipway just outside the point where the breakwater joins the land. Both anchorages are fully exposed to the east and you could get a swell coming in when the wind is from the south-west.

There are lights that can help guide you in at night and the chart shows leading lights to take you into the harbour in the deeper part of the channel, but I couldn't see these as marks during the daytime, so your sounder is your best guide. St Ninian's Chapel tower on the 'island's' headland dominates the harbour skyline and is a good guide to identify the place.

The Isle of Whithorn has a long history as a port, firstly as a fishing port before the pier was built and later as a port for steam packets and trading ships that came in from ports in England bringing in coal and fertiliser and taking out agricultural produce. The original pier was built back in the 1700s but it finally gave up the ghost in 1969 and collapsed. Now, it has been rebuilt and serves as the base for the inshore fishing fleet.

*The Steam Packet Inn* on the quay provides both food and drink so it is likely to be the focus of any visit, but there's also the active Wigtown Bay Sailing Club and a small chandlery and village store on the quay. **– DP**

▼ The drying harbour at Isle of Whithorn

# ACKNOWLEDGEMENTS

---

No book like this comes together without the help of lots of people. Among the many sailors and harbour staff who helped particular thanks go to John Elliott in Guernsey, Michael Kneale and his contacts in the Isle of Man, and Ray McGinty and Lester Sher of the Royal Northumberland Yacht Club. Richard Thompson did a tremendous job of interpreting a varied collection of sketch charts to create the simple and pleasing plans for each of the anchorages, as well as the overview maps to show their locations.

We would also like to thank Cath Pike, Dag's widow, for agreeing to the use of some of the many anchorage pieces he wrote for *Yachting Monthly*.

The idea for the book came about when Clara Jump of Bloomsbury and Theo Stocker of *Yachting Monthly* had a discussion about the long-running anchorage series in the magazine. Readers may recognise that a good number of the anchorages featured have already been published by *Yachting Monthly* in that series.

# PICTURE CREDITS

---

**P8–9** Alphotographic / iStock; **P34** John Worrall / Alamy; **P35** (bottom) Patrick Roach; **P62** Luke Carre / Alamy; **P74** (top) Angus McComiskey / Alamy; **P75** Patrick Roach; **P89** (top) Steve Taylor ARPS / Alamy; **P89** (bottom) Patrick Roach; **P93** (top) Allan Baxter / Getty; **P93** (bottom) Christopher Nicholson, Alamy; **P94-95** Peter Bailey; **P104** Nik Taylor / Alamy; **P105** Alan Curtis / Alamy; **P111** (top) Creacart / Getty; **P111** (bottom) Steve Roe – stephenroe.co.uk / Getty Images; **P115** Santiago Urquijo / Getty Images; **P122** Nigel Hicks/robertharding / Getty Images; **P123** Esther Hutchcroft / 500px / Getty Images; **P126–167** Geraldine Hennigan; **P170** C T Aylward / Getty Images; **P171** C T Aylward / Getty Images; **P178** David Grimwade / Alamy; **P179** HildaWeges / iStock; **P185** (top) Charles Hawes / Getty Images; **P185** (bottom) Alasdair James / Getty Images; **P190** Juliet Lehair / Getty Images; **P191** Patrick Roach; **P192** Dennis Barnes / Getty Images; **P193** George Standen / Getty Images; **P194–195** Christine Rose Photography / Getty; **P198** David Hodges / Alamy; **P199–202** Visit Isle of Man; **P203** (top) Isle of Man / Alamy; **P203** (bottom) Patrick Roach; **P223** (top) Keith Stewart / Getty; **P231** (bottom) Sebastian Wasek / Alamy; **P238** –Sue Middleton; **P244** (top) John Guidi / robertharding / Getty Images; **P244** (bottom) Chris Howes/Wild Places Photography; **P246** wanderluster / Getty Images. All other photographs were taken by the authors.

# INDEX

**A**

Aberdaron, Gwynedd 184–5
Acairseid Mhor, Rona, Highland 212–13
Alderney 60–1
anchorages, types of 5–7
Anglesey 188–9
Apple Cross Peninsula, Highland 214–15
Ardgroom Harbour, Co. Cork/Co. Kerry 144–5
Ardnamurchan Peninsula, Highland 233–4
Argyll and Bute 239–44
Arisaig, Loch Nan Ceall, Highland 228–9

**B**

Babbacombe Bay, Devon 94–5
Bantry Bay, Co. Cork 140–1
Bardsey Island, Gwynedd 182–3
Barloge, Co. Cork 134–5
Barmore Island, Lower Loch Fyne, Argyll and Bute 241–2
bars and spits 6
Beaulieu River, Hampshire 54–5
Beauport Bay, Jersey 82–3
Beer, Devon 92–3
Blackpool Sands, Devon 96–7
Blackwater, River 38–9
Bouley Bay, Jersey 79–80
Bristol Channel 120–1
Bryher, Isles of Scilly 112–13
Buck's Mills, Devon 122–3
Burtonport, Co. Donegal 158–9
Butley River, Suffolk 24–5

**C**

Caldey Island, Pembrokeshire 172–3
Canna, Small Isles, Inner Hebrides 222–3
Carbis Bay, Cornwall 116–17
Castle Haven, Co. Cork 132–3
Castletownshend, Co. Cork 132–3
Cawsand Bay, Cornwall 102–3
Cemlyn Bay, Anglesey 188–9
Chapman's Pool, Isle of Purbeck, Dorset 88–9
charted pools 5
Chichester Harbour, West Sussex 52–3
Cliff Reach, Essex 40–1
Colne, River 36–7

Cornwall 102–11, 116–19
County Clare 150–1
County Cork, Ireland 128–45
County Donegal 158–65
County Down 166–7
County Galway 152–7
County Kerry, Ireland 144–9
Courtmacsherry, Co. Cork 130–1
Crookhaven, Co. Cork 136–7
Crosshaven, Co. Cork 128–9
Crouch, River 40–1
Crowlin Islands, Inner Sound, Highland 216–17

**D**

Dartmouth, Devon 96–7
Deben, River 26–7
Derbyhaven, Isle of Man 201–3
Derrible Bay, Sark 74–5
Derrynane Harbour, Co. Kerry 146–7
Devon 92–101, 122–5
Dixcart Bay, Sark 74–5
Dorset 86–91
Drake's Pool, Co. Cork 128–9
Dumfries and Galloway 245–6
Dunboy Bay, Co. Cork 142–3
Dungeness, Kent 50–1
Dunmanus Bay, Co. Cork 138–9

**E**

East Coast, Herm 68–9
Eigg, Small Isles, Inner Hebrides 226–7
Elender Cove, Devon 98–9
Erwarton Ness, Suffolk 30–1
Essex 32–45

**F**

Falmouth, Cornwall 106–7
Fergus, River 150–1
Fermain Bay, Guernsey 62–3
Fort Belan, Gwynedd 190–1

**G**

Glengarriff Harbour, Co. Cork 140–1
Gola, Co. Donegal 160–1
Gower, Swansea 170–1
Great Cumbrae, Argyll and Bute 243–4

**248**

Green Bay, Isles of Scilly 112–13
Guernsey 62–5
Gwynedd 182–7, 190–1

## H

Hampshire 54–5
Harris, Outer Hebrides 206–7
Haverfordwest, Pembrokeshire 178–9
headlands, major 5
Helford River, Cornwall 108–9
Herm 66–9
Highland, Scotland 212–17, 228–36
historic highlights
    Bardsey Island, Gwynedd 182
    Buck's Mill, Bideford, Devon 123
    Caldey Island, Pembrokeshire 172–3
    Derbyhaven, Isle of Man 202–3
    Derrynane Harbour, Co. Kerry 147
    Dunboy Bay, Co. Cork 143
    Falmouth, Cornwall 107
    heritage centre, Old Leigh, Essex 45
    Lindisfarne, Northumberland 10–11
    Loch Moidart, Highland 231
    Lough Swilly, Co. Donegal 162–3
    maritime centre, Newbiggin Bay, Northumberland 25
    Newton Haven, Northumberland 13
    Piel Island, Lancashire 197
    Sea Heritage Trail, Rhos on Sea, Conwy 193
    visitors centre, La Grande Grève, Sark 71
Holy Island Harbour 10–11
Hope Cove, Devon 100–1
Hyskeir Lighthouse, Inner Hebrides 224–5

## I

Iken Cliff, Suffolk 22–3
Ilfracombe, Devon 124–5
Inishbofin, Co. Galway 156–7
Inishtrahull, Co. Donegal 164–5
Inner Hebrides 218–27, 237–8
Inner Sound, Highland 216–17
Isle of Man 198–203
Isle of Purbeck 88–9
Isle of Whithorn, Solway Firth, Dumfries and Galloway 245–6
Isle of Wight 56–7
Isles of Scilly 112–15

## J

Jersey 79–83
Jurassic Coast, Dorset 90–3
Jurassic Coast, Devon 92–3

## K

Kenmare Bay, Co. Cork/Co. Kerry 144–5
Kent 46–51
Kirby Creek, Essex 34–5
Kitchen Cove, Co. Cork 138–9

## L

La Grande Grève, Sark 70–1
lagoons, rocky 5–6
Lamorna Cove, Cornwall 110–11
Les Ecrehous 76–8
Lindisfarne, Northumberland 10–11
Llŷn Peninsula, Gwynedd 184–5
Loch Fyne, Argyll and Bute 241–2
Loch Moidart, Highland 230–2
Loch Na Cuilce, Skye, Inner Hebrides 218–19
Loch Na Droma Buidhe, Highland 235–6
Loch Nan Ceall, Highland 228–9
Loch Scadabay, Outer Hebrides 206–7
Loch Skipport, South Uist, Outer Hebrides 210–11
Lough Swilly, Co. Donegal 162–3
Lulworth Cove, Dorset 90–1
Lundy Island, Bristol Channel 120–1
Lydd-on-Sea, Kent 50–1

## M

Marmotière, Les Ecrehous 76–8
Martin's Haven, Pembrokeshire 178–9
Medway, River 48–9
Menai Strait, Gwynedd 190–1
Milford Haven, Pembrokeshire 174–5
Millport, Great Cumbrae, Argyll and Bute 243–4
Mizen Peninsula, Co. Cork 136–7
Morecambe Bay, Lancashire 196–7
Mull, Inner Hebrides 237–8

## N

Newbiggin Bay, Northumberland 14–15
Newton Haven, Northumberland 12–13
Newtown River, Isle of Wight 56–7
Norfolk 20–1
Northumberland 10–15
Norton Hole, Norfolk 20–1

## O

Ore, River 24–5
Orwell, River 28–9
Osea Island, Essex 38–9
Outer Hebrides 206–11

**P**

Paradise, Co. Clare 150–1
Pembrokeshire 172–81
Penzance, Cornwall 110–11
Percuil River, Cornwall 106–7
Petit Port, Guernsey 64–5
Piel Island, Lancashire 196–7
Plymouth Sound, Cornwall 102–3
Poll Creadha, Apple Cross Peninsula, Highland 214–15
Polperro, Cornwall 104–5
Port Erin, Isle of Man 198–9
Port Eynon, Swansea 170–1
Port Gaverne, Cornwall 118–19
Port Gorey, Sark 72–3
Porth Dinllaen, Gwynedd 186–7
Portmagee, Co. Kerry 148–9
Portmore, County Donegal 164–5
Prawle Point, Devon 98–9
Priory Bay, Pembrokeshire 172–3
Puilladobhrain, Seil, Argyll and Bute 239–40
Pyefleet Creek, Essex 36–7

**R**

Ray Gut, Essex 44–5
Rhos on Sea, Conwy 192–3
river mouths, minor 5
Roach, River 42–3
the Rocks, River Deben, Suffolk 26–7
rocky lagoons 5–6
Rona, Highlands 212–13
Rosaire, Herm 66–7
Roundstone, Co. Galway 152–3
Rozel, Jersey 79–80

**S**

St Catherine's Bay, Jersey 81
St Helen's Pool, Isles of Scilly 114–15
St Ives, Cornwall 116–17
Salcombe, Devon 100–1
sandbanks 6
Sanna Bay, Ardnamurchan Peninsula, Highland 233–4
Sark 70–5
Saye Bay, Alderney 60–1
Seil, Argyll and Bute 239–40
Sharfleet Creek, Kent 48–9
Shiant Islands, Outer Hebrides 208–9
Skomer, Pembrokeshire 176–7
Skye, Inner Hebrides 218–19
Small Isles, Inner Hebrides 222–7

Soay Harbour, Inner Hebrides 220–1
Solva, Pembrokeshire 180–1
Solway Firth, Dumfries and Galloway 245–6
South Deep, Kent 46–7
South Haven, Pembrokeshire 176–7
South Uist, Outer Hebrides 210–11
Spurn Head, Yorkshire 18–19
Stone Heaps, Suffolk 28–9
Stone Point, Essex 32–3
Stour, River 30–1
Strangford Lough, Co. Down 166–7
Studland Bay, Dorset 86–7
Suffolk 22–31
the Swale, Kent 46–7
swimming
    Beauport Bay, Jersey 83
    Blackpool Sands, Devon 96–7
    East Coast, Herm 69
    La Grande Grève, Sark 71
    Port Gorey, Sark 73
    Solva, Pembrokeshire 181
    Studland Bay, Dorset 87
    Wizard Pool, Loch Skiport, South Uist 211

**T**

Thames, River 44–5
Tinker's Hole, Mull, Inner Hebrides 237–8
Toberdenny Harbour, Co. Galway 154–5
Torquay, Devon 94–5

**W**

Walton Backwaters, Essex 32–5
Watwick Bay, Pembrokeshire 174–5
West Itchenor, West Sussex 52–3
West Sussex 52–3
wildlife
    Bardsey Island, Gwynedd 182–3
    Caldey Island, Pembrokeshire 73
    Cemlyn Bay, Anglesey 189
    Haverfordwest, Pembrokeshire 179
    Newton River, Isle of Wight 57
    Sanna Bay, Highland 234
    Shiant Islands, Outer Hebrides 208–9
    Skomer, Pembrokeshire 176–7
    Soay, Inner Hebrides 221
Wizard Pool, Loch Skipport, South Uist, Outer Hebrides 210–11

**Y**

Yokesfleet Creek, Essex 42–3
Yorkshire 18–19